D0923512

THE POSSESSED

Also by Brian McConnell

HOLY KILLERS: True Stories of Murderous Clerics, Priests and Religious Leaders

THE POSSESSED

True Tales of Demonic Possession

BRIAN McCONNELL

Brockhampton Press

First published in Great Britain in 1995
by HEADLINE BOOK PUBLISHING

This edition published 1997 by Brockhampton Press,
a member of Hodder Headline PLC Group

ISBN 1 86019 792 2

British Library Cataloguing in Publication Data

McConnell, Brian
Possessed
I. Title
133.426

Phototypeset by Intype, London

Printed and bound in Great Britain by
Creative Print and Design (Wales), Ebbw Vale

In memory of Edward McConnell, my father, an Anglican;
Edith, my mother, a Methodist; and
Valerie, my sister, a Roman Catholic,
who each had a different view
of demonic possession.

Contents

HEALTH WARNING

This is a book about evil, about lack of religion and surfeit of crime – and about whether or not it is possible to be possessed by the Devil. To the weak and the vulnerable, the young and the experimental, the mischievous and the ill advised, it should not be mistaken for temptation or invitation to dabble in matters which are dangerous. In these pages will be found a considerable number of cases which began with an innocent interest in ouija boards, in Tarot playing cards, in horoscopes and other so-called fortune-telling devices, seances and the occult, which are warned against in the Bible. Such trifling has led to unhappiness, tragedy, suicide, crime, murder and even serial killing. This is because the twentieth-century benefits of advanced education and technology have eclipsed so many fundamental religious beliefs. Many people in positions of power and influence are daily and publicly breaking the Ten Commandments. Their example and the sleaze factor in all walks of life are sending the disillusioned young to search for guidance, help and satisfaction in recently invented cults which promise a new paradise. This in turn has had apocalyptic consequences for hundreds, including Britons, in Jonestown, Guyana; in Waco, Texas; in Switzerland and Canada; and elsewhere. Meanwhile, some clergy and devout laymen and women are trying to reinterpret and even rewrite the Scriptures to follow rather than lead the crowd and suit fashionable thinking. Instead of doing good, they may well create more and more children of the Devil, the possessed.

BRIAN MCCONNELL

Introduction

The idea that the public are more interested in sex and crime than any other subjects is a half-truth. They are bewitched by illicit sex and law-breaking, but these are only part of a much deeper attraction to evil and wickedness of all kinds. The fact that evil conjures up the name of the Devil and invokes the question of religion makes it an embarrassment, a matter not for polite social discussion, even a forbidden topic of conversation. Secrecy ensures that people have an abiding interest in depravity and malignancy. And Satan, whether or not he exists as a person or an entity, his power, whether it is real or imaginary, has a very deep hold on the minds of the masses.

Ever since the people were told that Christ had met a man who lived among the tombs, who shrieked, tore his clothes and broke the fetters and chains which bound him, and that Christ drove the Devil out of him, people have been mesmerised by those they believe to be demonically possessed. Two thousand years have passed since Christ performed that simple act of exorcism, but the external signs of what is known as demonic possession have not altered. Extreme strength, frightening facial expressions, physical contortions and more tell the story of those who have been demonised. At the same time, belief in the phenomenon – that a person's body, mind and soul can be literally occupied, dominated, controlled and activated by an evil spirit – has much more recently been badly shaken by a series of tragedies, deaths, even murders, associated with exorcism, the Church ritual which is supposed to cure the afflicted. Even people who think it is nonsense are mesmerised by the argument.

Throughout the ages, writers, religious and secular, have supported the Biblical idea of possession. William Tyndale, the English translator of the basis of the Authorised Version of the Bible, first told us in 1526 of possession by the Devil in St Matthew's Gospel.

Bishop W. Barlow, one of the earliest interpreters, spoke of it in his *Three Sermons* (1596). William Shakespeare in *Twelfth Night* (1601) has the line: 'If all the devils in hell be drawn in little, and Legion himself possessed him, yet I'll speak to him.' Thomas Dekker, the playwright, used the complaint in 1612, 'I am possessed by the Devil and cannot sleep.'

In the next century, historians offered the idea that Abel, Cain's brother, slew a serpent that had been possessed by the Devil, showing that other creatures as well as human beings could be demonised. While some clerics, notably Balthasar Bekker and Jesuits Adam Tanner and his disciple Friedrich Spee, developed a more liberal attitude towards evil, Martin Luther and John Calvin promoted the essential belief in the pervasive and manifest power of the Devil which was then developed to excess.

Washington Irving, the father of American literature, in the Moors' *Conquest of Granada* (1829) wrote about 'one of those fanatic infidels possessed by the devil'. And if anyone doubted the power of the Devil to barter for men's souls, as happened in the story of Faust, the *Quarterly Review* of October 1886 defined 'the traditional demonic proposal' as 'I will be your servant here and you shall be mine hereafter.'

Christian belief in the Devil as the enemy of mankind and the prime source of all evil has remained constant despite the fall in church attendances, even if the identity of Satan and the extent of his powers have been disputed. In the early Church and still among Roman Catholics and some Protestants, the baptismal service contains references to exorcism and a renunciation of the Devil and all his evil works. Similarly, the water, salt and oil used in divine services are first exorcised to ensure their purity before being blessed and consecrated.

Exorcism is really a prayerful command addressed to evil spirits to force them to abandon an object, place or person they have in their power. Primitive peoples since time immemorial have retained a universal belief in unseen spirits, some good, some bad, and have devised certain rites to ingratiate themselves with the good and ward off or expel the evil ones. There has always been an argument as to whether such practices belong in the fields of religion, magic or witchcraft.

After Christ's demonstration of exorcism, in which he expelled demons by the word of God, his followers and others drove out demons 'in His name'. In the first two centuries after Christ, exorcism was regarded as a special gift which could be bestowed by the Church on both lay people and clergy. Around the year AD 250 there appeared a special class of minor clergy, called exorcists, who were entrusted with this ritual function.

Exorcism of people, places and objects is carefully regulated by the Roman Catholic Church under canon law and the extremely elaborate rite is contained in the Rituale Romanum instituted by Pope Leo XIII (1810–1903). The class of exorcists still exists as a minor category of clergy, but its duty to 'cast out demons' has become obsolete and the preparation for exorcism is carefully monitored by bishops on the advice of psychiatrists as well as priests. A priest must not perform an exorcism without special authority from the bishop, and that authority is given only to those who are experienced, pious, prudent and of proven moral integrity. Before conducting an exorcism, they must make a careful and thorough investigation into each case to decide whether or not it is one of genuine demonic possession. Even so, as we shall see, there have been appalling disasters arising from such rituals.

Not surprisingly, the arts, both classical and commercial, have found the demonically possessed an ideal subject for literature, music, cinema, theatre and opera. Faust, the chief character in the famous German story, is portrayed as selling his soul to the Devil for power or knowledge, for immediate gain in return for eventual surrender. The historic argument as to whether he died around 1540 or whether he was really two people (Georgius and Johann Faust), an astrologer, soothsayer, sodomite, necromancer or demi-god, has been lost in the essential moral of his story – that the Devil has unlimited power and that Faust, in order to regain some office from which he had been deposed, agreed to serve him and gave him in return a sealed denial of the existence of Jesus Christ for later use if he so wished.

This story was by no means new. St Augustine (354–430), who brought Christianity to England and became the first Archbishop of Canterbury, borrowed the story from historic Jewish chants and used it as a warning to the faithful.

Dramatists Christopher Marlowe and Goethe, poets like Byron and many others took up the theme; Gounod composed the best of many operas. Further evidence of the never-ending popularity of the subject came from many film interpretations of the Faust story to suit every age, including *All That Money Can Buy* (1941), *La Beauté du Diable* and *Alias Nick Beal* (both 1949), *Marguerite de la Nuit* (1955), *Damned Yankees* (1958) and many more extravaganzas, including Richard Burton's *Dr Faustus* (1967).

Burton's prowess in the classical role of Faust had already achieved great acclaim when he played the stage part at Oxford University. A year later he recruited some talented Oxford amateurs to appear with him in this film version of Marlowe's 400-year-old story in verse. It was a little-known fact that British universities house many societies devoted to Satanic study, if not pursuits.

The cinema overall has largely entertained and horrified rather than educated us in such matters. Despite the claims of publicity blurbs that the events depicted in some features actually occurred, the vast majority have been very fictional – *The Amityville Horror*, for example, which is the story of the Lutz family, who bought a house in Amityville on Long Island, New York, at a knock-down price because of its bloody history. According to the family, flies swarmed in where they shouldn't, pipes and walls oozed ick, doors flew open and priests and psychically sensitive people cringed and fled in panic. Within twenty-eight days, the Lutzes fled too. The truth was more prosaic, as will be seen in Chapter 11.

The Exorcist, based on a novel by William Blatty, was founded on an actual incident of documented possession, but the plot was changed to protect identities and, despite claims to the contrary, the cinematic embellishments made its authenticity extremely doubtful.

Sequels such as *The Exorcist II: The Heretic*, *The Exorcist III* and *Amityville II: The Possession* merely whetted the appetites of the entertainment-seeking public and encouraged the gullible to believe in cases of Satanic possession where they did not exist, serving only to confuse faithful believers and embarrass the churches.

Television has brought into our homes real-life ceremonies of exorcism in which priests have tried to expel evil forces from the possessed, but they seem to have stopped short of showing, as cinemas have done in fictional works, the extreme manifestations; the demonised writhing on the floor like snakes, levitating themselves from their beds, their faces and bodies thrown into horrible contortions and their voices speaking in languages never previously heard.

Despite warnings about the dangers of exorcism, a series of ill-advised rituals ended in tragedies, including some particularly horrible deaths. A Yorkshire husband, the subject of an all-night church exorcism, returned home and choked his wife to death with his bare hands. A pretty young university student starved to death during a seven-month-long exorcism. As a direct result of such tragedies, churches have imposed stricter controls on the conduct of clergymen, who in turn have become more and more divided on the whole subject. They have even begun to question the Scriptural definition of possession, the whole theology of evil; even to doubt the possibility of a person ever being possessed by Satan. Some want the words 'possessed' and 'exorcism' banned and substituted by the words 'evil' and 'deliverance'.

One of those who believed in mass 'deliverances' and 'healing services' (every Tuesday and Friday) was the Reverend Matthew George Frederic Peiris, of Hertfordshire. He had been ordained at St Albans, became a priest at St Francis of Assisi, Welwyn Garden City, and later curate at Hatfield Hyde. When he returned to his native Sri Lanka to become vicar of St Paul's, Colombo, he began writing a book, *Damn The Bloody Exorcist.* At his packed services he would appear hands upraised, showing the stigmata wounds of Christ on his palms, as he drove out devils as Our Lord had taught the disciples.

He fell in love with his secretary, Mrs Dalrene Ingram, and in order to make her his wife he first persuaded her husband, Russel Ingram, and then his own wife, Eunice, that he had been warned by the Archangel St Michael that they were both ill and had been doomed by Satan. They attended his healing services where he falsely diagnosed in both of them hypoglycaemia, low blood sugar level, and ministered to them Euglucon, which would increase any deficiency in the blood stream. The false diagnosis and dangerous remedy killed them both and the vicar and secretary were both tried, convicted and sentenced to death by hanging, a punishment later commuted to life imprisonment.

Whether or not priests administer private or public exorcism or deliverance, there is a danger that they include in their number the merely amateur who refuse to heed professional medical and other advice, as well as the grossly wicked.

So often forgotten in the religious disputes and debates over demonism are the other really evil people of this world, such as the cultists who usurp the all-powerful role of God and even serial killers who claim that they have heard voices and been directed by Satan to commit murders. Then there are the Satanists, dressed in ecclesiastical robes, using altars and bejewelled gold and silverware intended for holy communion, mouthing the black mass, a mockery of Church rites, as part of ritual sex and ritual sexual abuse of children, complete with drinking infants' blood from chalices. What of the incestuous, the paedophiles? Are these people possessed and bad or sick and mad?

In the Gospels, Jesus cast out devils and gave His disciples powers to carry out similar acts. But he also distinguished between the wicked and the mentally afflicted, between healing the sick and casting out devils. 'Heal the sick, raise the dead, cleanse lepers, cast out demons,' he said (Matthew x, 8). Today, the argument about how to differentiate between the ill and the possessed still rages.

For centuries, clergymen said that such people were possessed and exorcism was the only answer. Doctors insisted that they suffered from schizophrenia, a major psychiatric disorder, and should be in hospital on medication. The police and lawyers sometimes said they are criminal and should be punished or penalised. Who is correct? Or could each of them be right in different cases?

The twenty-first century is nearly here and more and more people are asking whether demonic possession exists. Who else but the demonically possessed could become cult leaders with one solution to life – mass murder and mass suicide; or serial killers; or Satanists; or sectarians slaughtering people in Northern Ireland because they belong to another religion; or religious people ethnically cleansing their fellow human beings in the former Yugoslavia; or tribal rivals committing genocide in holy places in Rwanda?

Strangely, many churchmen, faced with dwindling congregations and rebellious priests of the new theology, including women ordinands, have decided that there is no Satan, or Devil, or evil, as we and the Bible know it. To them, Jesus did not drive out demons from the possessed, and ritual exorcism of evil spirits is not only out of date but positively dangerous.

My book, *Holy Killers*, about clergymen and other religious faithful who broke the Sixth Commandment, 'Thou shalt not kill', and killed other human beings, prompted me to ask whether they were bad or mad and how the two could be separated and identified. Curiously, many of them who went to court even went into the witness box and claimed on oath that they heard voices from Satan, mistaken for God, sometimes in cemeteries, ordering them to kill. If that is so, were they not possessed by the Devil? Could they not have been exorcised and, as the churches put it, saved?

Despite the fact that some clergy, unable to maintain literal belief in demonic possession, wish to reinterpret the Biblical definition, others adhere strictly to the Good Book. Recently I was asked to edit a newspaper which would be based entirely on the Bible but set in the late twentieth century. The wealthy promoters, from the Bible Belt in the south of the United States of America, insisted on one condition: the literal teachings of the Bible were not in any way to be altered or edited. If the Bible said that people could be possessed by demons and that those demons could be driven out by priests, as the disciples of Christ, then it must remain so. The same rule applied to every other passage. The newspaper has yet to be published.

But can we really justify the belief in possession this late in the twentieth century? The behaviour and words of the candidate for exorcism are often the sole evidence that he or she is possessed. Symptoms include violent, unusual movements, shrieking, groaning and uttering disconnected or strange words to be found in no vocabulary. Sometimes a normally pious member of a religious community becomes incapable of prayer, swears and blasphemes, or exhibits terror or hatred at the mention of Christ, the appearance of sacred persons like priests and nuns or objects such as crucifixes and icons.

Scientists and clergy continue to argue. Christians insist that these cases are subject to a superior outside influence or cause. Many doctors believe equally strongly that they are either the work of imitators and attention-seekers or psycho-physical peculiarities which can and should be treated by medicine or by counselling from social psychologists. Curiously, there are today quite a number of priests who are also medically qualified psychiatrists and they often see links between demonic possession and epilepsy, hysteria, sleepwalking, schizophrenia and other forms of natural illness.

Different churches among different races interpret possession in various ways. In some communities, a person who has committed some sin or spiritual transgression is regarded as ill by their religious community. To be cured, he or she must confess and offer some recompense or sacrifice for the offence. In other beliefs, the possessed person is seen as an intermediary between spirits and humans who is able to diagnose and heal people afflicted by offensive spirits. In such cases the medium uses auto-hypnosis to put him or herself into a trance, helped by drugs, drumming or collective hysteria among the congregation. He appears genuinely insensible to ordinary activity, energy or other stimulus. Fakers have been known.

On the other hand there is a belief that exorcism can include, besides a cure, a form of religious ecstasy offering a mystical satisfaction and psychological release from mental disturbance.

Whatever the answer, demonic possession has been known and accepted among both civilised and primitive peoples from the ancient Greeks and early Chinese dynasties to Western Europeans and North Americans. Some communities encourage possession cults, even within the Christian Church, like the Voodoo Christians of Haiti. Their beliefs were originally (and still are in some places) a combination of Roman Catholicism and African animism. Voodoo, which is a term used loosely as a synonym for black magic and practices usually associated with witchcraft, is really a system of interrelated cults centred on Haiti and owing much to the beliefs of slaves brought there from Africa in the seventeenth and eighteenth centuries.

The poor, ill-educated and unemployed people of Haiti are prey to many influences. Some 80 per cent of Haitians are Roman Catholic, 10 per cent are Protestant and 75 per cent of the population practise voodoo. In that atmosphere of competitive devout religion, the churches are trying to wipe out voodooism. Catholics and Protestants have been accused of destroying people and sacred property. Catholic lay workers fired temples, a parish priest burned voodoo drums, an essential part of voodoo ritual. The Bureau of Ethnology in Haiti takes the view that many Catholic, Protestant and voodoo *hougans* (priests) and *mambos* (priestesses) are involved in supporting each regime, no matter how oppressive the regimes are.

Voodoo is a mixture of superstition, magic, witchcraft, even serpent-worship, encompassing both pagan and Christian beliefs. Critics dismiss possession among believers as delusion and hysteria. But possession by good and evil spirits is essential to voodoo belief and involves individual and collective trances and appeals to the supernatural being to free the possessed from evil spirits.

The last thing that the Haitians need is a religious war, but then – at least according to demonologists – where else would the Devil set to work except in a place where possession cults are actively encouraged?

Anyone in any doubt about the prevalence of possession cults has only to look at the international popularity and the apocalyptic demise of Jonestown, Guyana, and of the fortress of the Branch Davidians in Waco, Texas. The adherents of both cults chose their belief in Doomsday, accepted instruction and died in mass murder and suicides. And just as the last was about to be forgotten another possession cult took its place.

The Order of the Solar Temple, founded by Julien Oregas, a former Nazi Gestapo officer, ended in another mass murder and suicide in October 1994. Five houses in Switzerland and Canada belonging to the order were booby-trapped to erupt in flames automatically when a telephone call was made to each of them. Who is to say that the instigators of this tragedy were not demonically possessed?

The profusion of home-grown religions that have sprouted like spring wheat in the United States has been rivalled, if not superseded, by the mushrooming of cults in Europe. On the verge of a new millennium Europe appears to be an even grander supermarket of salvation than California ever was.

Intensive research would be required, particularly through the charity commissioners in Britain and similar agencies in other countries, to discover the definitive position. While traditional churches lose influence, religious cults are attracting followers across Europe. Professor Rodney Stark, who occupies the chair of sociology and comparative religion at Washington University, reported for the Institute for the Study of American Religions that France has the highest number of cults, 800 against Britain's 604, America's 425, Switzerland's 108, 57 in Sweden and 3 in Iceland. In an article in the *Journal for the Scientific Study of Religion* he reported that the 18 nations of western and southern Europe were home to 1,317 known cults, far more than the 425 identified in the USA. Even that figure is likely to be conservative: the true number of Euro-cults is probably far higher, for most are by modern definition secret societies. 'Compared with the United States,' says Professor Stark, 'Europe is awash with non-standard religious movements.'

Sanitised Switzerland's high cult rating has mystified many experts, but that country attracts money, and non-taxable money at that. Besides, historically it provided a refuge for Calvin, the French-born leader of the Reformation in Geneva and pioneer of Presbyterianism.

The American-based Church of Scientology and the Unification Church of South Korea have made inroads, not without difficulty, in Britain and other parts of Europe, but most Euro-cults are of local origin. One of the fastest growing in Britain is the Jesus Army, the recruiting arm of an evangelical Baptist sect. Some 2,200 of their troops, mostly young men wearing combat fatigues, hunt for converts at rock concerts and pop festivals. They live communally, believe in celibacy and refuse all drugs, nicotine and alcohol.

Crying out for an answer, though, is the question why so many Europeans are searching for salvation far, far from the beaten path of established religion. Why have so many apocalyptic cults, promising death on an early Judgement Day, succeeded in attracting so many people? And if all these cults are for the good, is this why the pervasive interest in evil and the demonically possessed remains constant, if not higher than ever before?

The truth is that the so-called age of reason and enlightenment has robbed the mainstream churches of their mysticism and sacredness. The rootless society has sought refuge in other beliefs. The collapse of communism and the erosion of the welfare state have left many people feeling vulnerable, with no one to turn to and no one on whom to lean. And as the traditional churches lose their authority, the cults have invaded the main ground to fill what they see as a spiritual vacuum.

The new religions may help to fill this vacuum but no matter how attractive their paradise, neither they nor the denominations they have tried to replace have so far satisfactorily explained a new concept of evil, or a way of combating it or preventing people from becoming demonically possessed.

There will never be total agreement on the subject. But then, truth is seldom pure and never simple. It is hoped that at the end of this work the reader will be better able to understand what it is to be possessed by devils – be they human or be they supernatural.

Brian McConnell
Dulwich Village
London
February 1995

1

Bad Luck Of The Devil

The Devil divides the world between
atheism and superstition.
G. Herbert, *Outlandish Proverbs,* 1640

If we think the Devil does not exist, why do we keep talking about him? We use exclamations like 'Good God!', 'God Almighty!', 'Jesus Christ!', 'Jesus wept!', 'Holy Mary!', 'Holy Mother of God!' in wonderment, surprise, shock, condemnation or just as oaths to punctuate our dialogue. How many more times do we call up the name of the Devil, or his many aliases? 'Go to the Devil!' we cry in anger to an enemy, or direct him to the flames of the bottomless pit: 'Go to hell!', sometimes almost without thinking. They are all oaths, made more or less universally acceptable by common usage and the passage of time.

Yet how strange it is that in all the popular opinion polls of what we believe, our faith in God remains the highest, in the 70 or 80 per cent-plus range. Our belief and disbelief in Satan fumbles around the 50/50 mark. Yet we still call him up more frequently to curse or otherwise decorate our language.

That is because we subconsciously fear the Devil and our references are a tribute to that dread. We are mesmerised and obsessed by him. And that is only a step away from being possessed by him.

'Men, women and the Devil are our three degrees of comparison,' according to the adage. Gather in company and someone will approach and say, even in fun, 'If only the Devil could cast his net now . . .' The speaker is saying that the Devil is alive and well and living very close. He is seldom out of our minds or off our tongues. 'Talk of the Devil and he'll appear' is the rejoinder.

'The Devil always leaves a stink behind him,' people say, and because he always takes advantage of the disadvantaged, 'The Devil wipes his tail on the poor man's pride.' For the unthinking,

'Idle brains are the Devil's workshop'. Hence 'The Devil finds work for idle hands' and 'Needs must when the Devil drives.'

How well he tempts us. Shakespeare's *Othello* is often quoted: 'You are one of those who will not serve God, if the Devil bid you.' Others warn of temptation: 'Beware of the Devil, because he who sups with the Devil should have a long spoon.' In any case, 'Where the Devil cannot come, he will send.' The Devil is all-seeing. The saying 'When the devil is blind' means never.

The Bard touched popular prejudices when he wrote, 'Now I understand the Devil understands Welsh,' and warned, 'Set a beggar on horseback and he'll ride to the Devil.' Some say, 'He'll ride to the gallows.'

'The Devil looks after his own,' we sneer in jealous mock-praise of someone's good fortune. This light critical tone masks our deep-rooted fear of the Devil, tinged with an attitude that we can do little or nothing about him. We readily use phrases like 'Devil-may-care', meaning reckless; 'Let the Devil take the hindmost,' when fleeing from an unpopular situation; 'The Devil dances in an empty pocket,' a criticism of the spendthrift. For those who desperately hang on to their money, 'The Devil lies brooding in a miser's chest,' and when someone is too mean to pay his share, 'The Devil has deep pockets.'

We warn the young about staying out late until 'the Devil's dancing hour' and others about 'leading the Devil's own dance' of endless trouble. Beware the danger of gambling with dice – 'the Devil's bones' – or playing cards, 'the Devil's picture book'.

The Devil's capacity for wickedness is reflected in the proverb, 'It is easier to raise the Devil than to lay him,' and there is resignation in the warning about the Devil's different disguises: 'Better the devil you know than the devil you don't.'

Our principal bogeyman has in fact become decidedly familiar, even matey, an everyday acquaintance, almost without us realising it. His name is not used only in everyday speech: the whole or the entirety of anything is 'the Devil and all'. When we are in difficulty we use his name to illustrate dilemmas, like 'between the Devil and the deep blue sea' – the 'devil' in this naval context being a danger water-level mark on the side of a ship.

Many popular superstitions, divinations, spells, cures, charms, signs and omens, rituals and taboos have emerged through the ages and still linger, all with Lucifer's name attached to them. When we sneeze, for instance, we think we are ridding ourselves of the Devil rather than germs. We say, 'Bless you!' to the sneezer in prayer to rid him of the Evil One. Remember, too, the rhyme, 'Sneeze on Sunday, your safety seek/The Devil will have you the whole of the week.' And the simple gesture of putting one's hand over one's mouth when yawning originally had nothing to do with politeness, hiding one's teeth or dentures or tonsils, or keeping in the germs, but was a habit formed in childhood. An adult hand would make the sign of the cross and close its mouth when a baby yawned, to stop the Devil getting in.

The colour black, about whose connotations the race-conscious are so alarmed, owes its evil reputation to the fact that it has been the Devil's colour, certainly since Virgil's time (70–19 BC). The greatest Roman poet refers to this in the *Aeneid*. The Devil is generally supposed to be a black man and has appeared thus in many artists' impressions through the ages. This superstition still lingers in many parts of the country where, if people see a black man, they turn right around to rid themselves of the bad luck he brings. Yet there is a corollary, a widespread belief that to touch a Negro brings good luck.

Sir John Graham Dalyell, in *Darker Superstitions of Scotland* (1834), wrote that 'if black is a mystical colour in Scotland, it has always been in combination with the metamorphoses of Satan, or his imps, as a black dog, as a black cat, or a black cock'. In Weardale, County Durham, there is a superstition that a possessed person can acquire salvation by giving Belial something black when he appears – a black hen, a black dog or a black cat, for example.

Folklore, the journal of the Folklore Society, once told the story of a fisherman from Banff, Aberdeen, who was having a poor herring season. His son had a black rabbit which, he decided, must be at the root of all the evil. The fisherman secretly killed it. We do not know if his luck changed. C. Oman tells us in *Oxford Childhood* (1976): 'We all gave her [the Scottish nanny] the presents we had made and she went off resignedly saying she knew her stay would not be for long since she had seen a black pig at the station somewhere on her journey south.'

In Gaelic the black beetle, *dharrig dhael*, literally means 'black Devil', the darkest object in creation. If you kill him with the thumb of your right hand before he cocks his tail, you will be forgiven the Seven Deadly Sins. In Ireland the beetle is considered to be unlucky and the faithful believe that it betrayed Our Lord. When the insect is seen in County Tyrone, Northern Ireland, people utter a reminder to imaginary Roman soldiers with the words, 'He went that way,' while pointing in the opposite direction to Gethsemane.

All around us are the geographical marks attributed to the Devil: the Devil's Arrows, the ancient monoliths in Yorkshire; Devil's Bridges across the River Mynach in Wales and the River Lune at Kirkby Lonsdale, Cumbria; the Devil's Causeway, the old Roman road which runs to Hadrian's Wall in Northumbria; the Devil's Chair atop the Slipperstones at Minsterley, Shropshire; the odd Devil's Chimney on Leckhampton Hill, Cheltenham Spa, Gloucestershire; the dolmen which form the Devil's Den near Marlborough, Wiltshire; the seven-mile earthwork known as Devil's Ditch at Newmarket, Suffolk; Devil's Dykes – the earthwork at Garboldisham, Norfolk, and the 700-foot beauty-spot near Brighton, Sussex; the Devil's Jumps, the three curious hills at Frensham, Surrey; the Devil's Kitchen at Nant Ffrancon Pass (3,263 feet) in Snowdonia; the deep combe of the Devil's Punchbowl at Hindhead, Surrey; the three stones known as the Devil's Quoits at Stanton Harcourt, Oxfordshire; the steep one-in-four Devil's Staircase hill at Abergwesyn, Powys; and Devil's Water, which flows into the River Tyne near Corbridge, Northumbria.

There are also named geographical oddities like the Devil's apron strings, batch, bog, book, chains, doors, fingerprints, footprints, frying pan, fruit, gallop, glove, grave, hills, hoofmarks, hopscotch, jumps, mustard pot, lime kiln, neck collar, plants, road, stone, thunderbolts, toenails, tor and well.

Long before such peaks and troughs, earthworks and monuments and the like were named, the Devil was blamed or credited for their creation. He was sometimes merely a giant, a Robin Hood or some other local hero or anti-hero who used his supernatural strength and ability to mould every strange feature of the landscape.

Many such landmarks carry their own special legends and beliefs. Local tradition has it that the great cleft in the Sussex Downs south of the village of Poynings was dug by the Devil. The enthusiasm of the Sussex people for religion made him decide to drown them all by digging a ditch through to the sea. As he reached the halfway-mark an old woman rushed up the hill with a lighted candle and a sieve. The light woke the cock, which began to crow, and the Prince of Darkness, seeing the candle through the sieve, thought the sunrise was upon him and fled.

The Devil's Bridge across the River Mynach at Bryn Garv actually comprises three bridges built close together where they cross a deep gorge. According to local legend, the lowest was built by the Devil when an old woman's cow became stranded on the other side of the gorge. He appeared and promised to build her a bridge if he might own the first creature to use it. She agreed but when the bridge was built she cunningly threw a piece of bread across it. Her dog ran after the bread and Satan, unwittingly, became the owner of the dog while the old woman went home happily with her cow.

Some legends gave rise to popular commemorative customs, most of which have now vanished. One notable exception is the

Helston Furry or Floral Dance, held every eighth of May, when the streets are decked with May flowers and the inhabitants dance through the streets in their finest clothes. It is the Feast of the Apparition of St Michael the Archangel, patron saint of the parish. One version of the legend says that he fought the Devil for possession of the town. St Michael took refuge on St Michael's Mount, near Marazion. The Devil flung the great stone that sealed the mouth of hell after him but it landed nine miles short, in the yard of what is now the Angel Hotel. The town then took the name Helston or Hell-stone. Part of the stone can still be seen and since St Michael protected the people, generations of them have continued to dance in thanksgiving.

Fruit-pickers will not eat blackberries after Michaelmas (29 September) not because they will be soured, out of season or past their picking date but because of the widespread belief that the Arch Fiend has cast his club, his cloven foot, his poisoned paw or his tail over them or spat on them. The Church also teaches us to always carry holy bread, *panem benedictum*, on such outings, journeys and enterprises to ensure that such unclean spirits are kept away.

Gardeners know that the root of the Devil's-bit scabious was used as a treatment for many ailments. The Devil was supposed to be so concerned that it might banish illness altogether that he bit off the end of the root, leaving only the truncated stump which remains for all to see. We may laugh, but the story still exists, even if the literal belief in it does not. Nigella or love-in-the-mist is partly hidden by leafy bracts and is also known as Devil-in-a-bush. Look at the flower sideways and you can see the Devil's horn, which becomes more conspicuous as the seed pods form.

The prickly poppy (properly *Argemone mexicana*) is naturally the Devil's fig. And the summer-flowering oplopanax variety known botanically as *O horridus* is similarly dubbed the Devil's club.

The Devil was never out of our customs and traditions. When new churchyards or burial grounds were brought into use in the last century, no one wanted to be the first to be interred there. The relatives of the dead would be anxious to make alternative funeral arrangements for the simple reason that the soul of the first to be buried in a particular place was thought to constitute a tithe, or tax, payable to the devil. At Loudon in Ayrshire, villagers once stopped a passing funeral and abducted the corpse to inter in their new burial ground to ensure that it was officially opened by someone else.

When the dead were buried salt was sprinkled on their coffins, as it is at exorcisms, to prevent the Evil One, who cannot abide salt, from seizing the souls of the departed. In some churchyards, black dogs were buried in patches where there were no other graves in the belief that the Devil would think that the animals, his demons, had already done their work.

Many churches in Britain are thought to have been resited during building operations due to the interference of Lucifer. Workmen would find that overnight he had removed their building tools to other sites, where they would eventually erect the holy places.

Not all superstitions involving the host of hell are negative. The idea that it is lucky for a baby to cry during its christening stems from the custom of exorcism. It was still included in the Anglican Church in the first prayer book during the brief reign (1547–53) of King Edward VI (son of Henry VIII and Jane Seymour, who died at the age of fifteen) and is still commonly observed in the baptism services of the Roman Catholic Church. When the Devil is going out of a possessed person – and the child is reckoned to be possessed until freed of the evil spirit through baptism – he is believed to leave with reluctance.

St Mark's Gospel (ix, 26) says, 'The spirit cried, and rent him sore, and came out of him: and he was as one dead.' So the tears and struggles of an infant in the arms of the priest, a perfect stranger in ecclesiastical garb, were held to be convincing proof that the Evil One had departed. Fundamentalists believe that the holy water used in baptism drives out the Devil. Just to make sure, in Ireland a nurse used to pinch the child to make it cry to evidence that the Prince of Darkness was being expelled.

The habit of keeping an ashen faggot from a Christmas fire and hanging it on the wall to use for lighting the fire the following Yuletide is based on the belief that it will keep the Fiend from causing mischief throughout the intervening year. We know from texts printed by Caxton (circa 1422–91) that church bells were rung in times of trouble, thunder, tempest, storm and man-made outrage to keep away wicked spirits. A vicar of Upton Grey, Hampshire, in the twentieth century corrected his sexton for using only the passing bells and told him to ring both the passing bells and the tenor bell because some demons are frightened by some bells and some by others. Ringing all of them would ensure success.

Sailors and fishermen, who are among the most superstitious creatures, dislike having clergymen on board their vessels. They believe that they tempt fate and that Davy Jones, a corruption of *duppy*, West Indian for devil, and Jonah, the devil of the deep, would do anything to snatch a dog-collared passenger. As a result, Royal Naval personnel would go to any lengths once they were at sea to avoid meeting the ship's chaplain on the voyage. Similarly, fishermen believe that the presence of a clergyman prompts the Common Enemy to frighten away the fish, which means a small catch.

After Samuel Pepys wrote in his diary in 1663 that he was vexed when his wife used the word 'devil', it became for many years a taboo word. When it was used in churches in north Wales, congregations used to join in a universal stamping of feet and spitting in disgust at the evil spirit. More recently, in spite of the fact that the Devil has given his name to so many geographical points, a woman at Devil's Bridge, Dyfed, objected to a visitor calling it by its name. She preferred *pont y gwr drwg*, the bridge of the Evil One or the wicked man. In the Orkneys, rather than 'devil' the spirit is referred to as the Old Child of Sorrow and Ill Health.

Clearly, in former times fear of the Devil was more real than it is today. Yet even in this century, farmworkers ploughed crooked furrows deliberately so that the wretch would not be able to see where the crops would grow and blight them. Householders would draw elaborate and intricate chalk patterns round the doorways of their homes to stop the Devil creeping in. They had to make sure there was no gap or interruption in the work round every step, doorpost and lintel which might permit entry.

Horseshoes still hang in many homes to protect the inhabitants from Satan. According to fable, St Dunstan, a farrier, was asked by the Devil to shoe his single cloven hoof. Recognising his customer, Dunstan gave him so much pain that the Evil One screamed for mercy. The saint agreed to stop torturing him providing the Devil promised never again to enter a house where the horseshoe was displayed.

Mistletoe is hung in houses at Christmastime after the fashion of the Druid belief that it kept away evil spirits. The monkey-puzzle tree offers similar protection. Children are taught never to speak while passing such a specimen out of respect for its complicated network of branches, which protect it from the Prince of Guiles. Fenland folk reckon that if you plant one by a graveyard it will inhibit the attempts of the Devil, hiding in the branches, to watch a burial for the purpose of body- or soul-snatching.

The *Malleus Malificaraum* (the Devil's Handbook) says:

> The stars can influence the devils themselves. [This is proved by the fact that] certain men who are called Lunatics are molested by devils more at one time than at another; and the devils would rather molest them at all times, unless they were deeply affected by certain phases of the Moon.

Proverbs and rhymes forbid cutting hair or paring nails on a Friday – because Christ's crucifixion was on Good Friday – or on a Sunday, the day of rest. Both are likely to invoke the Devil. So people recite, 'Friday's hair and Sunday's horn/Goes to the devil on Monday morn.'

The noise made on New Year's Eve is not merely jollification fuelled by alcohol. Ringing bells, clanging dustbin lids, bread bins or milk cans, beating dried cowhides, marching round the streets singing and shouting, firing shotguns and maroons and hooting sirens have a common original purpose: to drive out evil spirits and demons – although few in the West would admit that they are copying the much older banging-out celebrations of the Chinese.

No one was to go gathering nuts instead of going to church on Holy Cross Day, Holy Rood Day or Rood Mass (14 September), for they were bound to see a tall man in black with cloven feet. Sometimes he would hold the bough for the nut-collectors before taking their harvest.

Parsley has been described as an uncanny herb and was supposed to need to be sown nine times before it would flourish. It goes to the Devil, who controls it nine times before it comes back. Others say only the wicked can grow it.

The Devil is no doubt a thief. That is why, if you mislay or lose something, you should stick a pin in a cushion or in the padding of a chair or settee and say, 'I pin the Devil.' Before you know it, the missing object will be found.

A ritual that refers especially to reactions to the deranged or demonically possessed was described by Theophrastus (319 BC): 'If he sees a maniac or an epileptic man, he will shudder and spit into his bosom.' Similarly, Theocritus (275 BC) said, 'To avoid the evil eye, I spat thrice in my breast.' West Country people believe that if you meet the Devil you can make him instantly disappear by spitting over his horns. They also believe that they can cut him in half with straw!

Country folk fear some birds, notably the swift. Their local names for the creatures are all demonic: deviling, devilet, sker-devil, screech-devil, black swallow and devil bird. If farmers do not scare them off their land, their crops and livestock will suffer.

Henry Bourne, the eighteenth-century curate of All Saints, Newcastle, said that such superstitions were the 'product of heathenism' and the 'invention of the Devil'. He added:

> The observations of omens, such as the falling of salt, a hare crossing the way, of the dead-watch, of crickets, are sinful and diabolical. For by observations such as these, the parishioners

are the slaves of superstition and sin.

On the other hand, if a preacher did not tell his flock how to defeat the Devil, they would be bound to invent methods of their own, even if they were mere superstitions. If lessons are not clear, pupils will find their own explanations. In these circumstances, once the Devil was planted in the minds of people, there had to be a way to drive him out. Exorcism was the answer.

Calling [illegible]

(The [illegible]
to [illegible]
[illegible]
[illegible])

Having [illegible] that [illegible]
living [illegible] to [illegible]
look like, how [illegible]
of demiurges [illegible]
essential [illegible]
mythology [illegible]

The Evil One [illegible]
Vitra and Indra, the [illegible]
Prometheus and Zeus [illegible]
tempted Buddha and [illegible]
ian captivity [illegible]
to the Christians.

The writers of the O[illegible]
god of the Phoenicians [illegible]
bearer of morning star [illegible]
he was cast out of [illegible]
Muslims [illegible] by Allah [illegible]
under different [illegible]
the Gospels of Mark [illegible]
species – 200 of them [illegible]
celestial [illegible]
and fallen for the [illegible]
as belonging to the [illegible]
thrones, dominions, [illegible]

2

Calling Old Nick Names

*[The saint's] temptations were numerous;
day and night the demons varied
their snares. How often when he
lay down did naked women
appear to him.*
St Jerome's *Life of St Hilary*, circa AD 390

Having established that the Devil is alive and well in our minds and living very close to them, we should know whence he came, what he looks like, how he is dressed, how he will behave. In classical cases of demonisation, the possessed seem remarkably agreed on the essential details but how they evolved is a fascinating tapestry of mythology, fable, teaching and invention.

The Evil One has appeared in all the mythologies, as the Hindu Vitra and Indra, the Persian Ahriman and Ormuzd, the Greek Prometheus and Zeus and the Scandinavian Loki. In India he tempted Buddha and moved to Persia, where the Jews in Babylonian captivity blended him with their own Satan and handed him on to the Christians.

The writers of the Gospels identified him with Beelzebub, the fly god of the Phoenicians (Matthew xii, 24). As Lucifer, the light-bearer or morning star, known to both Jewish and Christian writers, he was cast out of heaven because of his envy of man, as was the Muslim Elbis by Allah. There was not one devil, though, but many, under different names, demons and legions of demons, as told of in the Gospels of Mark and Luke. They were given classes and categories – 200 of them, according to the Jews – and since they were celestial mutineers who had hankered after the daughters of Eve and fallen for the embraces of earthly women, they were identified as belonging to the ninth order of angels, cherubim, seraphim, thrones, dominions, principalities, powers, virtues, angels and archangels. Satan was supposed to be a cherub, Lucifer a seraph.

Given the complicated nature of mythology, legend and tradition, it is not surprising that a whole series of writers and poets tried to interpret the origins, failings, powers and responsibilities of the demons. We owe our non-Biblical image of Satan very much to the portrayal in John Milton's *Paradise Lost*. Elizabeth Barrett Browning equated devils with Greek gods; Byron, Shelley and Swinburne were all so impressed with Satan that they also attempted to vindicate him.

How many demons were there? If the Biblical phrase 'We are legion' is taken literally, that means the equivalent of the Roman legion of 600 soldiers, but other authors have either multiplied them to absurdity or reduced them to manageable figures. Washington Irving gave them 'various names', Shelley made them 'senseless and shapeless', Coleridge and Emerson turned them into geniuses.

Many other writers vied to name the most and nicknames began to appear – Old Horny, Old Hairy, Black Bogey, Black Jack, Black Man – and occupations, like the Baker, who tends the furnaces for bread as if he were keeping the flames of hell burning. New Testament chroniclers had the Devil as the Accuser of the Brethren, the Adversary of the Almighty, the Angel of the Bottomless Pit, the Ape, the Archangel Ruined, Arch Fiend, the Bad Man, Beast, the Black Archangel, the Dark Son of the Night, the Dog, the Deceiver of Mankind, the Dragon, Enemy of Mankind, the Genius of Evil, Spirit of Evil, Malignant Spirit, Unclean Spirit, Father of Lies, Father of Iniquity, Foul Fiend, Genius of Evil, Great Dragon, the Grim Gentleman Below, Infernal Rival, Liar, Lying Spirit, Father of Lies, Prince of Darkness, of Devils, of Hell, of Princes, the World, the Powers of the Air, the Crooked Serpent, Infernal Serpent, Murderer, Piercing Serpent, the Roaring Lion, the Spirit That Denies, That Worketh in the Children of Disobedience, Tempter, Tormentor and the Great Worm . . .

Britons, as royalists, mocked him as the Infernal Majesty, scholars as the Deuce, a corruption of the Latin *deus*, and Americans as Old Hick, Little Dick and Lusty Dick whence they took the phrase 'what the Dickens!' – not, as is sometimes supposed, from Charles Dickens. Nick and Old Nick come, as is mentioned elsewhere, from Niccolo Machiavelli, the Italian statesman whose principles of convenience became identified with those of the Devil.

Any doubt that he could appear in whatever form he chose was removed in earliest times. St Paul said he could transform himself into an angel of light; Thomas Cranmer, burned at the stake by Mary Queen of Scots, that he could appear as Christ himself; Timon of Athens that he could be in 'all shapes that man goes up and down in', and of either sex. He could wear Christ's crown and adopt his former bearing as an angel. As part of his role to represent physical ugliness and moral evil, he would assume any guise that would instil the greatest fear in the beholder. In addition, 'The devil hath power to assume a pleasing shape,' according to Shakespeare in *Hamlet.*

But, as his nicknames implied, he also took on the role of dog, dragon, roaring lion, serpent, wolf and inhabited an elephant. Students of folklore picked up the belief from Russian Nikolai Gogol's 1830 story 'St John's Eve' that if people wished to see the Devil as he really is they should stand near a mustard seed at midnight on that Christian feast. Sir James Frazer, (1854–1941) in *The Golden Bough* suggested that this was because the Prince of Darkness might be attracted on earth by the warm mustard in the chilly air.

The superstition that a black dog presages disaster or tragedy dates from Cornelius Agrippa (1486–1535), the sceptical philosopher and mediaeval magician, who was accompanied by the Devil in the shape of a black dog. As the guardian of hell, Beelzebub assumed the form of the three-headed dog, Cerberus, who, in Greek mythology, guarded the entrance to Hades. More often he represented the satyr, the Greek woodland god, sometimes with horse's ears and tail, sometimes with goat's ears, tail, legs and budding horns, more often than not half human to represent a lustful or sinful man.

Nor should anyone be surprised that even late in the twentieth century, those possessed by the Devil see themselves or are seen by others to be accompanied by the Devil's historic accomplices, particularly fat flies, cats, bats or a winged dragon or serpent. Sometimes the serpent appears with a woman's head. Artists have added to this picture so that when the Devil appears on canvas in human form he combines the head of an elephant, camel, pig or bird covered with thick hair resembling serpents, the ears of an ass, mouth and teeth of a lion, beard and horns of a goat, bull or stag, wings of a bat, long tail of a dragon, claws of a tiger, feet of a bull, horse, goat or cock. Sometimes one foot has a claw, the other a hoof.

In the form of a serpent, the head is that of a woman. Most of the adopted forms are to be found in the Bible: the dog appears in Philippians and Revelations, the dragon in Revelations, the worm in Isaiah and St Mark's Gospel, the wolf in the Acts of the Apostles, and the lion in St Peter's Epistle to the Romans and again in Revelations.

The Devil usually appears clad in black, sometimes red, and often has a flame-coloured beard. While white people regard him as black, West Africans portray him as white, Orientals say he is red. The Italians prefer yellow for infamy, the Spaniards green, because it was the battle colour of the Moorish invaders, and the French blue because the oath *sacré bleu* is in fact a euphemism for *sacré Dieu*.

There is no Biblical tradition for a black devil, but Satan appeared as a Moor or an Ethiopian in the writings of the early Church fathers and racism did the rest. He was black in colour in the Acts of the Martyrs, the Acts of St Bartholomew, and the writings of Augustine and Gregory the Great. Reginald Scot's *Discoverie of Witchcraft* (1584), John Bunyan's *Holy War* (1682), Washington Irving's *The Devil and Tom Walker* (1824), Robert Louis Stevenson's *Thrawn Janet* (1881) and Anatole France's *Le livre de mon ami* (1884) have all perpetuated the Devil as a black bogey. Scots still believe he is a black man.

Satan is also often portrayed as being thin as a rake, so that he casts no shadow, and deformed. He limps because of his fall from heaven, is hump-backed as a result of carrying sacks of people to hell. His garb is sometimes that of a priest or a monk (in sympathy with the anti-clerical feeling after the Reformation), a university scholar in cap and gown or a barrister in wig and gown. Victorian novelists portrayed him as extremely noble, dignified and gallant, the perfect gentleman in manners and conversation, the perfect impersonation of manhood, leaving just a whiff of suspicion that he was a conman.

Both Old and New Testaments refer to people burning in hell in a furnace or pool or lake of fire. Jews believe that hell is both fire and water. Even in contemporary cases of possession, the exorcists confirm the stench of sulphur, which is the modern term for the pitch and brimstone used for burning the damned in hell which features in Isaiah and Revelations. This was underlined in Dante's *Inferno*, for which he took descriptions from mythology. The Roman Catholic Church's image of hell comes from the *Aeneid* of Virgil, who lived from seventy to nineteen years before Christ.

Another characteristic common to the possessed and the inhabitants of hell is that they grind their teeth. Christ told in St Matthew and St Luke's Gospels of a 'gnashing of teeth', which has been interpreted as chattering rather than grinding. And St Tertullian and St Jerome suggested that this is caused by hell featuring places of extreme cold as well as areas of burning heat. Modern scholars take these opposites to represent the different interpretations of people of all races, depending on whether they hail from warmer or colder climates.

Where exactly is this infernal region? Most races believe it is in graveyards, hence the legend of the Devil trying to steal the souls of the newly dead. Hebrews and Arabs believe it is in the desert, where the hermit saints were tempted at night by the Devil in the guise of naked women. Many claim that the place of torment is 'in the north'. Biblical figures thought all evil came south from Babylon to Judah. This vague geographical reference to the 'north' has been used by Goethe and Milton. Guernsey people indicate a region described by Victor Hugo as the Ortach Rocks in the Norman Archipelago between Aurigny and the Caskets. Cornish people believe it is further north still. Churches are still built so that the north is to the left on entering, a traditional right-wing political reference to the opposition. In the past the northern section of graveyards was often reserved for suicides.

Others have suggested particular cities. Dublin was nominated as the boundless pit by William Dunbar, the Scottish poet, and his fellow countryman Robert Burns. Théophile Gautier, the French romantic poet, was just one of many of his compatriots to insist that the place of the damned was, in fact, Paris.

As for the devils themselves, they appear to have an order which is a mockery of that in heaven. Some say demonologists gathered all the information on the beaten and scattered army of demons and reorganised them into some form of parliament or hierarchy. Writers have always been interested in the Devil. Winkyn de Worde, the early printer who operated from the site of St Bride's Church in Fleet Street, London, produced a metrical tract called *The Parliament of Devils* in 1509. The expression 'printer's devil' for an apprentice in the trade is attributed to Aldus Manutius, the great Venetian printer, who towards the end of the fifteenth century employed a black slave who was supposed to have been an imp from hell. He was a good slave, and is reputed also to have inspired the phrase 'The Devil is not as black as he is painted.'

Then, the Devil was supposed to have invented printing. Heinrich Heine (1797–1856), the German romantic poet, said that printing was an art which had triumphed over faith, started doubts and revolutions, and was clearly the work of the Satanic force. When Johann Gutenberg (circa 1400–68) invented printing from movable metal type, he was promoted and financed by Johann Fust or Faust, who, because of his sorcery, gave Goethe the idea for the archetypal Devil for his masterpiece *Faust*, which, as we have seen, was imitated by many other literary and musical figures.

The Devil was also held to be the patron of lawyers. This was because when they went from their historic chambers in the Temple to lunch, they often headed for the Devil Tavern at number 2 Fleet Street, which was part of the same premises as Child and Co.

bankers, next door. For those who might want to find them in a hurry they left messages on their chambers doors, which gave rise to the popular phrase, 'Gone to the Devil'.

Religious belief in the Devil had to be maintained at all costs. The Anglican Church declared that 'a denial of the Devil's personal existence constitutes in man a notorious evil-liver and a depraver of the Book of Common Prayer'. John Wesley (1703–91), founder of English Methodism, declared, 'No Devil, no God.' Samuel Butler (1835–1902) said, 'God without the Devil is dead, being alone.' And for the best part of the twentieth century, the pulpit wits have added that Christianity without Satan would be like playing *Hamlet* without Hamlet.

Stanton Coit, who in 1888 founded the South Place Ethical Society, now in Red Lion Square, Bloomsbury, London, once said, 'We may not believe in the Devil but we must believe in a devil who acts very much like a person.' There were, of course, those who dissented. Devout Catholics believed in the Devil, some Protestants did not. A Protestant pastor was jailed for eighty days in Poland and heavily fined for denying the existence of the Devil and a candidate for Spurgeon's Baptist College was advised not to apply if he did not believe in a personal devil.

Some revisionists found a way of settling the argument by declaring conveniently that they had evidence in religious writings that the Devil was dead. In Scotland, they used to sing, 'The Devil is dead and buried in Kirkcaldy.' Breton fishermen, on the other hand, believe that after the fight with the archangel St Michael, the Evil One was buried under the mountain which faces Mont St Michel.

Writers, composers and orators have campaigned through the ages to make it easier for people to believe in the Devil for fear they may think he is no longer with us. In some versions of the famous children's Punch and Judy show, it is the Devil as well as Judy who is killed. Anatole France (1844–1924), the Nobel Prizewinner for literature, took his baby daughter to see a show which ended in the death of the Devil. France mused, 'The Devil being dead, goodbye to sin.' In this century, a puppet-master of the show had religious scruples about murdering the Devil and let him live, but the 'good' audience were so attached to this good-versus-evil Scriptural ending that they beat up the offending marionette player.

The Campaign for the Ordination of Women Priests and the individual females who have succeeded to the ministry have declined to help in this study of the possessed. One explanation put forward by a Methodist woman minister is that they may be still formulating their new liberal theology of demonology. There still remains a very real fear among people, from ignorance, legend and literature, that ever since Eve offered the apple to Adam in the Garden of Eden, woman has been the Devil's creation, accomplice, and eternal instrument of temptation. This ignores the Biblical text in Genesis, 'The seed of the woman shall bruise the head of the serpent.' It is also countered by writings that Satan mocks all human love. The Devil lures Faust through woman but she also frees him.

The suspicion that women were the creation of the Devil made them an obvious target in history when the spectre of witchcraft was raised to rally Christians against the Devil. Heathen religions long since dead and forgotten were recalled to provide much of the evidence. The old fertility rites were alleged to have been revived. The goat, which represented the Devil, was the animal which Priapus, the Greek god of vegetable and animal fertility, took on her journeys. The broom, used to carry witches on their nocturnal visits, was also a fertility symbol. The wild huntsmen who led the avenging maidens of Odin, the Scandinavian god, flew through the air on magic horses in the form of swans. The Devil was supposed to have organised such midnight rides to take the riders to their convocations. They are said to have been favoured by Diana, the classical Greek mythological huntress, sometimes portrayed as a witch; Herodias, the wandering Jewess, a queen-witch; and Marianne, the wife of Herod the Great, who brought down the wrath of God for her contemptuous treatment of the Magi when they passed Jerusalem on the way to Christ's manger.

As long ago as 1862, Jules Michelet, the French historian, saw in the witches' sabbat the first seeds of rights for women, equality between the sexes and the modern social reforms which resulted in women being admitted to the priesthood. He maintained that they surrendered to Satanism because Satan lifted them from the lowly position in which they were held by the Church. Michelet's work *La Sorcière* was translated into English by A. R. Allinson in 1904 under the title *The Sorceress: A Study in Middle Age Superstition*, but was published only in Paris.

Scriptural references to women have been copied by demonic counterparts: the Queen of Heaven is matched by the Queen of Hell, Our Lady of Sorrows by Our Lady of Darkness. In addition there is even Freya, the Devil's grandmother in Germany, and Hecate, who had powers over heaven and hell in Greek mythology, is in demonic terms the goddess of witchcraft and magic.

The imitation follows the pattern of mirror-image duplication throughout: as Daniel Defoe said, 'Wherever man erects a house of prayer, the Devil always builds a chapel.' The chief ceremony in the consecration of a new church is the casting out of Satan from the building. This accounts for the images of the Devil outside churches. A particular example is the dejected squatting horned gargoyle on the west front of the Nôtre Dame cathedral in Paris. In olden times, to pay the Devil his price for the land on which the church was built, a child was walled up in the building. Much later, on Palm Sunday churchgoers were asked to put consecrated palm crosses in their purses to drive out the Prince of Darkness.

In this fight between the Creator and the Adversary, the Common Enemy sends his legions of demons or lesser devils to gain possession of the souls of the human race. They could slip into people's bodies along with the food they swallowed – as happens in the story of demons hiding inside an apple – and cases of such 'possession' became more and more numerous. Stories abounded about the Fiend trying to take control of both sexes and all classes of people. Charles Baudelaire, the great nineteenth-century French poet, warned against thinking 'that the Devil tempts only men of genius. He doubtless scorns imbeciles, but he does not disdain their assistance.' Satan targets good people rather than bad, in churches and convents in preference to outside, clergymen and sisters of mercy rather than lay people, and when he fails he goes for the generally pious and faithful. Lord Morley (1823–1908) told a story about the Arch Enemy taking the place of a preacher in a church, an incident which is supposed to have happened in Berwick-upon-Tweed among many other places. And B. H. Berti, the Manchester poet, wrote a poem about how an alert nun tricked the Devil when he tried to assume the role of the preacher.

The Prince of Devils made many gains by exploiting the divisions in the churches. Jews believed that Christ's miracles were assisted by Beelzebub. Calvinists thought Catholics were serving Satan. Martin Luther took the view that Catholicism emanated from the Evil Spirit, declaring that even the hoods of the monks were the disguises of the Devil, and Lutherans called Calvinists 'white devils'. John Wesley, the founder of English free-will Methodism, told George Whitfield, head of Calvinist Methodists, 'Your God is my Devil.'

It is not surprising that such bitter rivalries throughout the ages were accompanied by outrageous explanations for the existence of the Devil and Satanism. They served to foster the belief in and the condemnation of witchcraft with its accompanying torture and burning at the stake of those found guilty. The more evilly outrageous the allegations, the greater the likelihood they would be believed. Magic was a heresy: the Devil was obviously a magician disguised as an animal with horns and a tail. But what kind of woman, other than someone possessed, removes all her clothes, takes a swig from a magic bottle, sits on a broomstick, flies up the chimney and disappears? Witches met Satan every 30 April, the Eve of May Day, originally the great heathen spring festival known as Toodmas in Britain and later Christianised as Walpurgis Night in Germany. Other reunions took place on 31 October (November Eve, Hallowe'en or All Hallows Eve) and in between Candlemas (2 February) and Lammas or the Gule of August (1 August). Additional gatherings were held weekly. Known as sabbats, these were not secret but public gatherings and took their name not from the Jewish sabbath but from the French *s'esbattre*, meaning to frolic. While the sabbath was puritanical, the sabbat was joyful.

Whoever invented witchcraft, Church or Devil, wanted to get in first so sabbats were held on Wednesdays (after Woden's Day or Odin's Day, the Scandinavian god who presided over banquets of those slain in battle) before Muslims worshipped Allah on Thursdays, Jews Jehovah on Saturdays and Christians their God on Sundays.

This worship by witches of the Father of Evil, which was a survival of paganism, was ignored by the early Christian Church. Only in the ninth century did the clergy reprimand their flock for their credulity. Then in the Middle Ages, when the priesthood became a hierarchy, they made witches an excuse to eliminate Satanists in a wicked persecution. In 1484, Pope Innocent VIII ordered that witches should be burned at the stake, a penalty which remained for 300 years until the eighteenth century.

Witchcraft did include hysteria, as witnessed at Salem, Massachusetts, and witch-hunting, particularly in Europe, involved inventive and lying prosecutors. Even if witchcraft did not exist in its most evil form before the Inquisition, it certainly became more polished and organised after witch-hunting ceased. It incorporated superstition, sorcery, voodooism and many other quasi-religious beliefs and is still practised in many countries.

Practitioners in the black art can always point to some Biblical reference in justification of their activities. For instance, the ancient and widespread belief in the evil eye owes its credence, perversely, to St Mark's Gospel (vii, 21–3) in which Christ said, 'From within, out of the heart of men, proceed evil thoughts, adulteries, fornications, murders. Thefts, covetousness, wickedness, deceit, lasciviousness, an evil eye, blasphemy, pride, foolishness: All these evil things come from within, and defile the man.' A further reference can be found in Matthew vi, 23: 'If thine eye be evil, thy whole body shall be full of darkness.' Christ himself gave an example of the 'evil eye' when he cursed the fig tree so that it withered, in Matthew xxi.

The evil eye was feared in France, Germany and Italy. In Naples people shunned the *jettatore*, the owner of the evil eye. Whenever he approached, the streets would clear of men, women and children. In Greece, Turkey, India and China the evil eye can harm horses and cattle, too – Virgil, the Roman poet, talks of an evil eye bewitching lambs – while in Britain it was reckoned to be cast by farmers on their rivals to harm crops. The only way to counteract the curse that could kill at a glance was by using charms and gestures, usually of an obscene kind and often involving the phallus.

It was small wonder, then, that when the public, robbed of their pagan worship, could find no satisfaction or fulfilment in Christian worship, were disadvantaged or persecuted, they turned consciously or unwittingly, with or without the encouragement of the Church, to the snares of the Devil for comfort. And as a result, some of them became possessed.

3

Witch Hunt

The devil got into the body of man,
making use of the organs of the
body at his own pleasure, for the
performance of such pranks and feats
as are far above the capacity,
strength or agility of the party
thus bewitched or possessed.
Henry More, *Antidote Against Atheism*, 1652

The parsonage or presbytery bell rings. The caller reports an illness. The voice is urgent. Someone in the background is making sounds and movements like an animal, is uncontrollable and violent. Sometimes she speaks in a gruff male voice, not her own, sometimes in a language with which neither she nor her listeners are familiar. She writhes on her belly like a snake and turns her head through 180 degrees so she is facing backwards. Her tongue is protruding by as much as eight inches. She displays abnormal, even supernatural strength, using it to break things, yet she is usually so gentle. She is also normally pretty but is now showing frightening and distorted facial expressions. She is undoubtedly troubled by spirits, by an absolute and inner possession and residence in the body of someone or something so different from the person people know. She says she has made a pact with the Devil. Now she is blaspheming and using foul language. She has been persistently ill, falling into heavy sleep and vomiting unusual objects. Like toads, serpents, worms, iron, stones or man-made objects like pins or nails. She says she has illusions caused by witches. She wants to lead a wicked life, though she is usually a good, clean-living, pious woman. Yet now she smells to high heaven. She seems just tired of living. Do you know what we should do?

In this year of hopeful grace, 1995, as we head for the second millennium, what is the answer to those who think they are possessed by the Devil and who call on the Church for help? If there is one subject from which many orthodox priests retreat faster than any other it is the matter of demonic possession. And non-religious people, atheists, agnostics, rationalists and the like, who thought they knew their subject, are not far behind in the decampment. The Devil defies them all.

For centuries it has been thought that a person who is demonically possessed suffers a complete takeover of his or her personality by a diabolical entity which enables the entity to dominate. The victim becomes, mentally and physically, the demonic being. Then as now, some blame this apparent demonic possession on bewitchment, others on hysterical fantasies, physical and mental disorders and repressed sexual desires. In the Middle Ages, Christian theologians held that possession by spirits was heresy. Unusual behaviour or change in personality was automatically diagnosed as possession by the Devil. That is why Christians relied heavily on charms and amulets as well as prayers to keep the Evil One away. The Devil either passed directly into a victim or sent demons into the victim with the help of witchcraft.

Many supporters of modern theology, particularly women ordained in the Church of England and the Campaign for the Ordination of Women Priests, seem uncertain about the existence of Satan as a person or an entity. Yet the devil refuses to go away. The first embarrassment is that there are too many unequivocal references in the Scriptures to the Evil One and to the exorcism of evil spirits to ignore. So many instances of Christ coming across those who were possessed and driving the demons from them, even instructing his disciples to do likewise, cannot just be forgotten or swept under the carpet. No clergyman or woman can easily hold up the New Testament, on which his or her whole faith is based, and pick and choose which subjects he or she believes and which he does not, those which he can explain and those on which he prefers to remain silent. This merely leaves lay folk in bewilderment.

Churchmen of all faiths, to whom we turn for explanation and help, are divided amongst themselves for various reasons. For instance, they have to distinguish between possession and obsession. Possession comes from the Latin *posidere*, 'to take possession of', and obsession from the Latin *ob*, towards, suggesting a bearing from the outside inwards. Both are considered to be states of mind in which the victim cannot be held responsible for what he says or does. In obsession, the Devil is said to besiege or sit outside the body of the afflicted. In possession, he sits within the body. Shakespeare was one of the first, apart from the translators of the Bible, to use the word 'possess'. In 1642, Bishop Montague contrasted the power of Satan to 'move and actuate' (obsess) and to 'possess and really inhabit' his victim.

Saints, because they were pure, were in former times held to be immune from possession, but the early saints, who were hermits in the Egyptian desert, first described the wiles used by the Devil to try to corrupt them in their loneliness. They suffered only obsession, just as the Devil still fastens on those who are alone, bereft of company, destitute or depressed.

St Jerome's *Life of St Hilary* (circa AD 390) tells how the saint's 'temptations were numerous; day and night the demons varied their snares. How often when he lay down did naked women appear to him.' St Athanasius (AD 298–373) describes the attack on St Anthony, 'at night assuming the form of a woman and imitating a woman's gestures to beguile him'.

Experts have looked into the whole question of involuntary possession, different from the induced trances of shamans and spiritualists, and have noted how it resembles the symptoms of epilepsy and hysteria – writhings and facial contortions, vomiting strange objects (often an intended prelude to suicide) and the lowering of the voice by several octaves.

Philosopher Henry More (1614–87), in his *Antidote Against Atheism* (1652), said that these signs were proof

> that the Devil got into the body of man, making use of the organs of the body at his own pleasure, for the performance of such pranks and feats as are far above the capacity, strength or agility of the party thus bewitched or possessed.

In the *Anatomy of Melancholy* (1621), another philosopher, Robert Burton (1577–1640), who was copied by many later authors, discussed the question of whether the Devil acts on the human mind, which affects the body, or on the body, which then affects the mind. Some demonologists, noting the unpleasant smell produced by hysterical epileptics, took the latter view. Jean Bodin, who wrote *The Demonomania of Sorcerers* (1580), thought the stench was due to the Devil assuming control of the body as if it were already a corpse. Sir Mathew Hale (1609–76), lord chief justice of England, who encouraged the persecution of witches and allowed false testimony to be given against the defendants in court, thought the malodour came from 'the sympathy betwixt the body and the soul'.

Theologians took the view that God sent the Devil to tempt his people as a lesson in the fight between good and evil; demonologists thought that witches had the same delegated power from the

Devil and could possess the souls of people. Any kind of abnormality in a child, such as a strange fit, was a cue for neighbours to immediately start a witch hunt, since witches had obviously sent their demons to inhabit and plague the child from within. Witches who sought to demonise their victims tempted them with food. Henri Bouget (circa 1550–1619), chief judge of St Claude, France, found that the Devil could hide in apples and could thus be unsuspectingly digested into the body. 'In this way,' he said, 'Satan continually rehearses the means by which he tempted Adam and Eve in the earthly paradise.' In 1585, frightened passers-by pushed into the river at Annecy, Savoy, an apple that gave out

> a great and confused noise. It cannot be doubted that this apple was full of devils, and that a witch had been foiled in an attempt to give it to someone.

Demonic possession has always been more prevalent among women than men, and particularly those who are cloistered, like nuns in convents. It would only require one hysterical nun to infect the whole flock: by direct stimulation or auto-suggestion the entire nunnery could be plagued by devils, a horror which could only be ended by exorcism. Francesco-Maria Guazzo, an early seventeenth-century friar who believed that Martin Luther was the offspring of the Devil and a nun, noted that 'those especially afflicted were bound by a vow of virginity. It was wonderful with what wiles the Devil surrounded them to deter them from chastity.'

To students of the subject, the catalogue of mass demonic possession of both sexes through Spain, then Italy, then France is so impressive that it cannot be ignored. In 1491 nuns in Cambrai in Picardy, northern France, showed superhuman strength, barked like dogs and foretold the future. One of them, Jeanne Potier, an hysterical nymphomaniac, was denounced as a witch and removed from the convent, which then resumed its normal, quiet, cloistered life. In 1550, nuns in Wertet, in the vicinity of Brabant, in Belgium, climbed trees like cats, were pinched and beaten by invisible assailants and levitated several feet in the air without doing themselves harm. A scapegoat had to be found and a reputable woman of the town was tortured into confessing that she had bewitched the convent.

At Kentorp, near Strasbourg, the 1552 possession of a group of nuns ended when their cook, Elizabeth Kama, was identified as a witch and the daughter of a witch. Pope Paul IV wanted to banish all Jews from Rome in 1554 but was dissuaded by the large number of conversions to Christianity. Eighty-two possessed women, all converts from Judaism, complicated matters by accusing their relatives of sending devils into them as revenge for their apostasy. A year later, eighty children in an orphanage in the celestial city were also possessed.

In Spain, at Xante, in 1560, some nuns bleated like sheep, tore off their veils and had convulsions in church. Their behaviour closely resembled that of the nuns at Wertet nearly ten years earlier, about whom they could not have known, and this was taken as further proof of supernatural influence.

Confessions of sexual relations with the Devil were not uncommon. Nuns at the Nazareth Convent, Cologne, in 1565 had lovers but claimed that it was the devils, masquerading as dogs, who had sex with them. This type of explanation, obtained under threat of damnation in confession, or of torture in criminal courts during witchcraft trials, produced an abundance of incidents. The combination of prurient investigators and hysterical women undoubtedly resulted in accounts which could only have come from erotic fantasies and neurotic imaginations. But this did not negate the existence of demonic possession in the minds of the majority.

A year later, thirty Dutch boys in an Amsterdam foundling hospital were possessed and under exorcism they vomited 'needles, shreds of cloth, pieces of pots, hair and glass'. No one could trace the soft, romantic night music with which lascivious devils, disguised as dogs, courted the German nuns of Oderheim on Rhine in 1577.

But the most terrible cases were undoubtedly those of nuns in France at Aix-en-Provence (1611), Lille (1613) and Loudun (1634), which are dealt with in detail in Chapter 4, and the Louviers scandal of 1642, detailed in Chapter 7.

In Protestant countries, exorcism was not practised at all for many years and the activities of an unattached preacher, John Darrell (circa 1562–1602), England's first if not official exorcist, led the Episcopal Church to forbid the practice under canon law 72. The disagreement, then as now, did not stop. Occasionally, individual clergymen spoke out, for and against exorcism, but generally they followed the dictates of their own consciences. In 1958, at the Lambeth Conference, the Church of England's 'parliament', one priest maintained that what was seen as demonic possession could be explained by mental disorders. The Anglican community had tried to reject the hypothesis that the Devil was able to enter human bodies, but opinion was never unanimous.

Darrell, from Mansfield, Nottinghamshire, who was educated at Cambridge, crossed swords with Samuel Harsnett, later Archbishop of York, over exorcism, but he defied the Church authorities, was criticised by magistrates and eventually pronounced an imposter, unfrocked and jailed for a year. Darrell's exorcisms were enhanced and made credible by his ability to play the ventriloquist and thereby to supply the demonic voice. His first venture into exorcism was performed upon Catherine Wright of Derbyshire in 1586. After a day of prayer, at the prompting of Darrell, she accused Margaret Roper of sending a demon, whom she called Middlecub, to possess her. When Catherine discovered that her father-in-law, on whom she relied for her daily bread, suspected her of making up the story, she confessed that she had faked her fits and visions. The magistrates threatened Darrell with imprisonment.

For more than a century, examples of demonic possession, believed or not, feigned or real, possession or epilepsy or hysteria, continued. The most famous cases in England were those of the Warboys Witches (1595), the Burton Boy (1597), Leicester Boy (1616), Bilson Boy (1620) and Edmund Robinson (1633), all of which we shall look at in detail in Chapter 6.

In Scotland in 1654, Master Thomas Campbell became known as the 'Glenluce Devil'. He was apprenticed to his father, a weaver, and such indentured boys were required to maintain discipline and good behaviour or give up their apprenticeships. To avoid being made to follow his father's trade he occupied his time throwing stones at doors, windows and down chimneys, cutting the threads on his father's looms, ripping clothes, pulling off bedclothes, ransacking closets, spanking younger children and starting fires. Tom convinced people that he was possessed by the Devil.

This was followed by the case of the Bargarran Imposter (1697), in which Christine Shaw, the eleven-year-old 'possessed' daughter of the laird of Bargarran near Paisley, Renfrewshire, who appeared to vomit rubbish, caused twenty-one people to be indicted for witchcraft. As a result of allegations by her and three other children seven of the accused were hanged and some of them were still alive when they were burned at the stake. Christine grew up to marry a minister of the Church and later introduced machinery to make the Bargarran thread, which led to Paisley becoming a centre for the wool trade. Patrick Morton, a youth of sixteen, read the account of the Bargarran Imposter and repeated the allegations against the Pittenweem Witches in 1704.

In Ireland in 1661 Florence Newton, billed as the 'Witch of Youghal' in County Cork, was supposed to have bewitched a servant girl and caused the death of a boy. She was given what appeared to be a fair trial, without torture and according to legal rules, but she was jailed and, it is believed, ultimately executed. A poltergeist was thought to have been responsible for the incidents which led to the imprisonment of seven witches in the Magee Island witch trial in Carrickfergus, Country Antrim, in 1711.

Parallel examples were found in Belgium, France, Germany, Norway, Sweden and the United States of America. The best known American cases are those of the Connecticut Witches (1662), the Goodwin Children (1688), Ann Putnam (1692), the Salem witch trials (1692), Mercy Short (1693) and Margaret Rule (1693).

Belief in witchcraft was taken to colonial New England by English settlers, and in the winter of 1691–2 at Salem, Massachusetts, twenty people were executed, some after being tortured, mostly by hanging, although one was pressed to death by heavily weighted planks for refusing to plead guilty or not guilty. It was America's only mass epidemic of what was believed to be possession. Not until 1957 did the state legislature declare that proceedings against Ann Pudeator and certain other persons had been shocking and the result of a wave of hysterical fear of the Devil, even though they were lawful under the province's charter. In those days the people were puritanical, beset by Red Indian marauders, intolerable British taxes, piracy, a cruel winter and an epidemic of smallpox.

Because it all began among young women residents and visitors to the house of the Reverend Samuel Parris, one of the accused witches, William Barker, was believed when he declared in a confession, 'The design was to destroy Salem village, and to begin at the minister's house, and to destroy the Church of God, and to set up Satan's kingdom.' John Evelyn, the English diarist, wrote at the time, 'Unheard of stories of the universal increase of witches in New England; men, women and children devoting themselves to the Devil, so as to threaten the subversion of the government.'

What it amounted to was the 'subversion' of a group of mere children, who were always referred to with prejudice as young unmarried women. They had merely listened to the Reverend Parris's West Indian slave girl, Tituba, telling tales of her native folklore. As a result, the two youngest girls, the parson's own daughter, Elizabeth Parris, aged nine, and her cousin Abigail Williams, aged eleven, were so emotionally excited by these get-togethers, coming at the onset of puberty, that they went into fits of uncontrollable convulsions.

Abigail was said to have been seen running to the fire and throwing fire brands around the house. Elizabeth, brought up by a strict clerical father, shrieked, romped and disrupted prayers, and flung a Holy Bible across the room. According to the evidence, they both showed defiance of the adult world, lawlessness, disobedience, flouting of authority and delinquency.

Other cases in America from 1647 were limited to New England settlements, scattered and limited. There was a slow progression of trials from 1647 to 1662 which resulted in eleven certain executions (nine women and two men) by hanging and two probable ones. According to one account, Mary Johnson, one of the convicted Connecticut witches, said that 'the devil appeared to her, lay with her, and cleared out her hearth of ashes, and hunted hogs out of the corn. She could not forbear laughing to see how he seized them about.'

Increase Mather, a Puritan minister who became President of Harvard University, and was one of the greatest Americans of the time, reported that Mother Greensmith, another witch, of Hartford, 'had had the familiarity with the devil.'

> She likewise declared that the devil first appeared to her in the form of a deer or a fawn, skipping about her wherewith she was not much affrighted, and that by degrees he became very familiar, and at last would talk with her. Moreover she said that the devil had frequently the carnal knowledge of her body. And that the witches had meetings at a place not far from her house; and that some appeared in one shape, and others in another; and one came flying amongst them in the shape of a crow.

She was executed.

A more typical and identifiable case of possession, which had parallels in many European cases before and after, was that of a sixteen-year-old girl, Elizabeth Knap, of Groton, Connecticut, who in 1671 cried out in fits and blamed a respectable woman neighbour for her affliction. According to those who had played key parts in the Salem witchcraft trials,

> she was taken after a very strange manner, sometimes weeping, sometimes laughing, sometimes roaring hideously, with violent emotions and agitations of her body. Her tongue for many hours together was drawn like a semi-circle up to the roof of her mouth, not to be removed, though some with their fingers tried to do it. Six men were scarce able to hold her in some of her fits, but she would skip about the house yelling and looking with a most frightful aspect.

Four of the six Goodwin Children, of Boston, Massachusetts, suffered epileptic fits, practised childish deceitfulness and were also condemned in 1688 as possessed. Cotton Mather, a minister like his father, Increase, found that 'nothing but an hellish witchcraft could be the origin of these maladies'. The children were two boys, aged five and eleven, and two girls, seven and thirteen, all brought up in a strict religious home. Their Irish washerwoman, Mother Goody Glover, was blamed for their devilish behaviour.

> Their tongues would be drawn down their throats pulled out upon their chins to a prodigious length. Their mouths opened unto such a wideness that their jaws went out of joint . . . and anon they would clap together again with a force like that of a strong spring lock. The same would happen to their shoulder blades, and their elbows, and hand-wrists, and several of their joints. They would at times lie in a benumbed condition, and be drawn together as those that are tied neck and heels; and presently be stretched out; yea, drawn backwards, to such a degree that it was feared the very skin of their bellies would have cracked. They would make most piteous outcries that they were cut with knives and struck with blows that they could not bear. Their necks would be broken, so that their neckbone would seem dissolved unto them that felt after it; and yet on the sudden it would again become so stiff that there was no stirring of their heads. Yea, their heads would be twisted almost round, and if main force at any time obstructed a dangerous motion which they seemed to be upon, they would roar exceedingly.

Mother Glover, who spoke only Irish, recited her prayers in Latin, and was steeped in Irish superstition and folklore, confessed very little and was condemned. Only when these cases were studied, often very many years later, was it understood that the accusations were migratory, that they had been transferred from Europe in the oral tradition of story-telling to fit any American person or place chosen.

Ann Putnam, the youngest and most precocious of the accusers in the Salem witch trials, was the daughter of the village constable who later became a judge. She was without doubt coached by her mother to give evidence. Among other things, she swore on oath that she had seen two ghosts with their bloody wounds stopped up with sealing wax.

Four years after the trials, she maintained her belief in witchcraft but acknowledged in a public confession that she had been deluded by Satan. She had, she said, 'been made an instrument for the accusing of several persons of a grievous crime, whereby their lives were taken from them.'

Mercy Short's father, mother, brother, sister and other relatives were killed by Indians at Salmon Falls, New Hampshire, in 1690. She was taken captive to Canada, rescued, and brought back to Boston, where she entered domestic service. For four months, until she underwent 'deliverance', she was subject to savage fits, behaved like a wild cat and could not be restrained even by several strong men. She would not eat for days, once fasted for fifteen days, imagined herself in a cellar where there was neither day nor night, would set her teeth, throw herself into torments, swallow pints of liquid and breathe heavily to make her abdomen swell 'just like someone poisoned by ratsbane'.

Despite her experiences, Cotton Mather blames her demonic possession on Sarah Good, one of the condemned Salem witches. Mather was sometimes suspicious of the descriptions of possession, particularly that of seventeen-year-old Margaret Rule. Her story was too similar to that of Mercy Short. They could have been describing each other.

She had spastic fits, clenched her teeth, refused food for days, gulped as if swallowing huge quantities of liquid, developed black and blue bruises as if she had been assaulted, found a small imp on her bed, produced from nowhere pins she had vomited and levitated from bed to ceiling. Like Mercy Short, she too had hallucinations of the inevitable black man or devil, but also of a white devil. Unfortunately, she made Mather suspicious when she complained that he had threatened and molested her.

Today, while the Church of England is divided to varying extents between the traditionalists and the liberals, Roman Catholic priests have fallen out over the continuation and the publicising of the ancient ritual of exorcism. The attitude of the Methodist Church is pragmatic and down to earth. The Church of Scotland, like many others, has sought independent outside expert help and remains canny on the issue.

As we shall see in later pages, the 'Satanist' trial of 1986, involving fraud, illustrated how seriously the issue is taken. A series of incidents showed that respectable, educated, intelligent, successful, wealthy people of high standing in the community believed in demonic possession and were prepared to put a great deal of energy and money into fighting it. They did not all come from the extreme fringes of the Christian faith, but they demonstrated the divide between those who are disposed to believe in possession and those who are not. The official or established churches have never universally disowned the idea, nor do the various commissions and committees of investigation they have set up from time to time. They usually take the safe and sane approach to the subject by recommending that clergy continue to seek psychiatric and spiritual remedies.

In the wake of the 1986 'Satanist' trial I have mentioned, the Church of Scotland's panel on doctrine urged the greatest possible caution before considering what it called 'unusual treatments'. The person who announces herself as suffering from possession can be assumed not to be so possessed but in need of medical help.

Mr John Allan, a lay specialist who prepared the panel's report, was sceptical. He noted how suggestion and expectation shape the behaviour of the allegedly possessed. When devils are driven out from Pentecostalists, the victims are inclined to produce an odd coughing sound. Anglicans make their bodies shake. When demons depart from charismatics they leave through the stomach.

The Church of Scotland report took the view that it was not the 95 per cent of cases of which self-deception and attention-seeking were suspected of being the cause which bothered the clergy. It was the 5 per cent whose experiences could not be dismissed. So the author remained sceptical but moved towards a liberal view by saying 'no' to the paraphernalia of mediaeval Roman Catholic exorcism, preferring an authoritative form of church blessing. He found that there are cases for calling for the 'casting out' of demons with prayer and quotes, but that as a rule of thumb, psychiatry should be considered first, exorcism second, psychiatry third.

This stance is borne out by the attention paid to cases of possession by psychiatrists and priests in mental hospitals, including those chaplains who are qualified both in religion and medicine, particularly mental health care. While psychiatry is an interpretive science, so often proved wrong, exorcism remains a phenomenon not yet capable of being adequately explained by reason or belief.

In a word beset with criminal evil, the worst excesses of man's inhumanity to man, could it be that the clergy and doctors are concentrating on a small, unrepresentative section of the community – the mentally ill, who have committed no criminal offences – and have overlooked the genuinely possessed, the serial killers of this world, for instance?

4

To Possess A Nun

[Sister Claire] fell on the ground,
blaspheming, lifting up her petticoats
and chemise, displaying her privy
parts without any shame.

Monsieur des Niau
La Veritable historie (de Loudon), 1634

Tests by doctors and priests through the ages have removed any doubt that while there are genuine demonics, there are also, as we saw in Chapter 3, examples of spurious possession. Neither real nor feigned instances are confined to individuals: mediaeval records are full of reports of whole communities being affected by the phenomenon, particularly those who lived in monastic conditions.

Many of these cases added another dimension to the debate on possession. First there was the problem of whether the demonic state could be explained in religious or medical terms or in both. For instance, why is possession so prevalent among girls reaching puberty and among isolated groups such as nuns? At the same time, such possession was said to occur in the practice of witchcraft, which had itself been promoted by the Church in the first place. In many such cases there recurred the sexual theme, the possessed being seduced by the Devil – or was it the priest? Or the Devil working through the priest?

Western Europe was well known for priestly parties in which dancing, kissing and other liberties, including seduction, were common. The licentious climate of the times permitted such *liaisons dangereuses* provided they were not complicated by allegations of witchcraft. Witches were always supposed to be possessed. Their supernatural powers, real or imaginary, proved that they were in league with the Devil. The church regarded it as its duty to put witchcraft down, by torture and burning at the stake, but a later age of reason argued – and put on the English statute book the 1735 Witchcraft Act – that since witchcraft was an imposture and a fraud, to pretend to be a witch and obtain money by witchcraft was a criminal offence. The Church, having adopted the concept of witchcraft to instil discipline in the people, regarded it with the utmost seriousness and punished it with severity.

In many of the cases doctors dignosed hysteria. Sister Jeanne Fery, an inhabitant of the war-torn Belgian town of Mons, was possessed for thirteen years, from around 1573 to 1585, by eight devils. She had been seduced by Satan when she was fourteen. From then until she was twenty-five, when she was exorcised, she suffered from hystero-epileptic fits, convulsions and delirious frenzy. The devils were described at the time as *malins esprits* and were identified as *Hérésie, Traitre, Art Magique, Béléal, Vraye Liberté, Namon, Sanguinaire* and *Homicide*.

To reduce the seizures she was given holy baths, during which she regurgitated through the mouth and nostrils 'a great quantity of filth, like hair-balls of goats and other animals in the form of hairy worms', accompanied by a horrible stench. Often, to try to rid herself of the odour, she flung herself into the nearby river.

The frenzies usually occurred between sleeping and waking. She had visions of hell, repeating parrot-fashion what she had heard in sermons and hallucinating. She saw, heard and experienced 'fire, burning sulphur, darkness and a stinking abominable smell'. Pains in her stomach were like a gnawing serpent and she confessed, 'For relief I consented to rejoin the devils, just to stop the unendurable agony.' She used filthy language and alternated between continuous sadness and great joy. When she was in despair she suffered greatly but when she was in ecstasy she could neither talk, eat nor feel any sensation or pain from her self-inflicted injuries, for which she blamed the Devil.

Her explanations sound adult, but Jeanne could revert to the true simplicity of infancy and forget all her knowledge of God, becoming incapable of articulating more complicated words than Father, Jeanne, sweet Mary, and pointing at objects around her. Sometimes she behaved like a naughty child and at others played with the statue of St Mary Magdalene like a girl with a favourite doll, 'as if she wanted to give it her breast' at feeding time. Was that possession or a phantom pregnancy?

All this was published by the Archbishop of Cambrai, François Buisseret, in 1586, along with this description of how, on 24 May 1585, Jeanne was allowed out of the hospital to hear mass. Then her torments began and she suddenly uttered an unhappy cry.

A priest found her on her knees, with the rest of her body bolt upright, transfixed into immobility, her complexion pallid and sallow, much altered, her eyes wide open and riveted on the holy statue of St Mary Magdalene above the altar.

Some time later, he saw the nun bend her body and laugh very softly to herself, remaining all the time in ecstasy with trembling, shaking her whole body and with excessive weakness, pounding of the heart. Not being able to declare by words, because of her extreme weakness, she made signs with her hand. One of the nuns rubbed her hands which had become stiff and dry like wood. A little later, still trembling, she was led to her room, and warmed in front of a fire, whereupon her debility passed slowly from her.

In Aix-en-Provence in the south of France in 1611 Sister Madeleine Demandolx de la Palud and Sister Louise Capelle accused Father Louis Gaufridi of seducing them and bewitching them. He claimed they were possessed by the Devil.

Sister Madeleine, who came from a rich and aristocratic Provence family, had been among the first to enter the Ursuline convent school at Aix in 1605, when she was twelve. She became very depressed and returned to her family home, where she met Father Gaufridi. Some two dozen women had selected him as their father confessor, and although he came from a much humbler background he was immensely popular. Six of the women were thought to be in love with him.

Father Gaufridi, who was thirty-four, visited Madeleine, often when nobody else was in the house. The head of the Ursuline convent school warned her mother and, when questioned, the girl said that the priest had 'stolen my most beautiful rose'. The mother superior of the convent to which the school was attached warned Father Gaufridi about his rumoured conduct.

When Madeleine entered the convent as a novice she confessed the priest's intimacies with her. She was promptly transferred to another convent where Father Gaufridi could not visit her. When she was sixteen or seventeen she displayed severe shaking fits and convulsive cramps and had visions of devils. Shortly before Christmas she smashed a crucifix.

Father Jean-Baptiste Romillon, the Jesuit spiritual director of the convent, decided to exorcise but the ritual was a failure. He and another priest warned Father Gaufridi about her symptoms and later questioned him about his conduct with Madeleine. He denied having had sexual relations with her.

Under exorcism she claimed he had denied God, given her a

'green devil' as a familiar and had copulated with her since she was thirteen. Later she changed her story to claim she had been only nine. She even quoted the priest as saying, 'Since I would enjoy your favours, I will give you a drink made of special powder to make sure that any babies you may get by me won't look like me. In this way, no one will suspect me of immorality.'

Sister Louise Capeau (or Capelle) was jealous of the attention being paid to Sister Madeleine so she tried to rival the other's tales of demonic possession. Sebastian Michaëlis, the grand inquisitor from Avignon, who had a reputation for savage justice and had had eighteen witches burned, was called in to conduct a public exorcism of both girls. This failed. In another ceremony, Louise revealed in a deep bass voice that she was possessed by 6,661 other devils. (Ever since the New Testament declared that 666 was the 'mark of the beast', demonologists have argued and multiplied that figure until one researcher claimed that the devils numbered more than half the population of the world.)

Louise publicly identified Madeleine's devil as Father Gaufridi. 'Thou was deceived by a priest who was thy confessor. He is of Marseilles and is called Louis,' she claimed.

The exorcists were convinced that the girls were possessed but they could not rid them of the devils. Madeleine, certified as 'no virgin', developed more manic-depressive traits – abnormal elation and pathological depression. She had visions, danced and laughed, sang love songs, and disrupted the mass by snatching birettas from the heads of priests and tearing their vestments. She told fantastic tales of witches' sabbats in which sodomy took place and children were eaten. She spat globules of frothy matter, which looked like a mixture of honey and pitch. Beelzebub, her principal devil, caused her bones to crack and grate against each other. In her paroxysm her bowels were displaced and turned topsy-turvy so that the sounds of unnatural motions could be heard. When these tortures were ended the devils were said to cast her into a deep sleep or lethargy in which she seemed quite dead.

The inquisitor took the priest and the nuns before the *parlement* of Aix to try to prove that Father Gaufridi was a sorcerer. Madeleine alternated between lucid and sane and wild and demented, accusing one day, retracting the next. She swooned for love of the priest. 'Oh! If only his tongue could bear to my ears a friendly word. What happiness!' At that she was seized by lascivious tremblings, representing the sexual act, with violent movements of the lower parts of her belly. She displayed 'Devil's marks' on her feet and under her left breast, into which the physicians stuck pins without drawing blood.

Madeleine, who twice tried to commit suicide, was eventually imprisoned because the marks on her, in other cases often claimed to be the stigmata of Christ's wounds, were held to be the Devil's marks. Although there was no independent evidence against Father Gaufridi, he was imprisoned in foul conditions and tortured until he confessed. Then he was ceremonially strangled and burned at the stake.

Two years later, in 1613, three nuns in Lille, in the Département du Nord in France, accused another of bewitching them. The possessed spoke in foreign tongues, had paroxysms and demonstrated that they had been introduced to shocking sexual orgies. Sister Marie de Sains said that on Mondays and Tuesdays, the witches copulated '*par voie ordinaire*' (in the usual way). On Thursdays, they practised sodomy.

> On this day everybody, men and women, commits the sin of the flesh in other than the vessel provided by nature. They pollute themselves in many strange and abominable ways, women with women and men with men. [On Saturdays] they have to do with all kinds of animals, like dogs, cats, pigs, goats and winged serpents.

On Wednesdays and Fridays they sang prayers to the Devil.

Again and again doubts about the veracity of the stories of possession are sparked by the impossible, in this case the suggestion that someone copulated with a winged serpent, a creature which does not exist.

Half a century later, Antoinette Bourignon (1616–80), who later became famous as a mystic, started a foundling home for fifty orphan girls and later a convent for them. When a pastor examined the thirty-two girls, aged from eight to twenty-two, on their religious beliefs, he heard them all declare

> that they had daily carnal cohabitation with the Devil, that they went to sabbats or meetings, where they ate, drank, danced and committed other whoredom and sensualities.

What had really happened was that the novices had discovered a way to exploit the credulity of their kindly founder. A thirteen-year-old girl explained: 'I was about to be whipped [for stealing] but I said to her do not do it and I'll tell you who it is that makes me do this mischief.' She was, she said, tempted by the Devil, who was 'a handsome youth a little bigger than myself'. A twelve-year-old escaped punishment for her bad behaviour by telling this story:

> When I was very young and playing with the girls in the village, they asked me if I would go to a sabbat: I was to have a good time and a sweetheart into the bargain. As soon as I agreed, my lover came up on a little horse, took me by the hand, asked me if I would like to be his mistress. I said 'Yes.' He caught me up into the air with the other girls and we all flew together to a great castle, where we played musical instruments, danced, feasted and drank wine.

Madame Bourignon at first wanted to expel the girls one by one, but she relented, thinking of the mischief they would do if set free among the population outside the convent. She founded the cult known as Bourignianism which grew and after her death infiltrated into Scotland. Her principal chronicler, Jack Cockburn, said she was famous for gaining secret knowledge of men's thoughts and predicting future events, and for the supernatural acquisition of knowledge without books or teachers. They were, he said, 'the effects of a melancholy head or crazy brain'.

When mass hysteria, accepted as demonic possession, struck a convent in Madrid in 1628, the Spanish Inquisition solved the problem and covered up any scandal by dispersing the nuns to other convents so that they could have no contact with one another.

The most famous of all cases of fake possession is that of the seventeenth-century nuns of Loudun, made famous by Aldous Huxley's 1952 book *The Devils of Loudun*. These sisters were used to accuse Father Urbain Grandier, parish priest of St Pierre-du-Marché, Loudun, of bewitching them.

At the time, Father Grandier was, like many priests, licentious, leading a scandalous life involving many 'marriages of convenience'. He was suspected of being the father of Philippa Trincant, daughter of the public prosecutor of Loudun, and he had openly made a mistress of one of his penitents. He might have survived all this and more but for the fact that he had made many political enemies, among them the powerful Cardinal Richelieu, who was temporarily out of favour with the court of Louis XV.

On 2 June 1630, after thirteen years as a parish priest, Grandier was charged with immorality before his enemy, the bishop of Poitiers, found guilty and suspended. Father Grandier appealed to Archbishop Sourdis of Bordeaux and was back in his parish within a year.

His opponents renewed their offensive through Father Mignon, confessor to the nuns of the Ursuline convent at Loudun. They persuaded a few sisters to undergo exorcism and swear that Father Grandier had bewitched them. The trio – the mother superior,

Sister Jeanne des Anges (Madame de Béclier) and a nun – went into fantastic convulsions, holding their breath to swell to a huge size and altering their looks and their voices. Sister Jeanne said they were possessed by two devils, Asmodeus and Zabulon, both sent by Father Grandier. The plot misfired and the only result was that the exorcists were prohibited by the archbishop from conducting any further such ceremonies.

But Father Grandier's immoral lifestyle came to an end when there came to town a relative of the mother superior, Monsieur Jean de Laubardemont. He was also an important friend of Cardinal Richelieu, who was now back in favour. The cardinal was himself related to one of the nuns at Loudun.

Since Grandier had published a wicked satire on Richelieu, the chance to humiliate the parish priest was not to be missed. Laubardemont was ordered to form a kangaroo court with two complaisant magistrates, a seneschal and the civil lieutenant to arrest, try and convict Father Grandier.

Under a new exorcism, more nuns made new accusations, helped by several of the priest's discarded mistresses. According to one chronicler:

> Sixty witnesses deposed to adulteries, incests, sacrileges and other crimes, committed by the accused, even in the most secret places of the church, as in the vestry, where the holy host was kept, on all days and at all hours.

The priests conducted the exorcism in public and great crowds attended to hear and see the evidence given.

Grandier took no steps to defend himself, believing that he could not be convicted of an 'imaginary crime'. He was thrown into jail and the Devil's marks were found on him by the trick of cutting the priest with a lancet on one part of the body, causing him to cry out in pain and bleed, and then touching another part of the body with the blunt end of the instrument so that it caused no pain and made no mark. Although use of this trick on his buttocks and testicles was exposed by a physician, the evidence of demonic resistance to pain was held to be proved. Nor did protests about the gross irregularities of his having been subject to a religious trial instead of a secular one carry any weight. Critics were frightened into silence by the explanation that this was an attack on the King and thus a treasonable offence. Those who would give evidence for the priest had to flee or were imprisoned on trumped-up charges.

Even under torture, Grandier refused to confess or name invented accomplices. His exorcists took part in his torture, smashing his legs. They argued that every time he prayed to God he was in fact talking to the Devil – 'his god'. Although he was given the privilege of being allowed to make a dying statement and to be strangled before being burned at the stake, friars prevented him from speaking by deluging him with holy water, smashed a heavy crucifix in his face (on the pretext of letting him kiss it) and fixed the hangman's noose so that it could not be tightened. One of his principal tormentors died within a month, claiming now that Grandier had not been responsible; a second died, insane, within five years; a third was so haunted by his false findings that he died in horrible delirium; and a fourth was banished from France for acting in collusion with bogus demoniacs.

The demoniacal possession of the nuns should, of course, have ceased when Father Grandier died, the Devil having left with him. Instead, the sisters continued their public displays and the town and convent became tourist attractions. The following description of the behaviour of the nuns is typical.

> [They] struck their chests and backs with their heads, as if they had their necks broken, and with inconceivable rapidity. They twisted their arms at the joints of the shoulder, the elbow, or the wrist, two or three times round. Lying on their stomachs they joined the palms of their hands to the soles of their feet; their faces became so frightful one could not bear to look at them; their eyes remained open without winking.
>
> Their tongues issued suddenly from their mouths, horribly swollen, black, hard and covered with pimples, and yet while in this state they spoke distinctly. They threw themselves back until their heads touched their feet, and walked in this position with wonderful rapidity, and for a long time. They uttered cries so horrible and so loud that nothing like it was ever heard before. They made use of expressions so indecent as to shame the most debauched of men, while their acts, both in exposing themselves and inviting lewd behaviour from those present, would have astonished the inmates of the lowest brothel in the country.

There was an ironic Anglo-French footnote to the Loudun affair. Lord Montagu, the English nobleman, was so impressed by the exorcisms conducted on Grandier by the Jesuit, Father Jean Joseph Surin, that he became a convert to Roman Catholicism. When Cardinal Richelieu's niece, the Duchess d'Aiguillon, visited Loudun she realised that the whole thing had been a fraud and told her uncle so. He replied that he had lost all interest in the matter and had stopped paying the nuns for their regular performances. Without this subsidy the nuns too lost interest and the cynics pointed out that money could always cast out devils when exorcism failed.

5

Selling Your Soul

The goat ordered her to make the sign of the cross with her left hand, and all present to venerate him. At which all kissed him under the tail.

Friar Francesco-Maria Guazzo,
***Compendium Maleficarum*, 1626**

The concept of someone being possessed by the Devil by agreeing to sell their soul to the Evil One in return for immediate temporary gain, wealth or power is as old as the Garden of Eden and was much used in history to prosecute those accused of witchcraft. Norsemen signed the pact in blood drawn by spears. Similar bargains were known to the Persians, the Babylonians and the Jews. The prophet Isaiah talked about the 'covenant of death' and 'an agreement with hell' (Isaiah xxviii, 14–18). Such a compact is mentioned in the Talmud, the collection of civil and religious Jewish laws and the most influential work on Jewish life. It is also dealt with in the Jewish Cabbala, literally, that which is accepted by tradition.

Christians know about it from the temptation of Jesus in the wilderness described in Matthew iv, 8–9.

> Again the Devil taketh him [Christ] up into an exceedingly high mountain, and sheweth him all the kingdoms of the world, and the glory of them; And saith unto him, All these things will I give thee, if thou wilt fall down and worship me.

By providing evidence of such a contract, real or imaginary, spoken or in writing, between the Devil and an accused witch, first the inquisition and then the courts found it a useful way to secure a conviction. An agreement with the Devil was against Christ's express wishes and could not, therefore, be ignored by Roman

Catholics or Protestants. The idea of a bond between Old Nick and a possessed person remains fascinating in both historic records and fictional accounts.

St Augustine (354–430), who brought Christianity to England, formulated the canon law which included the *pacta cum daemonibus*. He declared:

> All superstitions of this kind, either trivial or noxious, arising out of the damnable consorting of men and demons, as if formed by a faithless pact of treacherous friendship, are to be intrinsically repudiated.

St Basil the Great (330–379) recounts in his *Dialogues* how a senator's valet fell in love with his master's daughter. By signing away his soul, the valet won her. He was saved only by the assistance of the saint, who forced the Devil to give up the contract.

The most detailed legend of its kind is that of Theophilus, a sixth-century priest in Asia Minor. He was offered a bishopric but declined it out of modesty. The person appointed to the post, angry that he was second choice, deprived Theophilus of his priesthood. The first chosen enlisted the services of a Jewish magician to act as his agent and secure him an appointment with the Devil. Diabolos demanded from Theophilus a document signed and sealed with his own hand in which the deposed priest promised to deliver to the Devil his own soul to deny Christ and the Virgin Mary. The day after the conclusion of the contract, the bishop reinstated Theophilus.

After seven years of riotous and debauched living, believing he was going to die, Theophilus fasted and prayed to the Virgin for pardon. At first she turned a deaf ear but later she took pity on the repentant sinner and, descending from heaven, found him prostrate at the foot of her altar. Stroking his feverish brow, she assured him of pardon if he would deny the Devil and return to Christ. She then interceded with her Son on behalf of the penitent sinner. She demanded from the Devil the return of the parchment pact and placed it on Theophilus's breast as he lay asleep in church.

When he awoke and found the contract he threw it on the fire. Three days later, after publicly proclaiming his penitence, he died. The Church inscribed his name on the roll of saints as Theophilus the Penitent.

The story was told, translated, circulated worldwide, turned into poems and plays, satirised, philosophised and fictionalised. Copies of the contract were reproduced and in some the document was sealed not, as originally, in blood but with the mediaeval ring used so often in literature.

Jacob, one of the brothers Grimm, used the idea of a treaty in his *Deutsche Mythologie* tales. M. Gaster, in *Folk-Lore in the New Testament*, holds that it was passed on, like so many customs and beliefs, through migration. Other European examples include a Paris lawyer who was hanged in 1571 for having signed a contract with the Devil, and the Elector Augustus of Saxony, who in 1572 ordered death by burning for anyone who, 'forgetting his Christian faith, shall have entered into a compact, or held converse or discourse, with the Devil'.

Even as the world emerged from the dark Middle Ages, a 1643 Middlesex jury heard of a man who had sold his soul to an evil spirit for an annuity of £1,000. He was, however, acquitted. Increase Mather, the Puritan pastor of New England and President of Harvard, condemned 'cursed covenants with the Prince of Darkness'.

Educated people could hardly miss the theme in their reading. Chateaubriand in *Les Martyrs* (1809), Victor Hugo in *Han d'Islande* (1823), Edgar Allan Poe in *Bon-Bon* (1835), Alphonse Karr in *La Main du Diable* (1891) and Oscar Wilde in *The Fisherman and His Soul* (1891) are just some of the authors who used the theme in their work.

Were these stories about people entering into treaties with the Prince of Deceit true, legendary, superstition or invention? The *Golden Legend* of devilish pacts assembled by the thirteenth-century Dominican monk, Jacobus de Voragine, who became Archbishop of Genoa, quoted the Devil as complaining:

> The Christians are cheats. They make all sorts of promises so long as they want me, and then leave me in the lurch, and reconcile themselves with Christ as soon as, by my help, they have got what they want.

And the other version of the *Golden Legend*, by Henry Wadsworth Longfellow, the American poet, ends:

> It is Lucifer,
> The son of mystery;
> And since God suffers him to be,
> He, too, is God's minister,
> And labours for some good
> By us not understood.

The pact with the Devil was still taken most seriously during the witchcraft years. Even George Gifford, the Maldon, Essex, nonconformist minister who tried to rationalise the phenomenon, reflected public opinion when he wrote:

> A witch by the word of God ought to die the death not because she killeth men – for that she cannot, unless it be those witches which kill by poison, which either they receive from the devil, or he teacheth them to make – but because she dealeth with devils.

So making the covenant with Old Nick, not the evil doing itself, was, according to the critics of witch-hunting, the only offence. Take that away and there was no such thing as witchcraft.

Not surprisingly in those angry times, the Roman Catholics and Protestants formularised and published the contents and wording of the demonic pact. Thomas Cooper merely copied an evangelical ritual, substituting the Devil for God, in *The Mystery of Witchcraft* (1617):

> [The witch] must be covenanted solemnly in the house of God, there to make open testimony of her subjection unto him [the Devil], by renouncing all former covenants with the lord. And here, usually these things are performed in their order. Satan blasphemously occupying the place whence the holy oracles are delivered doth thence:
>
> First, require of the proselyte an acknowledgement of her covenant, causing her usually in her own person to repeat the form thereof: as, 'I, N., do here acknowledge that upon such conditions I have given myself unto Satan to be disposed of him at his pleasure.'
>
> Secondly: When this acknowledgement is made, in testimonial of all this subjection, Satan offers his back parts to be kissed of his vassal . . .
>
> Fifthly: For their confirmation, he yet enjoins them another ceremony, namely to compass about the font divers times, there solemnly to renounce the Trinity, especially their Salvation by Jesus Christ, and in token thereof to disclaim their baptism.

Even though he was violently anti-Papist, William Perkins, an Englishman, agreed and declared in 1608 that:

> The ground of all the practices of witchcraft is a league or covenant made between the witch and the Devil, wherein they do mutually bind themselves to each other.

German bishop Peter Binsfield wrote in the *Tractatus*, which ran through eight editions between 1589 and 1603:

> The witches abjure their baptism, the Christian faith, withdraw their obedience to God, and repudiate the protection of the Blessed Virgin, whom in derision they call *'La Rousse'*. Finally, they deny the sacraments of the Holy Church and trample under foot the Cross of Christ and the statues of the Virgin and other saints.

What should have caused little surprise was that the most famous ritual of all bore the name of Francesco-Maria Guazzo, the superstitious friar who believed that Martin Luther was the offspring of the Devil and who wrote the famous *Compendium Maleficarum* (The Handbook of Witches). In 1626 he classified parts of the ceremonial pact based on the Catholic liturgy, and even had seven of them illustrated.

1. 'I deny the Creator of heaven and earth. I deny my baptism. I deny the worship I formerly paid to God. I adhere to the Devil and believe only in thee.' Two hundred years later, inquisitor Nicholas Jaquier included trampling on the cross as an important part of the ritual.
2. Rebaptism by the Devil with a new name.
3. Symbolic removal of the baptismal chrism, the consecrated oil mixed with balm.
4. Denial of godparents and assigning of new sponsors.
5. Token surrender to the Devil of a piece of clothing.
6. Swearing allegiance to the Devil while standing within a magic circle on the ground. Another version had, as a token of this allegiance, the pact-makers putting their left hands behind their backs and touching the Devil as a mark of subjection.
7. Requesting the Devil for one's name to be put in the Book of Death.
8. Promising to sacrifice children to the Devil, a step which formed the basis of stories of witches murdering children. Children under three years of age were at one time specified.
9. Promising to pay annual tribute to the assigned demon. Only black-coloured gifts were valid.
10. Marking with the Devil's mark various parts of the body, including the anus in men and the breasts and genitals in women, so that the area in question became insensitive to pain. The mark might vary in shape – a rabbit's foot, a toad or a spider. Guazzo insisted that only those whom the Devil suspected were unreliable were so marked.
11. Taking vows of sacrifice to the devil. Promising never to adore the sacrament, to smash holy relics, never to use holy water or candles and to keep silent on one's traffic with Satan.

Ludovico Maria Sinistrari, the last of the inquisitorial demonologists, omitted some of the conditions and added throwing away sacred church medals, swearing allegiance on 'a full black book' and promising to proselytise others.

Guazzo told of a twelve-year-old girl, Dominique Falvet, who was accosted while picking rushes by a strange man.

> The girl was made to swear an oath to this man and he marked her on the brow with a nail as a sign of her new allegiance, and then he lay with her in the sight of her mother. The mother in her turn offered herself to be defiled by him in the daughter's presence.

The friar repeats another story about a young girl who confessed before the inquisitors of Aquitaine in 1594 that her Italian lover had taken her to a sabbat on St John the Baptist's Day (24 June). Having made a magic circle, the Italian invoked a large black goat, two women and a man dressed like a priest. When the devil-goat was told that the girl desired to become his subject,

> the goat ordered her to make the sign of the cross with her left hand, and all present to venerate him. At which all kissed him under the tail. Those present lit the candles they were holding from a black candle burning between the goat's horns and dropped money into the offertory bowl.

The sanguine credulity of youth, to use a Biblical phrase, must have taken over minds of all ages. Protestant demonologists often calmly adopted the same beliefs as Catholics. The contracts, people of both denominations said, were signed in blood and for specific periods of time. The practice of making such allegiances was to last for more than 200 years. In 1450, Jean de Stipulis gave blood from his left hand to the Devil so that Old Clootie himself could write the contract. The signatory died at the stake. In 1608 Guazzo gave a lurid account of a young man who sold his body and soul for twelve years of pleasure. When he came to sign the pact, 'The devil squeezed his left hand as he put it out, with such force that he filled his hand with blood pressed from the ends of three fingers.'

Nowadays documentary evidence for study is not too plentiful. Black witches of those times who could read and write were presumably few and most would hardly have known what they were signing. The educated ones, like the white witches of the late twentieth century, presumably copied out the contracts by hand and destroyed the originals for reasons of secrecy. Even so, very few examples even of copies have survived, throwing extreme doubt on the whole origin and veracity of the pacts. Inquisitors, demonologists and preachers had to fill the void and were rightly suspected of inventing or forging them or of falsely describing their details.

Even the Puritan Harvard University president Increase Mather boosted belief in the practice, but with a happy ending, in *Illustrious Providences* (1684). He cited the story of a young student of Caën, France, who, having squandered his allowance, was walking disconsolately on his own when the Devil, disguised as a stranger, gave him money on learning of his distress.

The money was soon spent, the discontent returned and the stranger came back and gave him more, this time on condition that the student signed the contract 'with his blood'. The student repented and asked some Protestant ministers to recover the contract. According to Increase Mather:

> The Ministers resolved to keep a day of fasting and prayer in that very place of the field where the distressed creature had made the woeful bargain, setting him in the midst of them. Thus they did, and being with special actions of faith much enlarged to pray earnestly to the Lord to make known his power over Satan, in constraining him to give up that contract, after some hours' continuance in prayer, a cloud was seen to spread itself over them, and out of it the very contract signed with the poor creature's blood was dropped down amongst them; which being taken up and viewed, the party concerned took it and tore it in pieces.

Thus Mather, who had so stoutly condemned 'cursed covenants with the Prince of Darkness', now negotiated by prayer for one to be returned and made void. Even the sceptic Reginald Scot looked at the two kinds of pact, the private *Professio Tacita* and the public *Professio Expresso*, and solemnly concluded that:

> That which is called solemn or public is where witches come together at certain assemblies, at the times prefixed, and do not only see the devil in visible form, but confer and talk familiarly with him.

Peter Binsfield (1540–1603), a German, said the pacts had become official and formularised because they were drawn up by lawyers, like a contract between two merchants or landowners. It should have come as no surprise that at the notorious 1633 trial of Father Urban Grandier for allegedly bewitching the nuns of Loudun, a document claimed to be his treaty with the Devil was produced. It was in two parts: one was the oath of allegiance to the Fiend which the priest was said to have vowed and the second the acceptance of the priest's allegiance by a committee of demons. The second part was written in Latin, backwards from right to left, since demons did most things in reverse to show their opposition to Christianity. It was signed Satanas, Beelzebub, Lucifer, Elmi, Leviathan and Staroth.

Whether or not people believed in the reliability of that document depended very much on whether they thought Father Grandier was guilty or innocent. Many took the view that the trial was corrupt and staged, a personal vendetta by Cardinal Richelieu and other political enemies against the admittedly worldly priest, and that the demoniacal agreement was a forgery.

We have been left one detailed and explicit devilish undertaking, drawn up by a lawyer and presented in evidence against a nobleman in Pignerole in 1676. The prosecution introduced it to explain 'this loathsome sin'. The twenty-eight clauses are worth repeating in full.

1. Lucifer, you are bound to deliver to me immediately 100,000 pounds of money in gold.
2. You will deliver to me the first Tuesday of every month 1,000 pounds.
3. You will bring me this gold in current money, of such kind that not only I, but also those to whom I may wish to give some, may use it.
4. The foresaid gold must not be false, must not disappear in one's hand, or turn to stone or coals. It should be metal stamped by the hands of men, legal and valid in all lands.
5. If I need a considerable sum of money, no matter when or for what purpose, you are duty bound to deliver to me secret or buried treasure. Nor need I fetch it myself from wherever it may be hidden or buried, but you must deliver it into my hands, without any trouble to me, to wherever I happen to be at the time, to dispose of according to my wishes and pleasure.
6. You are bound to cause no injury to my body or limbs, and do nothing to weaken my health, but preserve me from human illnesses and injury for fifty years.
7. If, contrary to our expectations, I should happen to become ill, you are bound to procure for me proved remedies to help me regain my previous good health as soon as possible.
8. Our agreement is to begin on this date . . . in the year 1676 and to end on the same day in 1727. You are not to tamper with this period or encroach on my rights, or make a false reckoning

(as you have formerly been accustomed to do).
9. When my time has finally run out, you are to let me die like all other men, without any shame or disgrace, and be honourably buried.
10. You are bound to make me loved and accepted by the King and all the aristocrats, by high or low, men and women, so that I may always be assured of goodwill and affection, and that everybody will grant without question what I may desire of them.
11. You are bound to transport me (and any other) without injury to the ends of the world, wherever I desire, no matter how far distant. You are to make me immediately so expert in the language of that place that I shall be able to speak it fluently. When I have satisfied my curiosity sufficiently, you will bring me back again, uninjured, to my home.
12. You are bound to protect me from all harm from bombs, firearms and other weapons, so that nothing may strike me and injure my body or limbs.
13. You are bound to assist me in my dealings with the King and help me prevail over my special enemies.
14. You are bound to provide me with a magic ring so that whenever I put it on my finger I shall become invisible and invulnerable.
15. You are bound to give me true and thorough information, without distortion or ambiguity, about any question I ask of you.
16. You are bound to give me advance warning of any secret plot against me, and to give me ways and means to thwart those plots and to bring them to naught.
17. You are bound to teach me whatever languages I may desire to learn so that I can read, converse, and express opinions as perfectly as if I had known them thoroughly from childhood.
18. You are bound to endow me with good sense, understanding, and intelligence, so that I can discuss all problems logically and can give an informed opinion about them.
19. You are bound to protect and look after me in all courts of justice and council chambers of King, Bishop or Pope, before whom I might be summoned.
20. You are bound to protect me and my household from injury, whether domestic or foreign, from theft and from harm.
21. I am permitted to lead my life in outward appearance like a good Christian, and to attend divine service without your interfering.
22. You are bound to teach me how to prepare medical pre-

scriptions and the correct use and administering of them in dosage and weight.

23. If, on any occasion, skirmish or fight, I should be attacked and set upon, you are to take up the challenge for me and produce help and assistance against all enemies.

24. You are bound to prevent anyone, no matter whom, from knowing about our accord and compact.

25. As often as I desire your presence, you are to appear to me in a loving and agreeable form, never in a frightening or horrible shape.

26. You are to see that each and every person shall do my bidding.

27. You are to promise me and bind yourself to keep unbroken these clauses, individually and collectively, and to comply assiduously with all of them. If you fail me in the slightest degree or display any negligence, then this pact and accord is null and void and of no force whatever.

28. In return for the foregoing promises, I swear and vow to deliver into your power several men and women. Furthermore I renounce God, the most Holy Trinity; I wholly renounce the vows made for me at baptism. I step forward with you in a new alliance and submit myself to you both in body and soul, forever into eternity.

The knight accused of entering into that contract was found guilty and imprisoned. What are we to make of this? Only a spoilsport would ask whence came the gold, how it was delivered and how other supernatural parts of the bargain were to be kept. For the times, the indenture was in the religious sense politically correct, obviously drawn up on behalf of the subject with only one clause of the twenty-eight to the benefit of the Devil. One is left with a suspicion that the Devil must have been a very easy-going person or entity to accept such a one-sided proposition. But above all it leaves open the question, were the nobleman or any of the parties to such agreements actually possessed by the Devil?

6

Phoney Exorcists

*I will not plead pregnancy to save
me from execution. It shall
never be said that I was a
witch and a whore.*
Miss Agnes Samuel, Warboys, Cambridgeshire, 1589

Demonic possession, as we have seen, was supposed to be at the root of witchcraft. The Devil, presumably a supernatural being, appointed witches to be his handmaidens to do his evil work on earth. Exodus, the second book of Moses, which condemns theft, damage, trespass, borrowing, fornication, bestiality and idolatry, also demands (xxii, 18): 'Thou shalt not suffer a witch to live.' Deuteronomy (xviii, 10) lists, among abominations to be avoided, 'There shalt not be found among you . . . a witch.'

There are plenty of other Biblical references. 'For rebellion is as the sin of witchcraft,' says 1 Samuel xv, 23. Manasseh, who reigned for fifty-five years in Jerusalem, used witchcraft and 'wrought much evil in the sight of the Lord, to provoke him to anger.' (2 Chronicles xxxiii, 6.) Again, in the New Testament, in Galatians, 'the works of the flesh' are manifest and include witchcraft which is listed (v, 20) alongside idolatry, hatred, wrath, strife, seditions, heresies, murders and drunkenness. 2 Kings ix, 22 talks about the whoredoms of Jezebel and her witchcrafts. Micah v, 12 says that the Lord will 'cut off witchcrafts', and in Nahum iii, 4 we are told of Nineveh, the ancient capital of Assyria, 'the well-favoured harlot, the mistress of witchcrafts, that selleth nations through her whoredoms and families through her witchcrafts'.

It is interesting that more rather than fewer people today believe in witchcraft, whereas fewer believe in demonic possession. But can the two be separated? During the centuries when alleged witchcraft was punished by unbelievably cruel persecution, witch-hunting, prosecution and punishment, the fantastic tales of demonic possession from France sometimes overshadowed those in Britain. There was a national difference: French nuns accused priests of immoral conduct and said that they must be demoniacal, while the priests said it was the holy sisters who were possessed by the Devil. The authorities, civil and religious, connived to solve the problem by condemning both priests and nuns, seldom legally or honestly, and sending them to their deaths. Britain, meanwhile, produced a different breed of accuser – children. With wanton mischief, often briefed and prompted by priests, they accused old ladies of being witches possessed by demons. Unlike the French, Britons did not regard exorcism as the answer to possession, and once they discovered that the late sixteenth-century exorcist John Darrell was himself the author of many of his spurious allegations of witchcraft, they took steps to curb the ritual ceremony of casting out devils. Canon law 72 of 1604 ordered:

> No minister shall without the licence or direction of the Bishop attempt under any pretence whatsoever, either of possession or obsession, by fasting or prayer, to cast out any evil or devils, under pain of the imputation of cozenage [fraud] and deposition [sacking] from the ministry.

Since then the whole question of exorcism has caused acrimonious debate. Before Darrell was born, a monk encouraged Elizabeth Barton, the 'Nun of Kent', to fake fits and pretend that she had been cured by the intercession of the Virgin Mary. The priest wanted his chapel to become a shrine, so that pilgrims would turn up in large numbers and he would reap an enormous profit. In 1533 Elizabeth confessed and said, 'Because the thing which I feigned was profitable to them, therefore they much praised me.'

But although Elizabeth's possession wasn't genuine, it had important ramifications. Her ecstatic behaviour and prophecies fermented public disquiet over the matrimonial policy of Henry VIII. She appeared to be a simple and sincere person, but her prophecies were political, and that led to her downfall and ultimately her execution.

Elizabeth was born in Aldington, in the Archbishop of Canterbury's manor, where she served as a maid in the house of the steward of the estate. She fell ill, showed physical and hysterical symptoms, went into trances and emerged uttering prophecies. Archbishop William Warham appointed two monks of Christ Church, Canterbury, to investigate. One of them, Edward Bocking, became her confessor and manager.

She became famous. Her pure and simple life was an example to all. Those who counselled her, both clerygmen and laymen, included Archbishop Warham and Bishop John Fisher – even Sir Thomas More was, for a time, taken in by her performance. Her prophecies, however, grew less and less mystical and more and more earthly and precise. Who but someone like her mentor, Bocking, could have persuaded her to predict that Henry VIII would suffer dire consequences if he did not drop his projected divorce from Catherine of Aragon and abandon Anne Boleyn?

After Henry's marriage to Anne had been declared lawful and valid, Elizabeth's utterances increasingly violated her allegiance to the sovereign, a treasonable offence. The next Archbishop of Canterbury, Thomas Cranmer, investigated her anew. She was examined and without torture confessed to having feigned her trances, having only pretended that she was divinely inspired, and was condemned along with those who aided and abetted her. She was executed at Tyburn on 21 April 1534 at the age of twenty-eight. Thus a woman of no education and little intellect, more hysterical than saintly, more deluded than sincere, went to her death.

Elizabeth Cross, known as the 'girl in the hole in the wall', who in 1544 claimed to be a clairvoyant, was thought to be possessed, but was also exposed as a sham.

In 1574, Agnes Bridges, aged eleven, and Rachel Pindar, who was twelve, appeared possessed and vomited pins, a well-known indication of demonic influence, but they were exposed as phoneys and confessed. So did Mildred Nerrington of Kent, who went into hysterics 'so strong that four men could not hold her down', another manifestation of the power of the Devil. She accused an old woman of being a witch but admitted her falsehoods when brought before the justices of the peace.

Anyone who has read Lillian Hellman's *The Children's Hour*, in which a neurotic child spreads a rumour about a lesbian relationship between two headmistresses of a private school, or Henry James's *The Turn of the Screw*, in which he deals with the developing consciousness and moral education of young girls, will understand the mediaeval origin of the much later fictional plots. Adults were taken in by the monstrous accusations of boys and girls. The accusers often came from wealthy families, and their victims the poor, whom they sent to their deaths. One of the most famous fraudulent cases is that of the Witches of Warboys.

Robert Throckmorton, a prominent squire living in Warboys, formerly in Huntingdonshire, now in Cambridgeshire, had a daughter, Jane, who was about ten years old. She fell sick, sneezing continuously for half an hour at a time, and would swoon, fall into a trance and swell to such an enormous size that no one could keep her down. Nor could they bend her limbs. She would shake one limb, then another, then her head. Her symptoms suggested that she had palsy, the original name for paralysis.

When a seventy-six-year-old neighbour, Mrs Alice Samuel, called to inquire after her health, the child said things like, 'Look where the old witch sitteth!', 'Did you ever see one more like a witch than she?' and 'I cannot abide to look at her.' Her parents ignored the outburst and remained confident that their daughter was in good hands and receiving proper medical attention from two well-known doctors, Dr Philip Barrow and Master Butler of Cambridge University.

Within two months, however, Jane's four sisters and seven of the servants all began to show similar symptoms. Because they were jealous of the attention paid to Jane, they said the same things about Mrs Samuel. They were, unfortunately, helped by Dr Barrow, who, unable to effect any progress in Jane's case, said, 'I have had some experience of the malice of some witches and I verily think that there is some kind of sorcery and witchcraft wrought towards your child.'

The parents at first refused to believe the charge, but as their daughters and servants all began to display the same signs, they challenged Mrs Samuel. At that moment, the children fell to the ground, strangely tormented. They scratched Mrs Samuel's hand to see if blood came from it and how quickly it would heal, another common test used in England to identify witches.

Mrs Samuel denied the denunciations and put them down to the 'wantonness' of the children. The Throckmortons became worried about the desperate plight of the children and their repeated accusations and behaviour towards the old lady. At first the children feigned fits only in her presence, but then they began to show the affliction when she was absent. The parents insisted that the old lady moved into the house so that they could keep a close watch on her.

Another of the children's mischiefs was to badger Mrs Samuel as she sat by the fire, pretending there was some sprite in the room, pointing at the imaginary figure and saying, 'Look, do you not see it sitting beside you? Now it is skipping and leaping.'

Lady Cromwell, wife of Oliver Cromwell's grandfather, Sir Henry Cromwell (the wealthiest man in Britain) and the most important lady in the district, called on the Throckmortons, saw the old lady and scolded her as a witch, knocking off her bonnet and slashing at her hair, which she ordered to be burned. Poor Mrs Samuel could only plead, 'Madam, why do you use me thus? I never did you any harm, as yet.' This encounter was later blamed for the bad dreams Lady Cromwell subsequently suffered. Her health declined and fifteen months later, in July 1592, she died.

In the December, to placate the family, Mrs Samuel pleaded with the children to stop their fits. The convulsions stopped. She could hardly believe it. In fact, she even began to doubt her own innocence of their accusations. She told the girls' father, 'Oh sir, I have been the cause of all this trouble to your children. Good master, forgive me.' The local parson, Dr Dorrington, was called. He heard Mrs Samuel confess. The next day she retracted her confession.

She was taken before the Bishop of Lincoln. Frightened, she repeated her earlier confession and expanded it to include the admission that she was possessed by demons in the form of three familiars – spirits given by the Devil – which she identified as dun chickens named Pluck, Catch and White. She was arrested and taken back to the county town of Huntingdon. Jailed too were her husband, John, and her daughter, Agnes, all to stand trial at the spring assizes on charges of witchcraft. There, the children relied heavily on the accusation that Mrs Samuel had caused the death of Lady Cromwell by witchcraft.

The girls even told the court that they would recover if only Mrs Samuel or her daughter, Agnes, would say, 'Even as I am a witch, and caused the death of Lady Cromwell, so I charge thee, spirit, to depart and to let us be well.' Of course, if the accused said, 'I am no witch,' the impudent adolescents would merely continue to pretend to be afflicted.

Mother Samuel did as requested in the forlorn hope that she would save her husband and daughter, but Agnes, urged to plead that she was pregnant to avoid execution, said, 'Nay, that I will not do. It shall never be said that I was a witch and a whore.' All three were hanged.

In 1596, the notorious John Darrell, whom we met in Chapter 3, conspired with fourteen-year-old Thomas Darling, of Burton-on-Trent, to fake confessions in an exorcism. Thomas, who became known as the 'Burton Boy', got lost in the woods while hunting with his uncle. When he returned home he became ill; he had fits, said he saw a green cat, green angels and later 'a man come out of a chamber pot, flames of hell and the heavens open'. A doctor who at first diagnosed worms suggested in the boy's hearing that he might have been bewitched.

His convulsions continued for a few weeks and then he suddenly remembered that he had inadvertently broken wind as 'a little old woman with three warts on her face' passed him in the woods. She had been annoyed and Thomas claimed she had bewitched him with a curse:

Gyp with a mischief and fart with a bell,
I will go to heaven and thou shalt go to hell.

A suspect was soon found. Alice Gooderidge admitted having been in the woods that day and said she had scolded another boy for breaking her basket of eggs. She claimed that Tommy had called her the 'witch of Stapenhill'. She had retorted:

Every boy doth call me witch,
But did I ever make thy arse itch?

Darling accused Alice face to face of bewitching him. When she was removed from his presence, his fits stopped. In the space of six hours in one day, he had manifested twenty-seven paroxysms, 'shrieking pitifully, blearing out the tongue, his neck so wrythen that his face seemed to stand backward'.

Every trick and ruse known to witch-hunters was used to try to make Alice confess. Then they turned their attention to her mother, Mrs Elizabeth Wright. When she was confronted by Tommy he pretended he was having a vision of hell, yelling, 'Yonder comes Mother Redcap! Look how they beat her brains out! See what it is to be a witch! See how the toads gnaw the flesh from her bones!'

On 27 May 1596, Darrell, using his considerable skills of ventriloquism, conducted an exorcism in which Thomas Darling was delivered from his possession 'by a spirit'. During the ceremony different voices were heard.

Small, soft voice: Brother Glassap, we cannot prevail. His strength is so strong, and they fast and pray, and a preacher prayeth as fast as they.

Big, authoritative voice: Brother Radalphus, I will go unto my master, Beelzebub, and he shall double their tongues.

Another voice: We cannot prevail. Let us go out of him, and enter into some of those here.

Holy voice: My son, arise up and walk; the evil spirit is gone from thee.

The exorcism was thought at the time to have cured Thomas of possession, although he suffered partial paralysis for the next three months. No more fits were recorded. But soon afterwards, Darrell was questioned by Samuel Harsnett, Archbishop of York, and confronted with damning evidence, including Thomas's confession, that the possession had not been genuine. Darrell claimed that the confession had been obtained from Darling only after seven weeks' imprisonment, threats to whip him and throttle him and then by giving the boy a blank piece of paper to sign for Harsnett to fill in the 'confession' later.

Alice Gooderidge, though proved innocent, died in prison before she could be freed. Her mother's plight is not known. As for the Burton Boy, he was eventually whipped and had his ears cut off for libelling the vice-chancellor of Oxford University.

Darrell's activities were coming to an end. In 1597, he went to Clayworth Hall, Leigh, in Lancashire, to exorcise seven members of Nicholas Starkie's household. In November that year he arrived in Nottingham to conduct public exorcisms. There he found William Somers, an apprentice, who had run away from his master and had been told he would have to work harder to make up the time he had lost. The boy pretended to be sick, caught a cold and huffed up his belly in the hope that his master would get rid of him.

Darrell gave him a pamphlet entitled *The Witches of Warboys* and the ideas of mock hysterics, gnashing his teeth, writhing his face and foaming at the mouth. He also fed Somers the story that he had been bewitched by an old woman because he would not give her a hat band that he had found.

Darrell announced that Somers was suffering for the sins of all Nottingham and asked for a public fast day. 'I desire all the people to refrain from the company of your wives that night and next day you will see strange things,' he said. The day after the fast day, Darrell preached a sermon enumerating fourteen signs of possession. At the mention of each, Somers obligingly demonstrated them. He spoke with his mouth scarcely moving, then apparently swallowed his tongue and, as signs of deliverance from demons, he cried, tore his hair and lay down as if he were dead.

At the end of the sermon, Somers did indeed appear to be dead, but Darrell hinted that the symptoms might recur, in anticipation of which he took a collection. At a later gathering Somers, confronted by thirteen so-called witches, proved not clever enough to feign a fit as each one appeared. When he was accused of deception, it was said on his behalf that 'the Devil would put in some such appearances of counterfeiting, to save the witches, and make God's work be believed'.

Eventually, in March 1598, Somers was taken to the workhouse, where the town council conducted an examination. Darrell insisted that he was possessed. The boy, warned that if it was all exposed as a fraud he would hang, insisted that the Devil controlled him.

But when the accused witches came to trial, he confessed and demonstrated his ability to feign his symptoms: 'By working the spittle in his mouth, he foamed till the froth ran down his chin.'

When both the exorcist and the boy appeared before the Archbishop of Canterbury, the Bishop of London and two senior judges, thirty-four of the forty-four witnesses were friends of Darrell and Somers. Even so, the exorcist was sent to prison. Darrell's father-in-law, whose own daughter had made a false accusation, said:

> I do verily think and believe in my conscience that William Somers did counterfeit all he did, that he was never possessed, dispossessed, nor repossessed; and that Mr Darrell dealt very unjustly in all his course.

In spite of his exposure as an imposter and subsequent slide into obscurity, years later Darrell still had supporters who continued to defend him. In 1659 Bishop Hall spoke of him as:

> a godly and zealous preacher, who undertook and, accordingly through the blessing of God upon his faithful devotion, performed these famous ejections of evil spirits which exercised the Press and raised no small envy from the gainsayers.

And, as late as 1715, the story of William Somers was repeated as if it had never been disproved.

In 1616, another fraud was exposed, largely as a result of the intervention of King James I, who was in fact responsible for much of the pursuit of witches. Early in his reign he exposed a woman who vomited pins as a fraud and denounced John Haydock, 'the sleeping preacher' of Oxford, as a phoney.

Then came the case of John Smith, a young son of Sir Roger Smith, an ancestor of the earls of Derby, of Husbands Bosworth, Leicestershire. He accused several women of bewitching him when he was only four or five years of age. He could whinny like a horse, simulate fits with such strength that several men could not restrain him, imagine and describe visions and display all the signs of possession so convincingly that by the time he was thirteen his word was good enough to secure the conviction and death of nine witches. According to contemporary accounts:

> Six of the witches had six several spirits, one in the likeness of a horse, another like a dog, another like a cat, another a *foumart* [polecat], another a fish, another a toad, with whom every one of them tormented him. He would make some sign according

> to the spirit as, when the horse tormented him, he would whinny; when the cat tormented him he would cry like a cat, etcetera. When he was in his fit, the witches were sometimes brought to him, and then were charged to speak certain words, and to name their spirits, and one of them to speak it after another, as thus: 'I, such a one, charge thee horse if I be a witch, that thou come forth of the child.' And then another by her spirit to do the like, and so till all had done. If any of them would speak a word contrary to that 'charm' the boy should be mightily tormented, but if they would speak as he first directed them, at the end of the last he would fall out of his fit as if one lay him down to sleep.

The nine witches had been hanged on his word on 18 July 1616, and another six were in prison. Little more than a month later, on 15 August, King James I was on his way to Leicester on one of his regal tours of the country. Since he was largely responsible for the enthusiasm for witch-hunting, first in Scotland and then in England, he took a great interest in John Smith. The King decided to examine the boy. He had learned that the lad 'upon a small entreaty would repeat all his tricks oftentimes in a day . . . whereupon the boy began to falter, so the King discovered a fallacy'.

The servants of the Archbishop George Abbott of Canterbury, who had believed the boy implicitly, in a short time discovered the whole deceit.

The six witches who remained in prison were given a new trial and a representative of the archbishop, well aware of the King's findings, was present. One of them had in the meantime died in her cell, but the other five were released. The magistrates responsible for sentencing them were overruled but not punished.

Still the deceptions continued. William Perry of Bilson, Staffordshire, accused an old woman, Jane Clark, of bewitching him. Judges at Stafford, alerted by the King's exposure of John Smith, dismissed his charges. But Perry, anxious for notoriety, repeated the allegations and could have sent the poor woman to her death if Thomas Morton, Bishop of Lichfield, had not taken an interest. He sent a trusted servant to spy on Perry. His emissary discovered the trick to one of Perry's party pieces, which was to produce black urine.

> Finding all quiet, Perry lifted up himself, and stared, and listened, and at length got out of his bed, and in the straw or mat under it, took out an ink-pot and made water in the chamber-pot. He then added the ink for a reserve. If he should be forced to make water before company, he saturated a piece of cotton

with the ink and put it into his prepuce, covering it with the foreskin.

By no means all such sharp practices were detected or exposed in time. During the infamous Lancashire witch trials of 1634, Mary Spencer, who was twenty years of age, was convicted because after going to the well for water she was supposed to have rolled her pail downhill and called for it to follow her. Her accuser, ten-year-old Edmund Robinson, also claimed that after he beat two greyhounds for not coursing a hare they promptly turned into a woman and a boy. In addition, he said he had seen six witches kneeling and pulling on ropes like bellringers as a result of which milk fell from above into waiting buckets. Yet Robinson later confessed that his stories had all been taught to him by his father and wholly fabricated for envy, revenge and hope of gain. By then three of those he had accused had died in prison.

7

Sex Scandals Of The Demonised

[The priest] habituated us to fondle one another with lustful embraces, and, what I dare not whisper, to give ourselves up to the most foul and sinful [lesbian] infamies.
Sister Madeleine Bavent, Louviers, 1642

Lurid sexual evidence in witchcraft cases was often so ludicrous it could not be believed by any reasonable human being, even though a lot of immorality took place. While the bishops insisted on rooting out such evil and publicly, with not overmuch regard for the truth, the anti-clerical sensation-seeking mob wanted more and more scandals to be revealed. Many more were invented to show that the church was keeping rigidly to its doctrine. The disgraceful case of the nuns of Loudun was barely forgotten when Father Pierre Barré, who conducted one of their earlier exorcisms, was disbarred as an exorcist and moved to another diocese. At Chinon, near Tours, he nevertheless continued this practice. Eventually, the Archbishop of Lyons warned him that girls 'believe themselves to be possessed on your word alone, so that the reason for their affliction is the confidence they place in your opinion'.

Barré ignored the warning and in 1640 connived with a Mademoiselle Beloquin to accuse a brother priest of being possessed and having raped the lady on the altar of his church. The altar cloths were examined and the blood produced as evidence was found to be that of a chicken. Barré was finally banished.

The scandals of Aix-en-Provence and Loudun examined in Chapter 4 were followed in 1642 by the affair at Louviers in Normandy. When the Bishop of Evreux, Monseigneur de Péricaud, heard that eighteen nuns from the same convent were possessed, he was cautious. 'It may be open to question whether the poor nuns are possessed,' he wrote. 'I have not examined them. But there can be no question that this state of affairs is a terrible scandal.'

Were their stories completely false, the fantasies of young women living in convents that forbade ordinary sexual activities? Were they completely true? Or were they somewhere between the two: reports containing some element of truth, misconstructions of occasional occurrences, or exaggerations of isolated cases of abuse? Since both the priests who advised the nuns of Louviers and the nuns themselves were suspect, the public were encouraged by both camps to take sides.

If the claims of the eighteen nuns were counterfeit, were they prompted by Sister Madeleine Bavent or Father Thomas Boullé or both? Madeleine was to tell the court at the eventual hearing that her testimony had been based upon nothing other than the vivid suggestions she retained from the interrogators' questioning. Her statements were supposed to itemise what she knew and what she did not know, and, in the end, in her autobiography, Sister Madeleine asked readers to 'distinguish what you think real from what seem to have been hallucinations'.

Madeleine Bavent was an orphan, brought up by an aunt and uncle in Rouen. When she was thirteen she was apprenticed to a dressmaker. While her employer, Dame Anne, busied herself catering for customers downstairs, Madeleine and some half-dozen other young girls in the upstairs workshop sewed church vestments and were often visited by priests who came ostensibly to examine their work. When she was about eighteen, Madeleine was seduced by one of the visitors, a Franciscan, Father Bontemps – ironically French for good times – who had previously been intimate with three other girls.

To allay any suspicions of her aunt, Madeleine decided to enter the little convent of the Franciscan Tertiaries at Louviers, a charitable home for the poor. She was deeply religious, so her decision came as no surprise. She spent three years as a novice under the chaplain, Father Pierre David, who sowed the seeds of a pernicious doctrine under the appearance of a saintly life.

The doctrine was that of the Illuminati, a heretical, mystical sect which, along with the Adamites and the Quietists, believed that a person filled or illuminated with the Holy Spirit could commit no sin; that he or she should worship God naked after the example of Adam and Eve, and that when he or she practised inward quietness or devotion any act was irreproachable. Small wonder, then, that when Father David died, the archbishop ordered all his papers and books to be burned.

The nuns at Louviers were, as a mark of their humility and

poverty, required to receive holy communion naked and then to fast for eight to ten days. Customs such as these, probably pure in their original intent, easily lent themselves to misunderstanding, misinterpretation, abuse and perversion. Father David actually ordered Madeleine as a novice to 'strip to the waist and communicate with breasts exposed'. When she tried to cover herself with the communion cloth she was forced to stretch up her arms to expose more of herself. In her memoirs, Sister Madeleine wrote:

> The most holy, virtuous and faithful nuns were held to be those who stripped themselves completely naked and danced before him [Father David] in that state, appeared naked in the choir, and sauntered naked through the gardens. Nor was that all. He habituated us to fondle one another with lustful embraces, and, what I dare not whisper, to give ourselves up to the most foul and sinful [lesbian] infamies. I have witnessed a mock act of circumcision performed upon a huge phallus, which seemed made of paste, which afterwards some nuns seized upon to gratify their fancies.

Father David, however, never had intercourse with Madeleine, content to take only immodest liberties, 'certain indecent caresses and mutual masturbation'.

Even when he was succeeded by Father Mathurin Picard and his assistant, Father Thomas Boullé, 'the obscene practices were continued and were held in great repute'. Madeleine claimed that she resisted these customs, and that the other nuns considered her stubborn. At an Easter confession, Father Picard revealed to her his passion for her and toyed with her:

> After that I never had any other kind of confession from him. Generally, all the time he handled the most private parts of my body, although I was always respectably covered, never, as the nuns maliciously report, was I undressed.

Madeleine always tried to refuse Father Picard the ultimate favour but sometimes he forced himself upon her and at last she became pregnant.

Other nuns were involved in the most diabolical practices. Father Picard was accused of making 'love filters' of sacramental wafers sopped up with 'several clots of menstrual blood' and burying them in the ground. (Menstrual blood does not clot.) The nuns were supposed to go to the sites of the burials and commit the most 'filthy acts' with him. For other charms he added the entrails of slain babies, broken limbs of dead bodies, and 'blood which trickled from the holy wafer'.

Once or twice a week, Madeleine went to the sabbat. 'About eleven o'clock I would lose consciousness and fall into a kind of trance or ecstasy.' Present at the sabbat were the two chaplains, Father Picard and Father Boullé, three or four nuns from her convent and some 'half-human and half-bestial demons'.

The priests recited the black mass, the parody of the church liturgy favoured by Satanists. There was a meal, which included, according to Madeleine, roasted human flesh. The nuns then copulated with the spectre of Father David or some other living priest. On one occasion Father Boullé seduced Madeleine while Father Picard watched and 'held my hands tightly while Father Boullé lay on top of me'.

Having said the black mass at the sabbat, said Madeleine, the priests took the consecrated hosts – larger than the usual wafers – cut out a round piece from the centre, trimmed it and fixed it to vellum or parchment, securing it in position with some greasy adhesive like shoemaker's wax. They then put this gadget over their genital organs, from which it reached to the stomach, and gave themselves to the women present.

Madeleine alleged that Father Picard had sexual intercourse with her five or six times at the sabbat but she added, with a note of either modesty or accuracy, 'but only once or twice in the manner just described'.

Anyone trying to honestly judge the accuracy of Madeleine's story must have come to the conclusion that she had sex with both humans and demons. She identified the two priests but she was also familiar with the Church's teaching that men can be tempted by an incubus, an angel who fell from heaven because of his lust for women. (The devil who appears to men in similar circumstances is a succubus.)

Madeleine was for several years visited in her cell by the Devil in the form of a very large black cat. She wrote:

> On no fewer than two occasions, having entered my cell, I found that damned incubus of a cat on my bed in the most indecent postures it is possible to imagine, exhibiting a huge penis just like a man's. I was terrified and tried to fly, but in an instant it leaped towards me, dragged me forcibly on the bed, and then violently ravished me, causing me to experience the most peculiar sensation.

One of the oddest features of the orgies is that they continued to take place regularly between 1628 and 1642, a period of fourteen whole years, yet neither whisper, complaint nor rumour reached the outside world. Madeleine explained that away by saying there was nothing untoward in priests visiting the convent to hear confessions. Besides, since she was the gatekeeper of the convent, whoever went in and out was known to her. However, she was the gatekeeper only as a novice. If her story were true, then presumably another corrupted novice kept the gate afterwards.

Only when Father Picard died and the nuns confessed to all this unbounded licence did the ecclesiastical authorities take notice. Père Esprit de Bosroger, provincial of the Capuchin fathers, wrote that after the events these apparently healthy young women in a convent had

> suffered the most frightful convulsions night and day during four years, and for three or more hours daily been subjected to exorcisms during a term of two years, although they have been subsisting in these paroxysms of constantly recurring frenzy, contortions, animal howling, clamours and outcries. And besides all these excessive torments, they have experienced the peculiar motions of their own demon, their special tormentor, three or four times daily.

Bosroger's test for possession named seven representative signs: denial of knowledge of any fits after the paroxysms had ended; incessant obscenities and blasphemies; circumstantial descriptions of the witches' sabbat; fear of sacred relics and sacraments; violent cursing at any prayer; lewd exposure; acts of abnormal strength and similar acts in other demoniacs.

Fourteen of the fifty-two nuns examined said they were possessed and confessed to everything that was asked of them. They were coached to put the blame on Madeleine Bavent. Churches were crowded to hear the public exorcisms of the nuns, who, perhaps flattered by the attention or frightened of the consequences, played their parts to the full. They roared their replies, shouted insults and contorted their bodies.

Dr Yvelin, a royal physician, claimed they were phoney and that their hystero-epileptic fits and confessions were rehearsed. The Bishop of Evreux had by then made up his mind that Sister Madeleine was responsible for much of the trouble and charged her with sorcery, attending the sabbat, signing a pact with the Devil, stealing the host and copulating with devils. She was held in an Ursuline convent at Rouen, where she was treated cruelly. She tried to commit suicide, stopped up her menstrual discharges with bandages, swallowed spiders and bribed a boy to bring her arsenic. In 1647, after five years in continuous solitary confinement in an underground dungeon, living on bread and water for three days a week, she died, aged forty.

One witness, burned as a heretic, confessed that he had prompted Sister Madeleine with 'merely gossips' twaddle' about the sabbats, the orgies and the black mass. Later he claimed he had been paid to give false evidence against her by the inquisitor in charge of the investigation.

Father Picard's corpse was exhumed and he was formally excommunicated for witchcraft and his corpse ceremonially burned. Father Boullé was imprisoned and tortured to persuade him to reveal the identities of his accomplices. He was eventually found guilty of witchcraft and burned alive and his ashes were scattered to the four winds. The nuns found to have been bewitched for immoral purposes by the two chaplains, Picard and Boullé, were dispersed to other convents to remove the 'dryness' of their souls.

And so the catalogue of possession and mass possession continued. The town of Paderborn in West Germany suffered mass hysteria which affected the whole diocese in 1656. The possessed, speaking many unknown languages, claimed that the Capuchin friars were responsible. Eventually, the burgomaster's maid was arrested for possessing articles used in sorcery – a toad, hair and needles.

Nuns at the Ursuline convent at Auxonne were subjected to far more meticulous investigation than many of their sisters in similar circumstances. They had made accusations of lesbianism against their mother superior, Sister St Colombe, or Barbara Buvée. Such charges were seldom made public and it emerged that the incidents had continued for five years before being made known in 1660.

The nuns appeared to be unanimous in their condemnation of the mother superior. Sister Henriette Cousin said that Sister St Colombe had put her hand on her bosom and passionately kissed her. When Sister Henriette protested, the mother superior claimed she thought she was kissing a holy statue. Sister Humberte Borthon had visions of hell in which the mother superior had put '*un serpent dans le partie*' and, having embraced her, lay down on her 'like a man with a woman'.

Sister Charlotte Joy had seen the mother superior kiss with the tongue Sister Gabrielle de Malo and place her hand under the petticoat, while the nun made 'reciprocal touchings'. Sister Françoise Borthon, often violated by the devil Asmodeus, swore that the mother superior had once made her sit on her knees and had put a finger in her private parts in the same way a man might have done. In answer to this charge, the mother superior insisted that she thought the nun was pregnant and had put in her hand and pried open 'her secret place, causing a lot of blood, both clear and clotted, to issue forth'.

Another nun had a vision of her superior holding in one hand a stolen sacred host on which was '*la partie honteuse*', the disgraceful thing, of a man. This artificial phallus, made of linen, was used by Sister St Colombe to perform 'impure acts' on herself.

Part of the truth of the case was that the mother superior had quarrelled with Father Borthon, a relative of Sister Françoise Borthon, and of two other nuns who accused her, and with his successor, Father Nouvelet. Eight nuns were said to have been sexually stimulated by him. On his account one of them suffered great temptations of the flesh. Father Nouvelet told her that he too must be possessed and that the mother superior was to blame.

Father Nouvelet conducted exorcisms in the chapel during which Sister Denise lifted a heavy vase, which two strong men could not move, with just two fingers. Other nuns worshipped the sacrament while lying on their bellies and raising their heads and feet to form an arc. Some of the exorcisms were conducted by Father Nouvelet while he was lying in bed with the girls so close that 'only the sister's veil separated her face from the priest'.

The exorcist had also spent a lot of time travelling with Sister Claudine Bourgeot, during which time they always slept in the same bedroom but, they insisted, in separate beds.

Sister St Colombe was formally charged with witchcraft, shackled in solitary confinement and then brought before the *parlement* of Dijon. Doctors disagreed with the verdict. One declared all the nuns to be frauds, though some may possibly have been sick. Another did say they were genuinely possessed by devils, but a third thought that nothing demoniacal had been proven. After all, they had not passed any of the standard tests – spoken in tongues, shown knowledge of hidden secrets, made revelations, levitated their bodies or made extraordinary involuntary contortions of their faces and bodies.

The mother superior was freed and went to another convent; the nuns were dispersed and the hysteria disappeared.

In 1669 at Mora, in Sweden, 300 children were reported to have been possessed and made to fly. Bishop Hutchinson said sceptically:

> Is it not plain that the people had frightened their children with so many tales that they could not sleep without dreaming of the Devil, and then made the poor women of the town confess what the children said of them?

Eighty-five persons were as a result of the accusations burned at the stake.

In Hoorn, Holland, a year later, children under twelve years old in an orphanage were reported to have been possessed. In Toulouse, France, in 1681, Marie Clauzette and four other novices were said to have been possessed and exorcised. The *parlement* which heard them said they had imagined it and were fraudulent. The novices, probably at the instigation of others, accused the government lawyers of having strayed from the true Roman Catholic religion and become dissolute, licentious and atheistic.

Mass possession was reported from Salem, Massachusetts – America's only epidemic of the kind – in 1682. Fifty nuns were similarly afflicted in Lyons, France, in 1687, and at Les Landes, near Bordeaux, Father Huertin, who wanted to perform miracles, exorcised young girls whom he thought were demonically possessed but failed to achieve the recognition that he so earnestly desired. In 1749, at Unterzell in Germany, nuns were found to have been possessed for several years, always manifesting convulsions, swellings and delirium. Eventually one of their number, Maria Renata, was held responsible and burned at the stake as a witch.

Although cases of mass possession, real or imaginary, naturally received more publicity, individual cases were occasionally elevated to *causes célèbres*. Charles IX of France went to Laon to watch the exorcism of Madame Nicole Autry by the monks of Vervins in 1566. During the ceremony she was publicly whipped 'to obtain through God the expulsion of the devils from her body'.

In Vienna in 1583, a sixteen-year-old girl suffered from cramps which were considered to be the creation of demons. Jesuits exorcised her, and after eight weeks had expelled 12,652 living demons, which they accused her grandmother of keeping in the form of flies in glass jars. The seventy-year-old lady was tortured into confessing that she had had sexual intercourse with the Devil in the shape of a ball of thread. She was found guilty and sentenced to be dragged at the horse's tail to the place of execution and burned alive. The Jesuits applauded the sentence of the courts and called on the judges to intensify their witch hunts.

Another French girl who claimed to be possessed attracted the attention of the superstitious King Henry III in 1586. He sent three physicians to Amiens to examine her. According to the girl's mother, the child had *des fleurs blanches* during menstruation. Doctors examined her and found she had venereal disease. Midwives confirmed that the girl was not a virgin. Two years previously, when she had first claimed she was possessed, a priest had found a way of getting to the truth by means of a trick. He read a passage in Latin from Cicero, the Roman statesman. The girl, thinking the passage was from the Holy Bible, feigned a fit. On this occasion she was ordered to be publicly whipped.

Even the genuine cases were not immune from being treated as frauds. In 1598, Mademoiselle Marthe Brossier of Paris claimed to be possessed. The Capuchin monks decided that her possession was genuine; the doctors said it was spurious. The Bishop of Angers pronounced as a matter of course that she was not possessed. The monks then referred her to the Papal court in Rome, but when the Jesuits took the same view as the physicians, the Capuchins dropped the whole case. Unfortunately, the poor girl and her father were left stranded in Rome with no money.

Although possession continued to take place through the ages, the celebrated individual and mass cases were publicised less and less by the end of the eighteenth century. The French became cynical about them after the case in 1816 of another girl from Amiens who created a stir. It emerged that she was not possessed but merely trying to divert attention from the fact that she was pregnant. She claimed that three devils, Mimi, Zozo and Crapoulet, infested her. When a Jesuit priest tried to exorcise her, Mimi left and Zozo broke windows in the church before flying away, while Crapoulet could not be banished. He was adjudged to have taken up a position in her pudenda. At that, the Jesuit was forbidden to continue the exorcism under threat of arrest.

8
Twentieth-Century Devilment

Why do you beat me? You know that
it isn't I, Germana, who is doing
this, but the one who is within me.
Does one beat a spirit? Is that
what a priest does?

The Devil speaking through Germana Cele,
Natal, South Africa, 1906

The eighteenth-century Age of Reason or Age of Enlightenment, during which philosophy was in vogue throughout Europe, saw the end of much nonsense. But the Devil didn't just vanish and people were still said to be demonically possessed. The Victorians, with their devotion to established churchgoing and medical innovation, were alerted to the phenomenon by reports in 1865 that two brothers had made pacts with the Devil in Illfurth, eight miles from Mulhouse in Alsace. Joseph Bruner, aged eight, and ten-year-old Theobald were behaving very oddly. Their father, a farmer, sought advice from the mayor and the parish priest.

Father Karl Brey began to take valuable notes. The boys, devout Roman Catholics, had suddenly developed a fascination for diabolical matters and an aversion to anything of a religious nature. The mayor of Mulhouse decided to visit the boys one Sunday with his councillors. One of them warned him, 'The Devil may influence us.' So the mayor, to be on the safe side, 'so the Devil will not be able to hold anything against us,' led them all to confession and communion before going to see the boys.

When they entered the children's room, one of the lads displayed amazing clairvoyance. Though neither had left the house, he said: 'Look at that! There's the mayor and others from the town council. Well, you didn't trust the weather and so you went to church yesterday and had them scrape the dirt from your conscience, right? But one of you didn't do it properly. He stole the turnips.'

One of the councillors was so shocked he blurted out: 'Yes, I took them but I put down money for them.'

The boy answered, 'But those people never got the money.' At that, the gentleman fled the house.

On another occasion the priest arrived with the mayor, but the mayor went upstairs alone and they could not have seen the priest. And yet they cried out immediately, 'The fellow in the black coat has come. We won't say a thing.' They then proceeded to jump up and down, back and forth, and to dance around.

For no visible reason, the boys' heads would turn rapidly through 180 degrees while they remained on their backs. They would thrash the bedsteads with their limbs, and the force was great enough to break the bedsteads. Afterwards they lay not merely exhausted but apparently lifeless. Next they developed an insatiable, wolfish hunger, their bellies began to swell and they vomited strange objects. Their legs entwined like flexible willows so that nobody could untwist them again. Suddenly, without warning, they would disentangle their limbs very rapidly with no ill effects.

Theobald was persecuted by a curious-looking animal which had a duck's beak and the claws of a lion, and whose body was covered with dirty feathers. As soon as the boy saw the monster flying over his bed he would cry out in terror. The creature threatened to choke him to death. The boy, in desperation, threw himself on the animal/bird and pulled out its feathers at least twenty or thirty times a day, all in the presence of hundreds of witnesses from all levels of society. The feathers had a repulsive smell and when burned left no ash.

On other occasions the children felt pricking sensations all over their bodies and would either secrete or vomit incredible quantities of foam, yellow feathers and seaweed – even though they were nowhere near the sea. This recurred no matter how often they changed their clothes. Sometimes Joseph and Theobald were lifted from their chairs by unseen hands and flung across the room into a corner.

The boys continued to fly into violent rages whenever any religious object was near them. Their parents tried to use holy water to cook their food without their knowledge, but they would refuse to eat it. They would then cry out in rough, male voices and would stop only when they were told they could cry as much as they liked to the glory of God.

The parish priest tried to understand the boys and comfort their parents. The children, who had previously been brought up with due regard to Christian morality, suddenly came out with abusive names for holy and consecrated objects. They talked of public events of which they could have had no knowledge. When they were asked questions in Basque, a language in which they had no education, they would reply perfectly fluently in French. They gave their names when asked and answered all normal, non-religious questions, and even said they did not want to go back to hell.

Several neighbouring families were kind to them despite the fact that their property as well as that of the brothers' family was subject to infestation by the Devil. Once, after there was considerable noise in the upper rooms of a neighbour's house, the neighbour visited the boys. The Devil, speaking through one of them, said, 'Did you hear us last night? Well, we certainly managed to carry on plenty!'

In bed, the children used to turn to the wall, paint horrible devil faces on it, and then speak to the faces as if they were in communication and at play with them. If, while one of the boys was asleep, a rosary was placed on his bed, he would immediately hide under the covers and refuse to emerge until the beads were removed.

At times the boys would behave like trained acrobats, standing simultaneously on their heads and legs, their bodies arched high. Unlike acrobats, however, they could remain in such positions without apparent ill effect for a considerable period of time, returning to a normal position only when, according to the priest, the Devil saw fit to give the objects of his torture some respite.

The brothers also displayed other uncanny examples of clairvoyance. Several times Theobald correctly predicted a death. Two hours before a local resident, Frau Müller, died, the boy knelt by his bed and acted as if he were ringing the mourning bell. Another time he did the same thing for a whole hour. When he was asked for whom the bell tolled, the boy answered, 'For Gregor Kunegel.'

Coincidentally, Kunegel's daughter was visiting the Bruner household at that moment. Shocked and angry, she turned on Theobald and told him: 'You liar, my father is not even ill. He is working on the new boys' seminary as a mason.'

Theobald answered her, 'That may be. But he has just had a fall. Go ahead and check on it.'

He was right. Her father had fallen from some scaffolding, broken his neck and died. This had happened at the very moment that Theobald had begun to imitate the ringing of the mourning bell. No one else in Illfurth, the scene of the tragedy, knew anything about it.

Joseph and Theobald were taken to hospital, where they were, for a time, quieter. They were now deaf, which made communication and understanding difficult. And they still avoided contact with any consecrated or religious object. An episcopal commission was appointed to examine the boys and report with a recommendation that they be exorcised.

Father Brey was already convinced that these bizarre manifestations meant only one thing: the brothers were the victims of demonic possession. The parents agreed. At first the boys were separated: Theobald went to the St Charles Hospital at Schlitigheim near Strasbourg, where the superior, Father Stumpf, and the nuns monitored his behaviour. For the first three days, he behaved apparently normally. On the fourth, he suddenly erupted: 'I have come and I am in a rage.'

One of the nuns asked, 'Who are you?'

A 'non-human' adult voice answered, 'I am the Lord of Darkness.'

Later, Joseph, whose symptoms appeared less severe, was sent to the same hospital. Once the boys were together again, they both displayed the same symptoms. For instance, both became infested with red-headed lice. The blood-sucking insects multiplied so quickly that three or four people working in relays with brushes and combs were unable to keep pace with the infestation. Then the priest poured holy water over them and said to each, 'In the name of the Holy Trinity, I order you to leave this child!' The vermin obligingly disappeared.

When Theobald was brought into the church so that he could undergo a session of exorcism he trembled all over his body, developed a fever, foamed at the mouth and blasphemed. When the priest recited the exhortation, 'I command thee to depart from here,' the Devil spoke through the child's mouth, 'My time has not yet come. I am not going.'

When the priest intoned, 'In the name of the Immaculate Conception,' the boy, in a deep bass voice, cried out, 'Now I must yield.' And at that he fell prostrate as if he were dead. After he came round, he rubbed his eyes and looked at all the people around him in astonishment. He knew none of them, although for four years they had been constantly around him. The only people he recognised and knew were his parents. His hearing returned and, by all accounts, he became again the decent, well-behaved boy he had been until he was possessed – except that he was four years older.

Some weeks later, Joseph underwent exorcism and was similarly cured.

Doctors and priests agreed that the affliction of the Bruner children was different from any known mental ailment or trance. They had been healthy to begin with, as was the whole family, until the sudden occurrence of abnormal behaviour, the incapability of priests (in the first instance) or doctors or hospitals to help, the

A demonised woman in a state of collapse expels clouds of demons from her mouth as a priest performs the exorcism. The line drawing is from the frontispiece of a brief work on the exorcism of a maiden, by Sebastian Khueller, Munich, 1574. *Credit: Fortean Picture Library.*

A classical nineteenth century engraving of a woman possessed by the Devil. Her eyes become slits, her tongue is extended to an abnormal length, and she tears at her breast and rends her clothes in typical distress. *Credit: Fortean Picture Library.*

A drawing of Sir William Crookes (1832–1919) the famous scientist (seated) with colleagues watching Daniel Dunglas Hume, levitating. This supernatural power which defies gravity – not uncommon among the demonically possessed – was said to have taken Hume out of one upstairs window and into another. *Credit: Fortean Picture Library.*

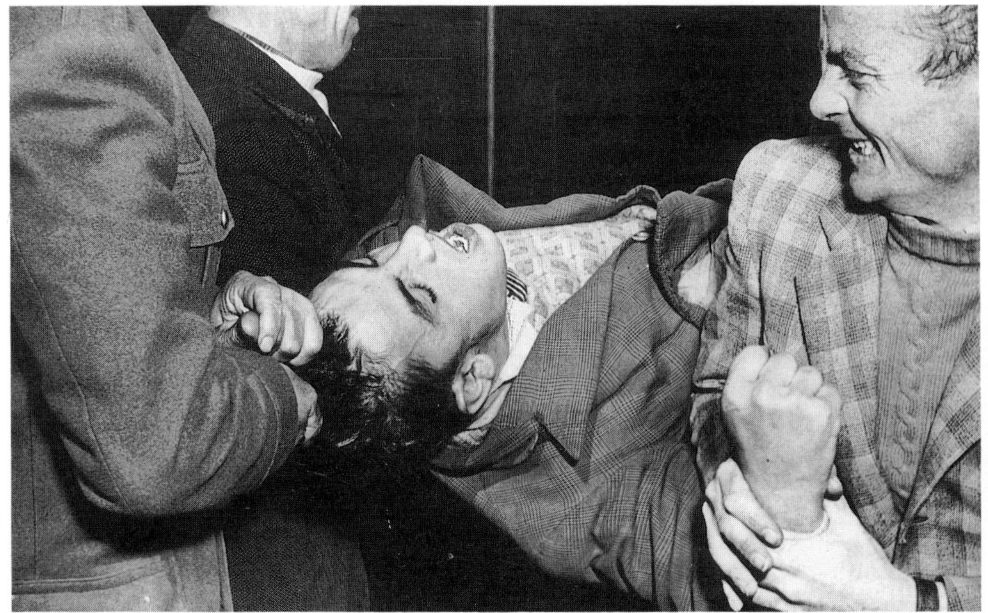

Leonardo de Arcadi, a demonised member of London's devout Italian community, is being restrained by his brother, Franco, right, and a physically strong male nurse, left, as he is taken to be exorcised at his church. *Credit: Keystone.*

Leonardo de Arcadi is so violent while being exorcised the priest has to 'collar' him with the restraining penitent ring of St. Vicinius and hold a consecrated wool pad to his heart while a powerful male nurse clutches his hair. *Credit: Keystone.*

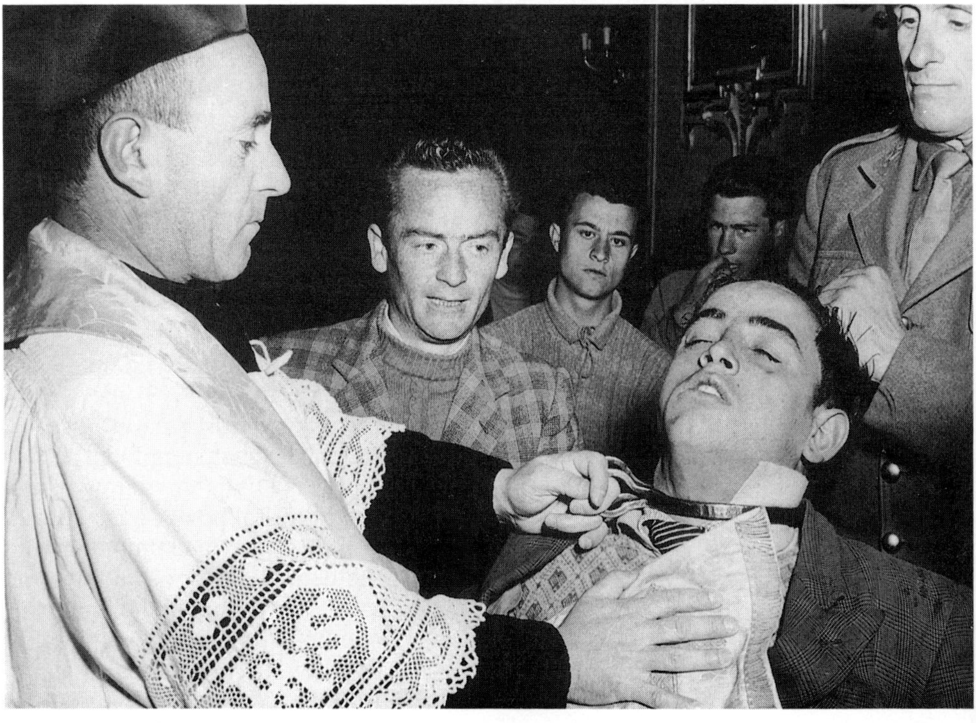

Detective Chief Superintendent Robert Fabian – the famous Fabian of Scotland Yard – investigated the brutal 'witchcraft murder' of a Warwickshire hedgecutter with a hay fork, an ancient method of getting rid of witches. He also warned of black magic rites, priestesses, hypnotised and blackmailed victims. See Chapter 10. *Credit: Mirror Syndication International.*

Exorcism – the power of the Church to drive out demons from those who are possessed – is demonstrated in the face of the Reverend Christopher Neil-Smith as he conducts the ritual at the high altar of his Hampstead, north-west London church. Priests know by their humility, piety, prayer, experience and gift when the devils are staying and when they are departing. See Chapters 13 and 17. *Credit: Mirror Syndication International.*

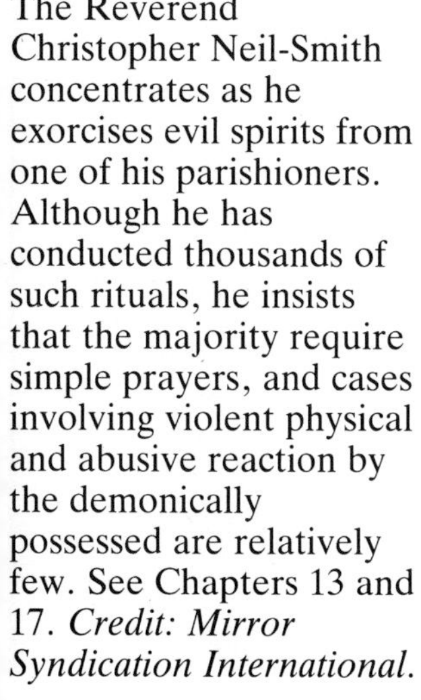

The Reverend Christopher Neil-Smith concentrates as he exorcises evil spirits from one of his parishioners. Although he has conducted thousands of such rituals, he insists that the majority require simple prayers, and cases involving violent physical and abusive reaction by the demonically possessed are relatively few. See Chapters 13 and 17. *Credit: Mirror Syndication International.*

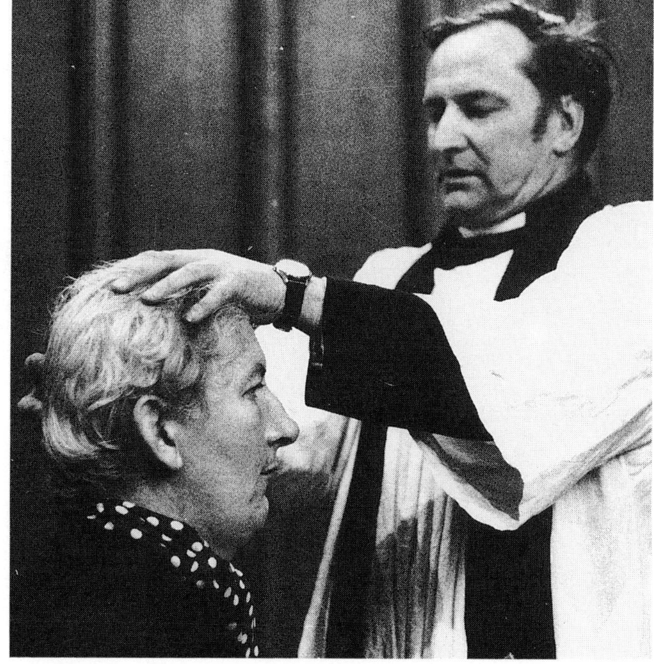

Denise, a 21-year-old alcoholic prostitute, screams and struggles violently. Three hundred worshippers from all over the country raise their hands, chant, sing and hand-clap. And the Reverend Trevor Dearing, vicar of St. Paul's, Hainault, Essex, casts out devils from another demonised person in a regular service of exorcism. See Chapter 13. *Credit: Keystone.*

A considerable number of young women take part in the regular 'healing ministry' sessions of the Reverend Trevor Dearing. Here they watch, sing and pray as the clergyman calls on the devils to leave the body and soul of another unfortunate demonised woman. See Chapter 13. *Credit: Keystone.*

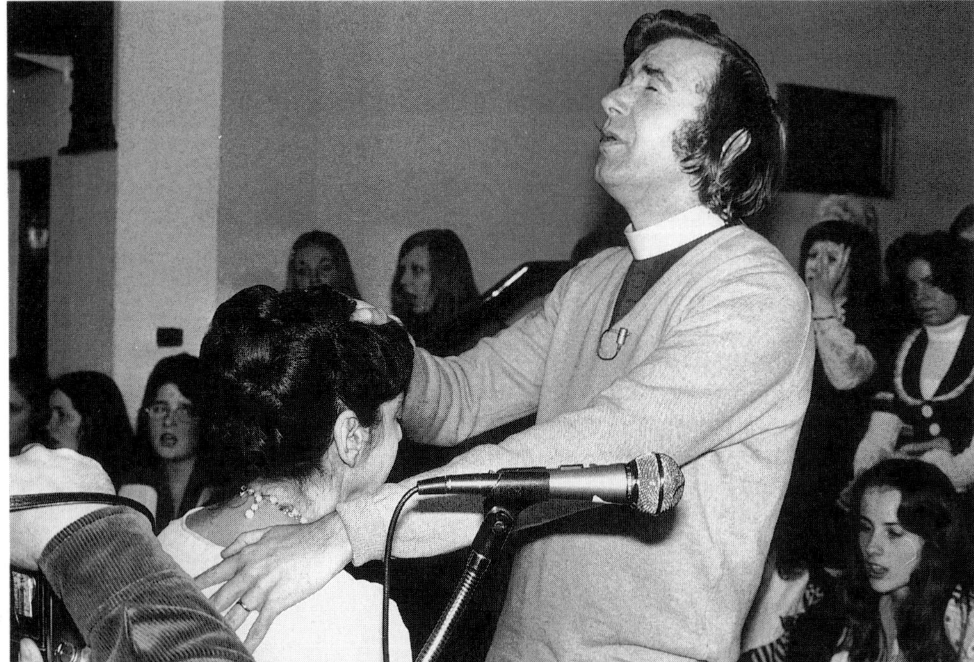

stinking feathers and the seaweed, witnessed by many, the strange loathing and fear of consecrated objects, the incomprehensible hatred of anything connected with religion, and finally their freedom from the Devil or his demons.

Theobald died on 3 April 1871, when he was sixteen. Joseph, born on 28 April 1857, who had been less afflicted, lived until he was twenty-five.

What had happened was no doubt supernatural, but the clairvoyance and the untaught knowledge of other languages, it was claimed, were not necessarily religious phenomena, being also known to psychics. The two schools of thought agreed to disagree.

After the case of the Bruner brothers, instances of demonic possession were recorded less hysterically, more accurately and more reasonably, helped by a greater understanding of both spiritual and medical matters. Such cases were not confined to the industrialised populations of Europe but were also found in the corners of the British empire.

After the turn of the century, news came from the Marianhill Order mission school in Umzinto, some fifty miles south of Durban, South Africa, of Clara Germana Cele, a Bantu girl born in Natal, South Africa, in 1890. Her parents had converted to Christianity but did not take their religion seriously. Germana had attended the mission school from the age of four. When she was sixteen, on 5 July 1906 to be precise, she handed to Father Erasmus Hörner a piece of paper which contained a written pact made with the Devil. From then on she behaved wildly, like a madwoman, crying out, 'I am lost! I have confessed and taken communion under false pretences! I must hang myself. Satan is calling me!'

There was no earthly explanation why a girl of her background, parentage, upbringing or education should behave in this manner. On 20 August, she tore her clothes, broke one of the posts on her bed, growled and grunted like an animal and seemed to carry out conversations with invisible people. When she was more rational and lucid, she called out to one of the nuns, 'Sister, please call Father Erasmus. I must confess and tell everything. But quick, quick, or Satan will kill me. He has me in his power! Nothing blessed is with me; I have thrown away all the [church] medals you gave me.'

Later she shouted: 'You have betrayed me. You promised me days of glory, but now you treat me cruelly.'

Two sisters who thought Germana was a fake were asked by the mother superior to guard the girl overnight along with three older girls. Germana, immediately aware of the plan, declared, 'I'll deal with them so they never forget it!'

At first everyone was in a good mood and the girls chatted

pleasantly among themselves. But suddenly Germana began asking contentious questions beyond her years and experience about God and faith. This led to a dispute. In the official record the incident was detailed thus:

> Before anyone realised what was going on, Germana stood before the sisters in blazing anger and upbraided them in a manner they would surely always remember about their lack of devotion and grace. When they made moves as if they might hit her, Germana streaked to the door like lightning, locked it and put the key in her pocket. Then she grabbed the two nuns by their caps, shook them and, with giant's strength, slammed one into one corner and threw the second into another corner of the room. Germana then severely beat one sister, tore the veil from her head, and left her in a daze; with that, she pushed her with one sudden push under the bed. With equal speed she was on top of the other nun, who was in a corner, choked and beat her. Next, she beat each one of them in turn. Of the three [older girls] none tried to touch her in this condition.

Up to that point, the nuns at the mission school had regarded Germana as a normal, healthy young person, somewhat erratic, perhaps, but no more than any other adolescent might be. As her condition worsened, the nuns and the priest began to record carefully the manifestations of demonic possession. When she was sprinkled with holy water or given it to drink it burned her head or mouth. When she was sprinkled with the ordinary water with which the font had been secretly filled, she instinctively knew and laughed at the deception. Whenever a cross was brought near her she complained noisily. Even when a small fragment of a cross was produced, heavily wrapped or otherwise concealed, she knew immediately what it was and protested vigorously.

On one occasion when she went into the kitchen, a huge flame suddenly leaped into the air. Everyone shouted in fear and ran out except for Germana, who just laughed and moved slowly away while the whole room filled with flames. On another occasion she was resting on her bed in the dormitory she shared with twenty or more other girls and suddenly cried for help. When Sister Juliana, who was sitting in a deckchair in the communal bedroom, went to her creaking bed and shook it, huge flames shot into the air. The flames subsided as the nuns sprinkled holy water on to the bed. Afterwards the boards and bedposts were found to be half burned but Germana's clothing and covers were unsinged.

The girl was moved to a private room in the house. Every night there were two or three thumpings in succession on the door. The cause of the noise was never traced. A reverend father and a monk, one of them armed with a gun, kept watch on Germana's bedroom from an empty room in the house. All remained quiet until:

> Suddenly at ten o'clock there was a sound like a thunderclap at the door. Inside, everyone cried out in fear and horror. We hurried outside to find out what was going on. Then again, one, two, five tremendous blows. We went out once more, and again there was nothing in sight. Banging and pounding could be heard on several doors inside the house. We went to investigate and found nothing. The noise and pounding continued in the rooms of the religious brothers, in the smithy, in the storage section, and even in the shed, where the animals had become restless, but nowhere was there anything to be seen. The noise stopped by eleven-fifteen.
>
> During the day when these phenomena occurred, Germana seemed oddly amused and laughed a good deal. The next day Sister Juliana had this to say, 'Last night around nine, Germana suddenly began laughing and said, "Just now the pastor and his brother are going downstairs to stand guard. He even has a gun with him. As if he could shoot a ghost with a gun! Is the baba [father] really that stupid? I'm sorry for the poor father, who gives so much to help me and others, but the one who is inside me is only taking a grim delight and pleasure in all this." '

Germana too displayed amazing clairvoyance. When Father Erasmus journeyed from Durban to Rome, she remained at the mission but was able to describe minute details of his journey and the names and addresses of places where he stayed. When a young man made fun of her condition, she shamed him by revealing scandalous details of his private life, complete with the names, times and dates of his liaisons.

While Father Erasmus was away and Germana was in a crisis, a young priest came, the Rituale Romanum under his arm and his stole round his neck, and started to pray. The girl began to interrupt. The priest ordered her to keep quiet. She became noisy, insistent and violent, whereupon the priest, who was obviously too young and too emotional to be much of an exorcist, forgot himself and slapped her.

Germana yelled at him: 'Why do you beat me? You know that it isn't I, Germana, who is doing this but the one who is within me. Does one beat a spirit? Is that what a priest does?'

This was too much for the short-tempered young man. He moved to slap her again. Germana knocked the Rituale out of his hand, tore the stole from his neck, ripped it into shreds, grabbed the priest by the neck, choked him and threw him to the ground. The man tried to fight back, there was a free-for-all and finally she threw him under the bed. Then she sat down in a corner and wept. The priest was badly hurt. His fingers were damaged and other parts of him covered with scratches and bruises.

Another of Germana's abilities under possession was to levitate. Levitation, literally something rising due to lightness, has, since the seventeenth century, been associated with spiritualism. 'Tables turn, furniture dances, men are levitated,' as the mediums used to boast.

Germana floated often three, four or five feet up in the air, sometimes vertically, with her feet downwards, and at other times horizontally, her whole body floating above her bed in a rigid position. Even her clothing did not fall downwards, as would be dictated by the laws of gravity. Instead, her dress remained tightly around her body and legs. If she was sprinkled with holy water, she came down immediately, and her clothing fell loosely around her on the bed. This extraordinary occurrence took place in the presence of witnesses, including outsiders. Even in church, where she could be seen by everyone, she would float above the pews. Some people tried to pull her down forcibly by her feet, but this proved to be impossible.

This phenomenon did not take place during periods of quiet and concentration or atmospheres of serenity but in those of raving and uproar at times so violent that Germana had to be handcuffed. It did not stop her levitating. The account recorded by the priests and nuns testifies that:

> Everyone sought to help, and still it took another three hours until we were finally able to put handcuffs on the girl as she was in a state of violent anger. Both her arms were stiff and immovable. At the same time and amid horrible noise and disturbance she was, over and over again, levitated off the ground while sitting in her chair.

One of the familiar signs of demonic possession exhibited by Germana was the ability to transform herself into a snake-like creature. Her whole body would become as flexible as rubber and she would writhe along the floor. At times her neck seemed to elongate, enhancing her reptilian appearance. Once, while she was being physically restrained, she darted like lightning at a nun kneeling in prayer in front of her and bit the poor sister on the arm. The marks made did not reflect the impression of Germana's teeth but were small red punctures resembling a snake bite.

On 10 September 1906, permission was given by the local bishop for an exorcism to be carried out by Father Erasmus, her confessor, and Father Mansuet, the mission rector. The rites commenced in the morning, lasted until noon, resumed at 3 pm and continued well into the night. The next morning they began again at eight o'clock and concluded at ten. The two exorcists put her under extreme pressure to renounce the Devil, and eventually the possessing demon said that he would signal his departure by performing, through Germana, a final act of levitation, an act of resigned defiance.

The Devil kept his word. The levitation occurred in the presence of 170 people in the mission chapel, who prayed and gave thanks for Germana's deliverance. But in January 1907 she had a relapse. While Father Erasmus was absent she made a new pact with the Devil and a new exorcism began on 24 April. It lasted for two days and this time it was successful. The Devil's final departure was signalled by an incomparably foul smell.

9

Crowley: Satan's Living 'Beast'

I administered a large dose of arsenic [to the cat]. I chloroformed it, hanged it above the gas jet, stabbed it, cut its throat, smashed its skull . . . drowned it and threw it out of the window.

Aleister ('The Beast') Crowley, *My Confessions*, 1931

Even in the 1990s, whenever a major case of demonic possession erupts in the media, the image of the evil Aleister Crowley is revived. Crowley was almost certainly possessed himself and he was unquestionably responsible for the physical and mental downfall of others. His outrageous behaviour can be traced through an interest in so-called esoteric studies to extreme wickedness.

When the Roman Catholic Church first looked upon freemasonry as a rival religion, the masons' secretive rites and anticlerical sentiments were attacked with blood-libel charges. Libel is a permanent form of publication or broadcast which tends to expose a person to hatred, ridicule or contempt. Blood-libel is usually the defamation of groups alleged to be guilty of murder and even genocide, often maliciously invented for political, racial or religious reasons. Freemasons were accused by word-of-mouth rumour of abducting babies and ritually murdering them. A Parisian journalist, Gabriel-Jogand Pagès, using the name Léo Taxil, fooled an international readership by inventing a conspiracy of masons directed from London, England, and Charleston, South Carolina, USA, which involved Devil-worship, bisexual orgies and ritual sacrifice of animals and children. His written hoax was so convincing that it embarrassed some British dabblers in the occult into abandoning their activities and disbanding their organisations.

To the astonishment of the Establishment, Taxil named William Wynn Westcott, one of Her Majesty's coroners for London, as head of the Satanic underground movement in Britain. The idea that a coroner, whose duty was to investigate how people died, should preside over ritual sacrifice sent a shudder through the corridors of power and the bereaved. Westcott was in fact a Rosicrucian, a member of an ancient, sometimes secret pseudo-masonic fraternity which dabbled in religious and occult practices.

Aleister Crowley, alias 'The Beast', turned Taxil's inventive accusations into reality. He combined the Rosicrucians' secrecy with the intellectual argument of Margaret Murray, the anthropologist, who held that the witches of Western Europe were the lingering adherents of a once-great pagan religion that had been displaced, but not entirely, by Christianity. As a result, witchcraft, Satanism, Devil-worship and associated attractions gained a new lease of life.

In 1931, Crowley wrote in the *Pall Mall Magazine*:

> I know that Black Masses are being celebrated today. On Friday nights there are special invocations to Pan and, on one occasion, a cat, which was considered to be an evil spirit, was sacrificed. It is even said that the blood of the cat was drunk.

Many dismissed tales of such devotions as nothing more than fashionable antics by people in embroidered robes decorated with hieroglyphics from Tarot cards and similar magic symbols. But Crowley had, since the age of eleven, dedicated himself to a life which was to embrace every excess from sexual perversions to live sacrifices. In his autobiography, *My Confessions*, he wrote about the family cat.

> I administered a large dose of arsenic. I chloroformed it, hanged it above the gas jet, stabbed it, cut its throat, smashed its skull and, when it had been pretty thoroughly burnt, drowned it and threw it out of the window that the fall might end its ninth life. The operation was successful. I was genuinely sorry for the animal; I simply forced myself to carry out the experiment in the interest of pure science.

Crowley's sexual appetite for women was first recorded when he seduced the kitchenmaid on his mother's bed while the family were at church. From then on he enjoyed a succession of prostitutes and mistresses, all of whom were fascinated by two characteristics: his hypnotic eyes and his animal virility. A titled woman who stopped to gaze into the window of a shop in Piccadilly was overcome by the reflection of his eyes as he stood behind her. They had never met each other before, yet immediately she booked into an hotel with him and stayed there for ten days. Women, Crowley thought, should be 'brought round to the back door like the milk'.

Crowley claimed that the secret of his sexual prowess was the 'perfume of immortality', an aphrodisiac made from a secret recipe which he rubbed into his scalp. It contained ingredients like musk from the male deer, ambergris from the sperm whale and civet, from the American cat-like mammal of that name. It was said that women whinnied after him like horses and men thought he had 'a sweet, slightly nauseous odour'.

Sex was a powerful ingredient of Crowley's evil beliefs. His first wife, Rose, is thought to have sealed his entry into the world of black magic when they visited the Cairo Museum together on 18 March 1904. She stood as if in a trance and said, 'Aleister, Horus is waiting for you. There he is.' And there, painted on a wooden obelisk displayed in a glass case, was the falcon-headed god Horus, in Egyptian mythology a solar deity, the son of Osiris and Isis. What shook Crowley was that the exhibit bore the number 666.

The Book of Revelations (xiii), talks about the Beast of the Apocalypse, the demon who bears the name 666, who 'came out of the sea, having ten horns and seven heads, and on his horns ten diadems, and upon his heads names of blasphemy,' and 'Let him that hath understanding count the number of the beast: for it is the number of a man; and his number is six hundred threescore and six.'

Crowley was convinced that the title was meant for him. He claimed that Horus immediately recognised him and sent him a spirit guide with prophecies for him to pass on to the world. Crowley affected a bizarre hairstyle which culminated in a waxed horn, making him look like either a fat unicorn or the great god Pan of Greek mythology, according to your point of view. His new diabolical religion was a ragbag of mysticism, poetry, prediction and pornography. It would, he claimed, lead mankind to a 'new dawn' – and he had been elected as its leader.

To convince the public, he introduced a series of publicity-seeking gimmicks. He filed two of his teeth to points so that he could give women the 'serpent's kiss'. One woman who was thus bitten on the arm claimed to have suffered blood poisoning. He defecated on drawing-room carpets and when his hosts protested claimed that his excreta was sacred. He appeared at the Café Royal in Regent Street dressed in wizard's robes and, not surprisingly, no one spoke to him. He boasted, 'There you are! That proves I can make myself invisible. Nobody spoke to me. That proves no one can see me.'

He was always accompanied by a 'permanent mistress' who was always described as 'The Scarlet Woman'. One of them, Leah Faesi, a New York singing teacher, had her breast decorated with the 'mark of the Beast', a cross within a circle, for which ornament Crowley claimed he had branded her with a dagger heated in fire.

In March 1920, Crowley founded the Temple of Black Magic, the Sacred Abbey of Thelemic Mysteries, in an isolated villa set amid olive groves near the fishing village of Cefalu, Sicily. 'My house is going to be the whore's hell,' he wrote, 'a secret place of the quenchless fire of Lust and the eternal torment of Love.'

The temple boasted an altar on which lay *The Book of the Law*, in which he had written down the prophecies he claimed had been handed down to him by the god Horus. Around it were ritual carafes, chalices, patens and 'cakes of light', a blasphemous mockery of the consecrated wafer made of oatmeal, honey, red wine and (he claimed) animal or menstrual blood. Behind the altar were the sacred thrones marked for The Beast and The Scarlet Woman. The temple walls were covered with Crowley's own paintings depicting every sexual act in every conceivable position and quite a few which are impossible.

The gross and perverted ceremonies performed inside the abbey terrified the locals, who were both deeply religious and superstitious. As they passed, the villagers crossed themselves in fear as screams, shrieks and wailing gibberish echoed from the building. Inside, in one drug-induced ritual, The Scarlet Woman committed bestiality with a goat, after which the goat's throat was ceremonially cut by Crowley and the blood allowed to run over another woman's back.

Wealthy, dissolute disciples flocked to the abbey to take part in orgies. Among them were Raoul Loveday, a twenty-three-year-old Oxford University graduate, and his wife, Betty May, an artists' model, who earned enough to keep them both. Before setting off for Sicily, they had visited the Egyptian Room of the British Museum, where Betty May had poked fun at the mummy of a high priestess of the wrathful ram-headed Egyptian god Amon-Ra. Her husband was terrified and warned her that Amon-Ra destroyed all who offended the priestess.

Loveday prayed that the curse would fall on him rather than his wife. It was she who noticed, looking through some photographs of her husband, that a mysterious, shadowy image of him lying horizontally, apparently dead, had begun to appear over his head in each of the prints. Even so, he insisted that they visit Crowley in Sicily as arranged. Betty May detested Crowley and was horrified by the sexual orgies attended by Crowley's children, legitimate and illegitimate. However, Loveday – who had undoubtedly been attracted to Satanism at Oxford – became Crowley's disciple. The self-styled Beast gave him the title 'Aud', which means magical light.

Drugs, dissipation and loss of blood caused by scourges of the flesh imposed by Crowley and self-inflicted wounds, part of an almost daily routine, sapped Loveday's strength. One night during a black magic ceremony, he was forced to sacrifice a cat. The Scarlet Woman lifted the 'Cup of Abominations' in readiness to catch the blood. Loveday slashed at the animal's throat. The cat wriggled out of his hands and ran around the room, blood pouring from its neck.

Loveday, trembling and overwrought, managed to catch the animal and kill it with a second blow, but he had to step outside the 'protection' of the magic pentagram to do so. The Scarlet Woman handed him the cup and he drank the blood. Within days, Loveday fell ill. A doctor was summoned and diagnosed acute gastro-enteritis. Crowley believed that his disciple had fallen victim to an evil spell. Betty May wondered if it was the curse of Amon-Ra after all, but Crowley said it was because he had unwisely stepped outside the 'magic circle'.

On 16 February 1923, Raoul Loveday died. His wife insisted that his body fell into the shape of the ectoplasmic image she had seen on the photographs. When the grieving widow landed at Southampton, reporters flocked to hear her views on Crowley. The *Sunday Express* referred to this 'maelstrom of filth and obscenity . . . horrible sexual debauchees . . . [and] the depths of depravity'. Other newspapers picked up The Scarlet Woman's oath from a 'record book' said to have been found in the abbey:

I will work the work of wickedness.
I will be loud and adulterous.
I will be shameless before all men.
I will freely prostitute my body to the lusts of each and
every living creature that shall desire it.
I claim the title Mystery of Mysteries,
Babalon the Great and the Number 156
and the Robe of the Woman of Whoredoms
and the Cup of Abominations.

Within three months, the Italian authorities had expelled Crowley from the country. He was deported to France and, for a time, Britain refused to re-admit him. His passport had expired and on some pretext or another it was not renewed.

When he did return, he had to content himself with publishing, usually at his own expense, pornographic books and pseudo-mystical works, including *Magick, White Stains, Snowdrops From a*

Curate's Garden and *My Confessions*. In *Magick*, under the heading 'Bloody Sacrifice', he wrote, 'A male child of perfect innocence and high intelligence is the most satisfactory and suitable victim.' A sharp-eyed editor studied Crowley's claims and added a footnote: 'He [must have] made this particular sacrifice on an average about 150 times every year between 1912 and 1928.'

Crowley knew how to make money through self-publicity and by at least one legal action, in which he was awarded £50 against a bookseller. In 1932, the writer Nina Hamnett's autobiography was published. Recalling her friendship with Crowley, she wrote:

> Crowley had a temple in Cefalu in Sicily. He was supposed to practise Black Magic there; and one day a baby was said to have disappeared mysteriously. There was also a goat there. This all pointed to Black Magic, so people said, and the inhabitants of the village were frightened of him.

Crowley spotted an ideal opportunity to gain more publicity and more money. He sued the publishers, Constable, and the author for libel. He pleaded that he was a harmless, misunderstood, misrepresented, ageing scholar. Even his friends and the fawning authors who had spread his fame could not dissuade him from pursuing the action. Mr J. P. Eddy, KC, his lawyer, advised Crowley's solicitors, 'I have no hesitation in saying that if the defendants are in possession of that book [*White Stains*] your chances of winning this action are negligible.'

The self-styled Beast was undeterred, and in court he smiled as his counsel described him as 'an altruist, a white magician, whose life has been a crusade against black magic'. The lawyer related how Crowley had inherited a £40,000 fortune and had devoted his life to poetry, art, travel, walking across the Sahara and mountaineering, climbing the Alps. As for the abbey at Cefalu, that, said Mr Eddy, was 'a little community for the purpose of studying white magic'.

At least, that was what Crowley had told his solicitors. Mr Malcolm Hilbery, KC, later Mr Justice Hilbery, counsel for the publishers, put it to Crowley in the witness box:

'Are you asking for damages because your reputation has suffered?'

'Yes.'

'For many years you have been publicly denounced as the worst man in the world?'

'Only by the lowest kind of newspaper.'

'Did any paper call you "The Monster of Wickedness"?'

'I can't remember.'

'Have you, from the time of your adolescence, openly defied all moral conventions?'

'No.'

'And proclaimed your contempt for all the doctrines of Christianity?'

'Not all the doctrines.'

'Did you take to yourself the designation of "The Beast 666"?'

'Yes.'

'Do you call yourself the Master Therion?'

'Yes.'

'What does Therion mean?'

'Great Wild Beast.'

'Do these titles convey a fair expression of your practice and outlook on life?'

'The Beast 666 only means "sunlight". You can call me "Little Sunshine".'

When the laughter had subsided, Hilbery read some erotic verses from Crowley's book *Clouds Without Water*, and then asked: 'Have you not built a reputation on books which are indecent?'

'It has long been laid down that art has nothing to do with morals.'

'We may assume that you have followed that in your practice of writing?'

'I have always endeavoured to use the gift of writing which has been vouchsafed to me for the benefit of my readers.'

'Decency and indecency have nothing to do with it?'

'I do not think they have. You can find indecency in Shakespeare, Sterne, Swift and every other English writer if you try.'

Here it became obvious that not only had Hilbery read the accounts of Mr (later Sir) Edward Carson's famous cross-examination of Oscar Wilde at his disastrous libel action against the Marquess of Queensbury, but so had Crowley. Carson had read one of Wilde's poems and demanded, 'Is that a beautiful phrase?' Wilde replied, 'Not as you read it, Mr Carson. You read it very badly.' Now Hilbery recited a piece of Crowley's poetry and asked: 'Is that not filth?'

Crowley replied: 'As you read it, it is magnificent.'

If Crowley was a pornographer was he also, as was suggested in the alleged libel, a practitioner of black magic? Hilbery quoted from Crowley's books on magic and the occult. 'You say here, "I had two temples: one white, the walls being lined with six mirrors, each six feet in height; the other black, a mere cupboard, in which stood an altar, supported by the figure of a Negro standing on his hands. The presiding genius of the place was a human skeleton—" '

Crowley did not let him finish, interrupting: 'Yes, the skeleton was from Millikin and Lawley's, the medical shop.'

Counsel continued to quote: ' "—which I fed from time to time with blood, small birds, and the like." Was that true?'

'Yes.'

'That was white magic?'

'It was a very scientific experiment.'

Hilbery again quoted from Crowley's work. ' "The idea was to give it life, but I never got further than causing the bones to be covered with a viscous slime." '

'I expect that was the soot of London,' Crowley responded.

Hilbery quoted the plaintiff on human and animal sacrifice, on transubstantiation, on his ability to invoke evil spirits and summon up supernatural darkness in the middle of the day. He read from an interview with Crowley in the *Sunday Dispatch*. ' "They have called me the worst man in the world. They have accused me of doing everything from murdering women and throwing their bodies in the Seine to drug peddling." Is that, then, your general reputation?'

'Any man of distinction has rumour about him,' replied Crowley.

'Does any man of distinction necessarily have it said about him that he is the worst man in the world, by way of rumour?'

'No, not necessarily. He has to be very distinguished for that.'

'You wrote, "James Douglas described me as a monster of wickedness. Horatio Bottomley branded me as a dirty, degenerate cannibal." You never took any action against any of the persons who wrote and published those things about you, did you?'

'No,' conceded The Beast.

'And then comes this silly little paragraph in this book, and you run to your lawyer with it, according to you, to bring an action for injury to this reputation of being the worst man in the world. Is that the case?'

'I also have the reputation of being the best man in the world.'

Mr Martin O'Connor, counsel for the book's author, Nina Hamnett, questioned Crowley about his debts and challenged him to make himself invisible as he claimed he had done at the Café Royal and to conjure up demons. Crowley declined.

Betty May, the widow of the Oxford graduate who had died at Cefalu, gave evidence of the perverted rituals, drugs, blasphemies and obscenities, animal sacrifices and pornographic paintings in Crowley's 'chamber of nightmares'.

By then, the jury had heard enough. They stopped the case and the judge, Mr Justice Swift, said, 'I have never heard such dreadful, horrible, blasphemous, abominable stuff and by a man who poses as the greatest poet.'

Outside the court, Crowley found some sympathy. A nineteen-year-old girl told him, 'That verdict, it's the wickedest thing since the Crucifixion.'

'Is there anything I can do to help?' asked the sixty-year-old Beast.

'Couldn't I be the mother of your child?'

Crowley obliged. He had already left his two wives in lunatic asylums; his mistresses to the gin bottle, the drug addicts' hypodermics or the streets to earn their money by prostitution. The Beast himself died ten years later in an obscure boarding house in Hastings, Sussex, a physical wreck and dependent on a heavy dose of injected heroin each day. Members of black magic circles in London, Lewes and Shoreham attended his pagan funeral.

Yet neither his lifestyle, the allegations, the confessions nor the libel action entirely convinced everybody that he was the epitome of evil – or that he was possessed. In him, genuine demonism and self-destruction could not be entirely separated from self-advertisement and money-making.

10
Devilish Murder

The girl had been hypnotised and exposed to occult obscenities so persistently that she was almost insane. Her own pet dog ran howling in fear from her. It took two years to restore her mind.

Detective Chief Superintendent Robert Fabian, Scotland Yard, ***London After Dark*, 1954**

Aleister Crowley waved the branches of the forbidden tree, and the vulnerable, the defenceless and the weak took the fruit and joined in Satanic worship. He had a crony and helper in Dennis Wheatley, who, although he denied ever taking part in Satanic rituals, whipped up the fascination for Satanic covens in a series of accurate fictional books, *The Devil Rides Out* (1934), *Strange Conflict* (1941), *The Haunting of Toby Jugg* (1948), *To the Devil a Daughter* (1953) and *The Satanist* (1960). By portraying fictional, wealthy, otherwise intelligent Devil-worshippers, often in league with the current British enemies, Nazis, Fascists and Communists, Wheatley turned Satanism into a popular, recognisable and acceptable 'baddy'. And, having excited popular interest, allegedly for the public good, he was always careful to warn the public not to dabble in such matters.

So great was the renewed interest in the Devil that an influential circle of Christian writers, the Inklings, devotees of J. R. R. Tolkien, exposed such evils in their own fictional works. C. S. Lewis, with the help of his considerable inside knowledge, confirmed the existence of many demonic cults in our universities by portraying one of them in *The Hideous Strength* (1946), which featured recruiting agents and mutilation rites. On the other side, Charles Williams, who had been a Rosicrucian and a confidant of Crowley, and whose knowledge of black magic was extensive, published a whole series of witchcraft novels. The best of these, *All Hallows Eve* (1948), received a literary accolade in the form of an appreciative introduction by the poet T. S. Eliot. Its central figure, a young girl who has been specially conceived to be a sacrifice to the Devil, is saved in the end by a Christian nurse who baptises her.

Whatever the motives of the writers, the effect of this trend was to encourage a bigger than ever popular interest in evil, in personal and institutional wickedness. Much of it was private and offended only moral codes, but incidences of related assault, violence, torture and reputedly murder at times attracted the attention of the police.

The emergence of criminologists, both academic and streetwise, in exposing organised baseness was as surprising as its efficacy was doubtful. Henry T. F. Rhodes, who was a student at the Institute of Forensic Science at the University of Lyons, France, under the pioneering Dr Edmond Locard, and who became general secretary of the British Association of Chemists, wrote a sympathetic study of occult witch hunts, *Satanic Mass* (1954), revealing that underground Satanic movements had been guilty of child murders up to the 1700s. There was, however, scant substantiation for his claims. He held that by the 1950s 'Satanism no longer looms large and terrible because it no longer exists as a kind of public mischief.' By then, it seemed to have degenerated into a 'commercial racket' by comparison with the evils of previous centuries.

Yet Detective Superintendent Robert Fabian of Scotland Yard – known to the popular press as Fabian of the Yard – painted a lurid picture of degradation in *London After Dark* (1954).

> The practice of Black Magic – of diabolical religious rites in the heart of London – is spreading steadily. There is more active Satan worship today than ever since the Dark Ages, when witches were burnt on Tower Hill . . .
>
> When a Sunday in December falls on the 13th day of the month (as it did in 1953) and is, therefore, the 13th day before Christmas, the moon may shine upon London's rooftops, but, in any case, men and women will congregate at midnight in secret temples of South Kensington, Paddington – and I believe Bloomsbury, too – to strip off their clothes and worship Satan with ritual and sacrifice that would shame an African savage!

Fabian described one private 'temple of Satanism' as being equipped with black candles, inverted crucifixes and other symbols of diabolical wizardry, including pentagrams daubed on walls and ceilings. During rituals, communion wafers were blasphemed and ritually soiled, orgies followed and susceptible young girls and boys were dedicated to Pan. The officer admitted, however, that the police had never made any arrests. The cults were very difficult to infiltrate, and any potential police witness who did see the obscene ceremonies might be hypnotised to invalidate any evidence he or she might have been able to give.

From a Scotland Yard file he cited one Satanic cult survivor, a twenty-one-year-old girl who had been taken by her mother to a lecture on Satanism.

> She was invited to a garden party at the house of a woman calling herself a 'High Priestess', who persuaded the girl to sing a 'magical invocation', in the process of which the girl was successfully hypnotised.
>
> She did not return home for months. When, with the help of the Yard, her parents finally recovered her, the girl had been hypnotised and exposed to occult obscenities so persistently that she was almost insane. Her own pet dog ran howling in fear from her. It took two years to restore her mind.

Fabian added that 'there was no prosecution because there was no evidence. The girl had been "willed" to forget how it happened.' He blamed 'psychic circles' which drew in the curious with 'harmless spiritualism' and then gradually seduced them, through hypnosis and drugs, into Satanism.

A very experienced police officer, Fabian had been head of the Vice Squad at Scotland Yard, but was called in to join the Murder Squad to help Warwickshire police investigate what became known as the 'Witchcraft Murder'. At twilight on 14 February, St Valentine's Day, in 1945, the body of Charles Walton, a seventy-four-year-old hedge-cutter, was found under an oak tree on Meon Hill, near Lower Quinton in Warwickshire, just off the road between Stratford-on-Avon and Cheltenham. His own pitchfork had been driven through his body with such force that it penetrated the earth for six inches underneath the corpse. It took the joint efforts of two burly policemen to pull it out. His hands and arms were badly cut, as if he had put up a fight for his life, and the rough sign of a cross had been slashed in his throat.

Walton had been an oddball character, a recluse, a heavy cider-drinker who reputedly talked to birds and animals and was said to have the evil eye, the power to harm or even kill with a glance.

The county police asked for Scotland Yard's help because in those days the Metropolitan police had superior skills in investigations and were not embarrassed by local fears and favours. In this case, however, the Londoners had reckoned without the local myths, legends and superstitions from which William Shakespeare – who was born, married and buried in nearby Stratford – drew much of his material. One legend has it that the Devil threw a huge clod of earth at the newly built abbey at Evesham, Worcestershire, intending to destroy it. Fortunately, St Egwin, Bishop of Worcester, who founded the abbey in the year 717, was watching. His prayers were able to stop the missile, which fell to the ground and become Meon Hill.

Walton had apparently believed that the evil eye could make cattle die and crops rot, and he had spoken volubly about it when a heifer was found dying in a ditch. Superintendent Spooner, the local officer in charge of the case, handed Fabian a book, *Folk Lore, Old Customs and Superstitions in Shakespeare-land* by J. Harvey Bloom, and pointed out a passage: 'In 1875 . . . a young man killed an old woman named Ann Turner with a hay-fork because he believed she had bewitched him.' He produced another volume, *Warwickshire* by Clive Holland, in which 'A man named John Haywood stabbed to death with a pitchfork an old woman, exclaiming that he would kill all the sixteen witches in Long Compton . . . His mode of killing was evidently a survival of the ancient Anglo-Saxon custom of dealing with witches by "stacung", or sticking spikes into them.'

The police made door-to-door inquiries in the village but the people lowered their eyes and talked about bad crops and the heifer dying in the ditch. When asked about Charles Walton, they shook their heads and would not answer.

Like so many country folk, the locals believed the legend of the black dog, which dates back to Horace, the first-century Roman poet and satirist, who held that the sight of a black dog, particularly with pups, was an evil omen. As we have seen, the Devil has often been portrayed as a black dog.

Fabian described how he was actually standing on Meon Hill when a black dog ran past. Soon afterwards a farm lad followed, and the officer asked him, 'Looking for that dog, son?'

'Dog, mister?' The boy went pale.

'A black dog.'

The boy ran away as fast as his heavy earth-clogged boots would carry him.

When Spooner was told of the incident, he explained: 'There's a local legend of a man who saw a black dog on this same hill. It turned into a headless woman who rustled past him in a black silk dress. Next day his sister died.'

'Who was the man?' Fabian asked.

'His name was Charles Walton.'

The police took 4,000 statements, traced dozens of gipsies and other travelling folk and sent twenty-nine samples of hair, clothing and other trace evidence to the area forensic laboratory in Birmingham, but the murder remained unsolved. When Fabian called at one house and said, 'I'm inquiring about the late Charles Walton,' the occupier snapped, 'He's been dead and buried a month. What are you worrying about?' and slammed the door. When the officers called at the village pub, the locals drained their glasses and left hurriedly.

The belief that this was a witchcraft murder was supposed to have been given credence by Margaret Mead, the American anthropologist and expert on primitive religions. She visited Lower Quinton in 1950, five years after the killing, and declared herself 'almost satisfied' that the murder was a witchcraft killing. Colin Wilson and Pat Pitman quoted her on the matter in their *Encyclopaedia of Murder* (1961). Unfortunately, they had received their information about her views from a highly suspect source, Gerald Gardner, the leader of a witchcraft movement.

Many years afterwards, I visited Lower Quinton as a result of an anonymous letter. A man tending the neat graves in the parish churchyard pointed to Charles Walton's grave and said, 'Him?' Turning to another tombstone, he went on, 'He were killed by him, and it was all over how much an hour Charles got for hedge-cutting. Nothing to do with that rubbish about the evil eye or witchcraft at all.'

Dr Hilda Ellis Davidson of the Lucy Cavendish College, Cambridge, a distinguished member of the Folklore Society between 1949 and 1986, had a pertinent recollection of another member, the flamboyant and somewhat sinister informant Dr Gerald Gardner, who wrote popular books on modern witchcraft and was himself an unashamed practitioner, keeping an extremely odd museum of witchcraft first on the Isle of Man and later in Cornwall. Dr Davidson told of Folklore Society dinners at which

> he [Gardner] would startle the waitresses by pulling out an evil-looking dagger or an exotic magic ring between the courses, or, even worse, offer postcards with naked witches portrayed on them. Mrs Lake Burnett [the society secretary] would sometimes speculate, as she viewed some almost illiterate letter received from him, how and where he could have received his doctorate.

There is little doubt that Gardner was in many respects a quack. He claimed to have been initiated into an underground coven of witches directly descended from one of the mediaeval cults which Margaret Murray, the anthropologist and sometime president of the Folklore Society, believed were driven underground by Christianity, even though by this time the theory had long been discredited.

One of Gardner's publications, *Book of Shadows*, was supposed to be so secret that those initiated into witchcraft were instructed by their mentors to copy out the ancient passages by hand. Each copy, Gardner explained, was to be burned at each witch's death. Inquiring scholars discovered that this was why there were no original manuscripts to substantiate the claim that his brand of religion was founded so long ago. Not surprisingly, Gardner was believed only by the extremely gullible, but they were many.

The revival of witchcraft and its diabolical rituals in the 1950s must have persuaded many sane people that the organisers were possessed. On 16 March 1958, a priest at one of London's most famous churches asked for protection by the police from a Satanic cult operating in the Chelsea district. Highly intelligent men and women in the group held rites in different houses once a week, culminating in a black mass to pervert men and girls away from God and into Devil-worship. A former cult leader claimed they indulged in blood-drinking and orgies, during which the leaders photographed members in compromising positions, thereby ensuring that none could return to the normal, decent society of fellow Christians. Faced with blackmail, the members either remained in the cult, vanished or committed suicide.

Church robberies were rife at that time, although the target was mainly lead guttering from roofs which could be sold as scrap metal. Occasionally, though, churches were broken into, and while regalia, gold, silver and jewelled items and collection boxes were the principal attraction, the idea that they were wanted for black mass ceremonies seemed far-fetched and no police confirmation was forthcoming.

In 1958, Leslie Roberts, a self-styled authority on the occult, told the Brighton Forum Society that there were numerous witchcraft covens in the area, and there is little doubt that that is as true thirty-seven years later as it was then. But he went on to claim that one of these gatherings, not necessarily limited to the usual thirteen witches, was led by a nurse who had 'access to blood, which is required at certain rites'. He offered to direct police to a private house where a black baby had allegedly been sacrificed during a black mass. Police found 'no substance whatsoever in the matter'. Roberts implied that the police were shielding the cults.

A second wave of Satanic panics focused on a series of grave desecrations. Among the most publicised were those near Clophill, Bedfordshire. In March 1963, children playing in the eerie ruins of the roofless, disused Church of St Mary on top of Dead Man's Hill found that several graves had been opened. Police found 'scattered feathers of a sacrificial cock' and discovered that the tomb of one Jenny Humberstone, wife of an eighteenth-century apothecary, had been torn open and her 200-year-old bones arranged in a circle around the gutted nave of the church – according to one local paper, 'in the pattern used for the black mass'.

Some locals wondered whether this was an attempt at necromancy, in which black witchcraft magicians are supposed to summon and speak with the dead. On another occasion, tombs were again smashed and graves desecrated as part of some fantastic ritual.

The local vicar, the Reverend Leslie Barker, recalled that someone had telephoned him the previous month to ask if the church had ever been used for occult purposes, and commented, 'It certainly looks as if a black mass was held there.' The churchwarden added: 'We think the gang were fanatics who have done this terrible thing for black magic rites, some kind of Devil worship.'

The police would not rule out the idea that occultists had disturbed the graves, but they noted that robbers might have been looking for jewellery or lead linings. The vicar disagreed. 'Satan-worshippers are known to always use a female at the centre of their ceremonies,' he said, and there were indications that a woman or women had been present. He also found two Celtic crosses on walls inside the church, one rather weather-beaten. Both had been painted red at different times, possibly with animal blood, indicating that the church had been used for occult rituals over a period.

By 2 April 1963, Jenny Humberstone's grave had been disturbed three more times and was attracting a constant stream of visitors from London and other urban areas. Women's Institutes, Rotary Clubs, Lions and other such clubs organised coach trips – in aid of charity, of course – to the site. Meanwhile, a former forestry student approached a local paper, confessing that he had taken part in a hoaxed 'black mass' two years previously. He and a dozen other students from an agricultural college had killed a cockerel, painted one of the crosses and left trails of blood and feathers for the police to find. An unexpected rain shower scattered the evidence, however, and the hoax failed. 'It was only a huge joke,' the student said, adding that he could guess who had conducted the more recent ritual. 'I'm fairly sure that the present ceremonial was a similar stunt.'

Fact or fraud? Curious pilgrims to such desecrated shrines are generally keener to believe that black magic and Devil-worship have taken place than that juveniles have been conducting practical jokes. The late Eric Maple, author of popular books on witchcraft traditions, visited Clophill and suggested that the bones found there had been used by black magicians as implements during psychic attacks on others. He reported:

> After being impregnated with *mana*, or magic powder, the bones are pointed in the direction of one who is to be destroyed, and he begins to suffer a mysterious bruising of the body known as 'the Devil's pinch'.

Maple later published a coffee-table book on witchcraft containing grisly photographs of the vandalisms he had visited. He wrote:

> Those who feel the inclination for a truly Gothic experience should visit desolate Clophill to savour its wilderness of desecrated and looted tombs, symbols of the revival of black magic in the twentieth century.

Many had already done so. When the Reverend Barker retired in 1969, he said that since 1963 'not a month has gone by without one of the graves or tombs in the churchyard being dug up and some sort of rite performed'.

These desecrations were followed in July 1969 by a series of apparent sacrilegious acts in Lancashire. On 7 December a bell-ringer went to the parish church of Westham, Sussex, to find four men lighting candles in the chapel and performing what he called 'a kind of mumbo-jumbo chant'. The men escaped and the vicar commented, 'I have no doubt that this was a black magic game. They have been practising in Somerset and are known often to set fire to churches.' John Kobler, an American writer, reported that by 1964 British police claimed to have linked more than 200 acts of graveyard vandalism to black magic.

When Gerald Gardner died in 1964, neo-pagans were as common in Britain as they were in the United States. A series of squabbles erupted over who was to lead the Wiccan movement of the 'only real witches', which Gardner said had been passed down through the ages. Schisms followed as several claimed the right to be Gardner's successor, having been either appointed by him or initiated into traditions superior to the one he maintained he had inherited.

All these witches – including Sybil Leek, Alex Sanders and Leslie Roberts – claimed to be white witches completely opposed to black magic. On 16 February 1964, they demonstrated their power and voice by turning up in force at a Folklore Society lecture at University College, London, to hear Dr Rossell Hope Robbins, professor of English at Colombia University, New York, speak on 'The Synthetic Sabbath', supported by his evidence that witchcraft was an imposture.

Dr Jacqueline Simpson, the current president of the Folklore Society, recalled the event.

> It was quite an experience. There was a pile of broomsticks in the corridor, brought, I hope and believe, by students, not witches. And I noted with dismay that female scholars and witches can look rather alike, both tending to dramatic jewellery and hats. As a newcomer I was spotted [by a fellow academic]. 'Let's sit together and be respectable,' said she. 'Glad to see you're wearing coral beads. They'll keep off the evil eye – we'll need them.'
>
> She was right. Dr Robbins, an American, was known for his hostility to Margaret Murray's view that the witches of history were a secret society of fertility cultists. He stressed that their confessions had been got by torture and deprivation of sleep, and were moulded by leading questions. There had never been any covens, sabbaths, or old gods and goddesses surviving – just victims of religious and judicial scapegoating. But by 1964 neo-pagans were common here and in the USA, and they claimed that a Murray-style old religion had been passed down through the centuries. About thirty of them had come to heckle Robbins, and had alerted the press.
>
> The most picturesque was Sybil Leek, high priestess of the New Forest Coven, who had a tame jackdaw, Hotfoot Jackson, perched on her shoulder. He squawked occasionally during the lecture, and sometimes so aptly that I suspected her of prodding him when she particularly disliked what was being said. There were also a few human cries of dissent, but on the whole the lecture itself passed smoothly.
>
> Question-time, however, was chaotic. Witches arose and harangued us. Dr Robbins became locked in verbal combat with an elderly warlock [Alex Sanders] who said he owned handwritten books of spells and rites centuries old, but they must never be shown to anyone outside the craft. Robbins said that he had seen such things himself, but the paper and writing were modern. Naturally, said the warlock, since a witch always copies out any grimoires she inherits or acquires, and destroys the originals. 'Very unfortunate, or maybe very convenient,' said Robbins.

Angrily, the witches asked how Dr Robbins could explain the close likeness between what they did and believed and what Dr Murray had described in her books. Simple, said he, modern witches had cribbed all their ideas from these very books, which had been around for forty years, and from later ones by Robert Graves and Gerald Gardner. None of these were historically sound.

It must have been bitter for the witches to hear all this; not only was their cherished self-image being denied, but Margaret Murray was being criticised by the very society of which she had been president, and which only a few years previously had affectionately marked her hundredth birthday.

Probably the Folklore Society Committee were feeling equally tense, dreading bad publicity and striving to make clear their academic standards. The long evening wore on; Hotfoot Jackson squawked; Peter Opie, the luckless chairman, sat with his head in his hands, speechless. Everyone's eye grew steadily more evil. But next day the press coverage was ample, and, as far as I know, reasonably balanced. As Mrs Leek told the *Daily Mirror*, 'Ours is the only true religion.'

The meeting, which I, too, attended, was indeed bitter. One of the hecklers demanded of Professor Robbins: 'What is your religion?' When he replied, 'Atheist,' the witches and warlocks thought intellectual victory was theirs and whooped with joy.

But the witches were not as white as they painted themselves. Alan W. Smith, who was then secretary of the society, recalls that one young man at the meeting, after satisfying himself that Smith was not 'one of them', provided him with a duplicated publication produced by some former disciples now disenchanted with Gardner's witchcraft. This included rituals involving flagellation and culminating in the 'Great Rite' (sexual intercourse), either real or simulated.

According to Smith:

> It is my firm belief that the late Gerald Gardner was the 'onlie begetter' of our latter-day Sunday newspaper witches, but that he did possess a real power insofar as he could persuade so many people to dream his dreams and act out his fantasies with him.

Ralph Merrifield, curator of the Guildhall Museum, City of London, once wrote an article about witch bottles. Gardner read it, called on Merrifield, and promptly anointed him on the wrist with oil from a witch bottle. Later his wife took one sniff and demanded, 'Where have you been?'

Gardner thought the curator a potential convert and invited him to a meeting where there would be dances. Asked what sort of dances, Gardner said, 'Foxtrots and other ballroom dances.' Seeing the disappointment on Merrifield's face, he hastily added, 'Of course, we take all our clothes off first.' The curator declined the invitation.

Merrifield was in Ghana at the time of that country's independence celebrations and by chance saw Gardner, who was there to give a lecture on witchcraft at the YMCA in Accra. The hall was packed to capacity and there was nearly a riot among those unable to gain admission. When Gardner visited the market he was mobbed by the market women with cries of 'Master, you give me baby?' Thoughts of announcements like 'To the Devil, a daughter' crossed many minds. 'I'm too old,' Gardner replied. Perhaps he did not want to be confused with Aleister Crowley and the nineteen-year-old girl who had asked the same question outside the High Court a quarter of a century before, and been obliged.

After Gardner's death, canvassing for a successor was more important to the witches than the argument about whether or not they were evil. Sybil Leek, Ray Boone, Doreen Valiente and Alex Sanders used the media to press their claims to being authentic witches. And several representatives of 'the craft' countered accusations of black magic by admitting that 'Satanic lodges' did exist, but that their own Wiccan circles had only honourable intentions.

Sybil Leek, billed as a world-renowned witch and occult scholar, admitted that she had seen three black masses and knew the person responsible for the Sussex desecrations, but said, 'I dare not disclose his identity.' Not to be outdone, Alex Sanders confessed that during the trying years after the Second World War he had given way to temptation and practised black magic to gain 'wealth, riches and power'. Later, he claimed, he had recognised his error and had purged his guilt through white magic ceremonies.

It seems strange how many of the 'white witches' confessed to knowledge of black witches, who were supposed to be their sworn enemies. Patricia and Arnold Crowther, leaders of a Sheffield coven, conceded that there might well be 'black' witches who practised in secret alongside them. The Crowthers, who had offered £50 in vain to anyone who could direct them to a real black mass, concluded:

> Anyone who . . . was able to celebrate the black mass throughout the country would have lots of followers and, no doubt,

> become a wealthy man. His followers would not be teenagers either, but so-called respectable people. You would be surprised if you saw the type of man who approaches witches to join the craft, hoping that it is connected with black magic and sex orgies. They are all too ready to become members, providing their names are kept secret and their wives and business associates know nothing about it. Their absence from home to attend meetings could always be blamed on business appointments.

It was no longer a question of whether or not black witchcraft existed. The Witchcraft Research Association, a network of Wiccans, warned against 'spurious covens' and declared: 'It is known that one such group is organised by thoroughly undesirable people practising the most horrible sexual and other deviations. Please be extremely careful.'

With all the public interest in black witchcraft, it is not surprising that in 1968 Hammer Films, the specialists in horror movies, chose Dennis Wheatley's *The Devil Rides Out* to launch a new series. Wheatley had always been ready and willing to offer sound 'hands-off' advice to any people tempted to dabble in witchcraft and to warn the police that they were wrong to ignore any report of Satanic evil, no matter how flimsy. Hammer Films, for their part, remained true to his theme that no matter how demonic the plot good must always triumph in the end.

They cast Christopher Lee, uncharacteristically, as the white occultist who combats the evil black magician to save the life of a young man, played by Patrick Mower. The movie became something of a cult classic among adolescents. In the Hammer films which followed, Lee returned to his more usual role as a Satanic vampire repeatedly brought back to life by drinking blood at Satanic masses.

Satanists continued to be blamed by the media for disturbing cemeteries throughout the 1960s. On the night after Hallowe'en in 1968, police found 'black magic symbols' around a newly opened grave in Tottenham Park Cemetery, north London. The following February, police near Tunbridge Wells in Kent blamed witchcraft when a cross was upturned and a mysterious sign daubed on gravestones. In 1969, the *News of the World* excited its readers with weekly exposés of witchcraft circles, researched mainly by reporters who had approached Wiccans and asked to be initiated. Ceremonies involving ritual nudity and flagellation followed but there were no prosecutions because the 'novices' had offered themselves voluntarily. The idea that young girls and children were being lured by occultists into their rituals was only hinted at darkly.

By 1970, police and clergy were convinced that unexplained desecrations were part of black magic ceremonies rather than teenage practical jokes and that cults were capable of 'hypnotising' and abducting unwary youths. Even occultists conceded that such evil cults probably operated alongside their own. Sexual perversions, especially involving small children, were alleged to occur frequently during celebrations of the black mass. And the members of such cults were, it was said, ordinary-seeming people who mingled freely with other Britons, except when a ritual was due to take place.

To this day imagination and fantasy play an important part in mystifying and attracting newspaper readers and television viewers to such activities. But what those who relish such stories do not readily appreciate is that when people are demonically possessed and exorcised, their condition is very often rooted in dabbling in the occult, black magic, witchcraft and like evils.

In November 1994, more than fifty years after Crowley's death (which some say was due to drinking the blood of a ritually killed cat), *L'Osservatore Romano*, the official Vatican newspaper, attacked the most famous pop group of all for pandering to Satanism. Father Corrado Balducci, an exorcist, said that The Beatles top 'Satan's hit parade' of bands responsible for the rising number of suicides among young people:

> One proof of the Liverpool boys' yielding fascination for Satan is the photograph of Aleister Crowley, the father of Satanism, on the cover of *Sergeant Pepper's Lonely Hearts Club Band.*

Crowley's picture is, it is true, readily identifiable in the back row of a group of famous people on the album cover. Father Balducci's article, which reflects the views of Pope John Paul, claims to see a Satanic message in the Beatles song 'Revolution Number 9'. The priest adds that the lyric of another Beatles record, 'Let's Rouse the Dead Man', is a blasphemous reference to the Resurrection.

The Beatles are not alone in being accused of 'destabilising youth with evil subliminal messages'. The Rolling Stones 'profess sympathy with the Devil and invite us to dance with Mr D.'; The Eagles offend with 'I Have a Little Thought for Satan'; Led Zeppelin with 'I Desire You, Mr Satan', and various other works by Iron Maiden and Pink Floyd are cited.

11

Hollywood Goes To Hell

Flies swarm where they shouldn't;
pipes and walls ooze ick, doors
fly open; and priests and psychic
sensitives cringe and flee
in panic.

***Variety Movie Guide*, 1992,**
describing *The Amityville Horror*

In the first year of the twentieth century, two decades before the palmetto trees of Hollywood were uprooted and the studios built, film-makers realised that the Devil was hot property at the cinema box office. They made the first of eight or more cinematic versions of *Faust* and the Devil began to make frequent appearances on the screen. Religious and moral censorship ensured that good always triumphed and that evil was curbed. Devil-worship did not creep in until 1934, when *The Black Cat*, influenced by the antics of Aleister Crowley, was made. Even then there was a gap of seven years before *The Seventh Victim* (1943), *Night of the Demon* (1957), *Back From the Dead* (1957), *The Witches* (1966), Wheatley's *The Devil Rides Out* (1968) and *Rosemary's Baby*, which started a rash of diabolically inspired children in *I Don't Want to Be Born, It's Alive, Devil Within Her* and *The Exorcist.*

Neither pains nor expense were spared to bring this morbidly attractive subject to the notice of filmgoers. *The Amityville Horror* (1979) was no exception. Offered as fact, it was challenged and proven to be fiction, but its success and rescreening on television indicates a flippant attitude towards the truth.

It all began when the eldest son of the DeFeo family was convicted of killing his parents, two sisters and two brothers in their house, known as 'High Hopes', at 112 Ocean Drive in affluent Amityville, a village which sprawls along the shore of Great South

Bay on Long Island, New York. Many of the 10,000 residents commute daily to New York City, thirty-five miles to the west. The very name suggests peace and contentment. Amity means friendship, harmony, good relations, and the only crimes previously reported there were vandals untying boats from their moorings in the bay.

On 3 November 1974, Ronald 'Butch' DeFeo, who was twenty-three years of age, was out all day. He had some drinks, shot some heroin – and when he returned home that night he ran screaming from the dreadful scene he encountered. His whole family lay dead in a welter of blood. A caller phoned the police department from a local bar and said, 'A kid come running into the bar. He says everybody in the family was killed. "You gotta help me. Someone shot my mother and father!" '

When the police arrived at the house, they found upstairs in the master bedroom, on their stomachs on the double bed, the bloodstained bodies of a man and a woman. In a smaller room, two boys were lying face-down in their beds. In a third bedroom was the body of a teenaged girl. She had been shot in the face. The grisly search ended in an attic bedroom, where an older girl was also lying, dead, face-down on her bed.

The bodies belonged to wealthy Ronald DeFeo senior, aged forty-three, chief of the family Buick car dealership in Brooklyn, New York, his wife, Louise, their two daughters, Dawn, who was eighteen, and Allison, thirteen, and two sons, twelve-year-old Mark and seven-year-old John. The only surviving member of the family, Butch, claimed that a Mafia hit-man, Louis Falini, had a grudge against his family and could be the killer. He also maintained that two weeks previously he and an employee of the family firm had been robbed at gunpoint as they drove to the bank with several thousand dollars in takings. His father hadn't believed him. Falini, the alleged Mafia hit-man, turned out to be a friend of the father's.

Neighbours reported that the family was given to incessant arguing. Butch and his eldest sister, Dawn, often quarrelled, particularly over her choice of pop music. He hated the soul sounds that she loved. 'They all screamed at each other,' said one neighbour. Butch had once pointed a gun at his father and squeezed the trigger, but it had misfired. He described his mother as 'a lousy cook' and his brothers as 'a couple of pigs'. So depressed and worried was his father at the constant schisms within the family that he sought succour by becoming a devout Catholic, building several religious shrines in the garden of 'High Hopes'.

The family came originally from Brooklyn, where Butch had been a high school drop-out, surly and uncouth, a drifter from job to job, fired from one post after another for absenteeism. He preferred to spend his time and money – generous hand-outs from his father of sometimes $500 (£333) a week – doing little or nothing. He told the police that he was an occasional drug-user, but eventually admitted to doctors that he had started with pills and marijuana, moved on to 'acid' (LSD) then progressed to hard drugs such as heroin and 'speed' (amphetamines).

When he stopped taking drugs, Butch would become violent. 'I would break up a place. I was like an animal. I had no problem with girls – then.' But in 1974, his drug addiction caused a problem. 'Women just started to turn me off – right before this [the killings] happened. I couldn't have sex.' To calm his fears about his sexual inadequacies, Butch returned to heroin and found that 'when I was on it I could do it with women'.

Gun experts found that all six victims had been killed with a .35 calibre Marlin rifle and that in Butch's bedroom was a cardboard box which had contained such a weapon. Other evidence indicated that he was a gun enthusiast and that he had been looking for a silencer.

When detectives spoke to DeFeo the morning after the bodies were found, he asked, 'Have you found Falini yet?' One of the officers replied, 'We have guys out on the street looking for him, but to tell you the truth I think you're the guy we want.'

What actually happened, according to DeFeo's own words, was that he had awakened in the early hours of the morning, gone to his room and loaded his .35 rifle. 'It all started so fast. Once I started, I just couldn't stop. It went so fast.' First he shot his father and mother. Then he shot Allison in the head. Standing between the beds in his brothers' room he had murdered Mark and John. Dawn had woken in the commotion but Butch had assured her that everything was all right. Then he had followed her into her room and shot her dead. The family's sheepdog, Shaggy, had been 'screaming'.

Butch then went to his room and wrapped the rifle in some pillowcases. He went round the house retrieving spent cartridges, returned to his room and changed, stuffing the clothes he had been wearing into another pillowcase. Next he drove his car to the dockside, dumped the rifle in the bay, and drove on to Brooklyn. There he put the rifle scabbard, spent shells and ammunition boxes into the pillowcase with his clothes and threw the lot into a sewer. His next port of call was a diner, where he ate a hearty breakfast and waited until the family business opened for the day – the business to which the head, his father, would never return.

Butch DeFeo, waiting in gaol for nearly a year for his trial, rehearsed his insanity plea. To a fellow prison inmate he boasted, 'I can beat this case. I have been going to psychiatrists all my life.' Once he had been freed, he said, he would have several hundred thousand dollars that he had looted from the house, plus his inheritance and insurance amounting to $100,000 (£66,000). To bolster his madness claim, he acted the part of a demented person, destroying his own mail, starting a fire in his cell, even threatening suicide.

When he stood trial, his psychiatrist, Dr Daniel Schwartz, testified that Butch was mentally diseased and had not known what he was doing the morning he slaughtered the other six members of his family. He had been in the grip of paranoid delusions, chief of which was that there were people who were going to kill him and that his only recourse would be to kill them first.

Butch spent three days in the witness box giving evidence, smirking and playing the bewildered madman. Shown a picture of his mother, Louise, lying dead in bed, he said he had never seen 'this person' before. Asked if he had killed his father, he replied, 'Yes, sir, I killed them all in self-defence.' Later he changed his story and said that his 'evil sister', Dawn, had decided to kill everyone in the house and had woken him, placing the .35 rifle in his hands. Not angry or mad, 'just very, very, very calm', he had gone to his parents' room and shot them. He dropped the gun but Dawn had seized it.

'I heard shots. Realising that she must have killed the other children, I pushed her down and I shot her.' He crowned his story by adding that his sister had had an accomplice.

Prosecuting counsel Gerry Sullivan asked him: 'Why did you tell people that you had called your house and couldn't understand why you had gotten no answer?'

At that, Butch lost his temper. He shouted back: 'I wasn't sure if they were all dead. I wasn't even sure if I had killed them. I ain't even sure if they are dead right now. One of them might come walking in here any minute, then we'll see who the laugh is on.'

Dr Harold Zolan, the prosecution psychiatrist, said that DeFeo was not a psychopath but a sociopath, not a psychotic but an antisocial personality. He was, therefore, sane. In striving to enhance his macho image he had 'finally reached a point of aggression where he committed the ultimate crime'. Zolan found no evidence whatsoever that DeFeo was suffering from mental illness.

Ronald Joseph 'Butch' DeFeo was found guilty on six counts of second-degree murder and sentenced to twenty-five years on each count. There was an ironic twist to the last question as the clerk of the court, taking down his personal details, name, date of birth, status as a citizen, asked, 'Are your parents living?'

Butch DeFeo sneered, 'No, sir.'

The scenario for an ordinary book and film were already there.

DeFeo's defence counsel, William Weber, had decided to write a novel based on the massacre when he met George and Kathy Lutz. They had bought the house on Ocean Drive from the DeFeo estate and told of all sorts of strange goings-on: ghosts, mysterious faces at windows – even an invasion of green slime. Thinking that all this would make an interesting epilogue to the novel, Weber interviewed the Lutzes.

At first, he considered asking for a retrial for his client on the grounds that the house and his client were possessed and that DeFeo could not therefore have been responsible for his actions. After forty-one hours with the Lutzes, though, he decided he didn't believe their story. But since what he was planning was a work of fiction, he decided to go along with the couple and even to invent some ghostly occurrences of his own. Weber said that the Lutzes agreed to work with him on the book.

But then the Lutzes got together with another writer, Jay Anson, and turned out *The Amityville Horror*. Weber sued the Lutzes, alleging that they had broken their contract to do the book with him. The Lutzes refused to comment on the charges.

During a television appearance to promote the national première of the film, they insisted that all the 'horrors' described in the Anson book had really occurred. Meanwhile, the Amityville police, fearing that the opening of the movie would attract new hordes of sightseers to the house on Ocean Drive, assigned a special patrol to the area. A police officer explained, 'We're going to see to it that people stay away from the house and that they don't trample on the lawns and shrubberies of the neighbours in the immediate vicinity.'

The couple who subsequently bought the house from the Lutzes, James and Barbara Cromarty, denied seeing any spooks or demons or any evidence that they had been there. They moved out after twenty months only because they could not put up with the sightseers, many of whom knocked on the door and asked for guided tours.

Then came *The Exorcist*. William Peter Blatty, a young undergraduate at the Jesuit Georgetown University, St Louis, Missouri, read in the *Catholic Review*:

> A 14-year-old Washington boy whose history of diabolical possession was widely reported in the press last week, was successfully exorcised by a priest after being received into the Catholic Church, it was learned here.
>
> The priest involved refused to discuss the case in any way. However, it is known that several attempts had been made to free the boy of the manifestations.
>
> A Catholic priest was called upon for help. When the boy

> expressed a desire to enter the Church, with the consent of his parents he received religious instruction. Later the priest baptised him and then successfully performed the ritual of exorcism. The parents of the afflicted boy are non-Catholics.

Blatty, who had thought of becoming a priest, turned writer and eventually struck a deal with the exorcist so that he could use the true story as a basis but would fictionalise it so that it was not recognisable. The real-life case concerned Robert, a fourteen-year-old boy from a suburb six miles from the capital, Washington DC. The boy's aunt, a spiritualist, introduced Robbie to the ouija board and taught him how to use the planchette, the small board on two castors which, when touched gently, operates a pencil or pointer which moves automatically towards letters or numbers in answer to questions. This device, used to contact spirits, was blamed for the boy's subsequent possession.

There followed a series of unexplained mysteries in the house: water dripping; automatic knocking on the walls, which could be started by verbal request; shaking mattresses; scratching; a flipping chair; a Bible falling out of a bookshelf; a coat on a hanger, an orange and a pear flying round the room; a chair which could not be easily moved tipping over of its own accord. Robert's bed began shaking for no reason and when he emerged from underneath it his face was badly cut. No one had been near him.

A Lutheran minister called in to help sought assistance from the local Roman Catholic priest, who gave him a blessed bottle of holy water and candles. When the water was placed by the boy's bed the bottle broke into small pieces. When the boy's mother tried to telephone the priest to tell him, the telephone table disintegrated.

Robert's father ripped out wall panels and made other structural searches but could not find the cause of the disturbances. The family called in turn on a doctor, a psychiatrist, a psychologist and a psychic, but none of them could provide an answer to the mystery. When the local Catholic priest, an Irishman, attempted an exorcism he was slashed from shoulder to wrist at the very moment he was commanding the Devil to leave the boy. The wound – probably caused by a loose spring from the bed – needed a hundred stitches. The priest retired from the case and to another parish.

The disturbances in Robert's life turned into physical violence. To questions of the kind put to the ouija board by the spiritualist aunt, answers came in the form of carvings in the boy's flesh. When the family were planning to go to the aunt's home in St Louis, Missouri, the word 'Louis' appeared on the lad's abdomen. When? The word 'Saturday' was seen. For how long? '3½ weeks'. When it was suggested that Robbie should return to school, 'No school' appeared. When questioned, he showed his wrists. On each of them was clearly written, 'No'.

Eventually, in a full exorcism at a Catholic mental hospital in St Louis, Robbie, even though he was strapped to a bed, showed horrific violence. He – or more accurately, according to the Church, the Devil, speaking through his voice – shouted, 'Get away from me you assholes', 'Go to hell, you dirty sons of bitches', 'You have a big fat penis', 'Stick it up your ass'.

The Devil, having slashed the local priest, now caused Robbie to urinate during the ritual, broke the nose of an assistant exorcist, Father Halloran, spat at Father Bowdern, the exorcist, hitting him directly between the eyes, and kicked him in the testicles. Robbie began to use obscene words he had never heard or used before and even spoke in Latin, a language he did not know. During solemn moments of the ritual he would sing 'Way Down Upon the Swanee River' and hum 'The Blue Danube' waltz, tunes he had never learned.

Eventually, when Robert, of his own free will, said he wanted to become a Catholic, asked for communion, took the wafer voluntarily and uttered the responses he had just been taught in Latin, he was exorcised. The Devil was driven out and the boy, now fifteen, stood smiling beside his bed.

Blatty, the student who turned that true story into a novel, agreed with the exorcist, Father Bowdern, to change Robert's name and sex to create Regan McNeil, a young girl. He added incidents from other exorcisms about which he had heard from Jesuits and some from his own imagination. *The New York Times* called his book 'a terrifying mixture of fact and fancy'. *Life* magazine dubbed it 'hair-raising entertainment'. The *Sunday Express* said the story was 'a hypnotic combination of morality tale and supernatural detective story'. The public had been warned.

William Friedkin's film of the novel was, by artistic standards, an expert telling of a supernatural horror story. The well-cast film made powerfully credible in laymen's terms what the film-makers described as the rare phenomenon of diabolical possession. The climactic sequences assaulted the senses and the intellect with pure cinematic terror.

Separating fact from ballyhoo in the film industry is never easy, but it cannot be denied that an unusually large number of accidents beset the shooting of the film, which took place in a New York warehouse. In fact there were so many that Friedkin asked Father Thomas Bermingham, a Jesuit and one of two priests acting as technical advisers, to exorcise the warehouse. Bermingham refused and told the director that there was not sufficient evidence of Satanic possession to justify such a serious ritual. Instead he blessed everyone and everything on the set, including Max von Sydow, who played the part of the Jesuit exorcist, and the accidents stopped.

During the weeks before *The Exorcist* opened in London in 1974, the media treated the public to an avalanche of blatant hype. The film was more successful than the book. There were stories of audiences queueing for hours to be shocked, fainting and vomiting, then giving way to mass hysteria; of the demonic infection of harmless housewives, of the audiences rushing screaming from the stalls; of doctors, nurses and ambulances, not to mention parish priests, being hired by cinemas to attend such emergencies.

Some British critics, with masterly knocking reviews, tried to ensure that UK audiences would remain distinctly underwhelmed by their own potential for demonisation. On the other hand, a few religious groups up and down the country gave out warning leaflets to cinema queues while one or two nervous councils refused to grant the film a certificate.

Father Bowdern and Father Halloran did not like the film. When they saw a girl being portrayed on the screen bouncing on the bed in simulated masturbation with a crucifix and later urinating on the cross, they were revolted.

The Times pronounced on the subject and some mainstream clerics got into the act, including Canon John Pearce-Higgins, a leading Church of England exorcist from the diocese of Southwark. He declared that the film was filthy, indecent, blasphemous and would produce 'a new crop of schizophrenics and a small number of cases of genuine possession'.

The film and the box-office takings struck a responsive chord with audiences. As Canon Pearce-Higgins had warned, *The Exorcist* did produce a rash of doubtful and downright phoney claims of demonic possession, some genuine ones and unfortunately some disasters. It also spawned a series of similar films involving young girls and copulating demons, none of which were a patch on Roman Polanski's pioneering *Rosemary's Baby.* This 1968 film version of Ira Levin's diabolical thriller, in which Mia Farrow is drugged to conceive a baby by Satan, succeeded in holding the audience's attention without resorting to explicit violence or gore. The rash of demonic films helped to confirm that public interest had expanded from mere sex and crime to include violence, religion and mystery.

The Exorcist also served to raise the general awareness of the public to the idea that exorcism was not something that had died with the Middle Ages and was still, behind closed doors and drawn curtains, a not uncommon fact of everyday life. Of course, the focus on the subject led to its vulgarisation. Obscure vicars were persuaded by some sections of the press to reveal details of exorcisms they had performed on teenage girls and suburban mothers; less obscure vicars rushed into autobiographical print; and any court case involving sex and violence during which the magic words 'possessed' or 'exorcism' were uttered received a disproportionate number of column inches in the next day's newspapers.

But then tragedy struck, and the warnings of the latter-day prophets of doom came true, showing beyond doubt how dangerous exorcism and films like *The Exorcist* could be.

12

Exorcised To Death

Mr Blatty's novel [The Exorcist] *is about 80 per cent accurate to the actual case which motivated it. Another 15 per cent can be documented from one or another historical case, leaving only a small portion of the novel which is purely imaginative.*

Father John J. Nicola, SJ, technical consultant to the film *The Exorcist*

The film version of *The Exorcist*, made by Warner in 1973, was still being shown and talked about on Sunday 6 October 1974, the feast of St Faith. That was the day Michael Taylor killed his wife. He had just undergone an all-night exorcism to drive the devils out of him, yet he slaughtered the most important woman in his life, his friend, lover, devoted wife and mother of his five sons, who were aged between six and twelve.

And for no easily understandable reason. With his bare hands he tore out her eyes and her tongue. He ripped her face almost from the bones and she died choking in her own blood. A psychiatrist was to say later that the case was unique in his experience of more than 1,000 murders.

The killing happened in Ossett, just outside the run-down coalfields of Barnsley, Yorkshire. But a tragedy arising from an exorcism that went wrong could, perhaps, have happened anywhere. The cry 'deliver us from evil' had not been answered.

Canon John Pearce-Higgins, who had denounced *The Exorcist*, was not a lone voice. Among the condemnations was that of Father Peter Vincent, vicar of St Thomas's Church, Gawber, Yorkshire. He said:

The one thing the film does not show is the Church's work of

> exorcism. If the cross means anything it means that Jesus was conqueror over the power of the Devil and his evil spirits. Exorcism is the casting out of evil spirits and Satan himself by the power and victory of Jesus, and when exorcism is carried out in the name and by the authority and cover of the blood of Jesus the spirits must go.
>
> The film is an exploitation of the gullible minds of the public, who like a bit of sensation and may get more than they bargained for, I'm afraid.
>
> No film can be good if it corrupts the mind and reverses the principle of good being more important than evil. I cannot warn you enough to avoid this kind of film. If you know of anyone who is disturbed by *The Exorcist* tell him to get in touch with me or Father Cheetham at Grimethorpe or the Reverend Ray Smith, and we can call on a team who will help.

Within three months of that warning Father Vincent carried out a ceremony of exorcism on Michael Taylor, a thirty-one-year-old resident of Ossett, eight miles away. The next morning Michael tore his wife to death with his bare hands. Criticism and condemnation has been heaped on those the law thought responsible, but no one seemed to stop and consider the whole picture of how the problem of demonic possession should be dealt with and whether or not exorcism was the answer.

A decade earlier, in 1963, an unhealthy and near-hysterical interest in witchcraft, magic and the occult prompted the Church of England to look again at the spiritual casualties so often involved in such bizarre matters and how to handle them. The Right Reverend Robert Mortimer, Bishop of Exeter, was disturbed by the number of requests he was receiving for help with and advice about exorcising places and people. He knew that few in the Church of England had any knowledge or experience of the subject.

The general attitude in the Church of England seemed to be that exorcism was an exercise in white magic or a survivor of mediaeval superstition. The bishop found that:

> It was seen as a purely negative action of expelling an evil force or cleansing an evil environment. Its positive aspect as an extension of the power of the Resurrection to overcome evil and replace it with good was overlooked.

He decided to call together a small inter-denominational group to consider how exorcism fitted into the theology, techniques and life of the Church. He chose experienced clergy: the Reverend Fathers

T. Corbishley and J. Crehan, both Jesuits; the Reverend Dr M. H. B. Joyce; the Reverend Dr E. Mascall; the Reverend Sir Patrick Ferguson-Davie, Bart.; the Reverend Dr D. W. Omand and the Anglican Benedictine monk, Dom Robert Petitpierre.

Bishop Mortimer's opinion was that the national press had generated the current interest in demonic possession and exorcism, rather than merely reflecting what was going on among the people. The idea that exorcism did not have a place in the regular ministry of the Church had taken root in Britain and other countries with a long historic tradition of Christianity. The Devil was not important and had already been conquered. But in countries which had been until comparatively recently pagan or primitive, exorcism was taken for granted as an everyday part of the clergyman's work. These distinct attitudes were to become blurred, not least because of the migration to Britain of people from those countries where Christianity was newer. The bishop explained:

> In Western countries today the widespread apostasy from the Christian faith, accompanied by an increasing recourse to black magic and occult practices, is revealing the presence and the power of evil forces and the contaminating influence of an evil atmosphere in particular places and environments. The need for the restoration of the practice of exorcism to its proper place is becoming more evident and more urgent.

Bishop Mortimer wanted to take the heat out of the subject, put it into perspective, explain the underlying theology of possession and offer practical help by providing specimen prayers, forms of service and specially chosen clergy who could undertake the task. They would be available to teach others in any diocese where the bishop thought they were necessary.

The findings of the commission only touched the tip of the demonic iceberg. Dom Petitpierre reckoned that there were 400 black magic groups in the country and at least one in every university. Even so, the Reverend Michael Perry, Archdeacon of Durham, thought that many parish priests felt out of their depth because they had no previous experience of such cases or because they felt threatened by the forces of evil which they were not confident they could control. It was one thing to have a 'flying doctor' sort of exorcist to hurry into each diocese and parish when called upon but there was no substitute for a trained parish priest who knew his flock and could counsel the afflicted on the spot.

Apart from the influence of *The Exorcist* in 1974, the Right Reverend John Robinson, Bishop of Woolwich and controversial author of *Honest to God*, thought that the Devil had 'turned into a figure of fun'. Billy Graham, the American evangelist, who had already brought his crusade to Britain, found that 'Everywhere you go today, the young are complaining about bad vibrations. Bad vibrations have shaken our youth.' In America, where so many trends are started and equally quickly abandoned, the United States Congress study commissioned to 'analyse and evaluate the needs and resources of the mentally ill' found that 42 per cent called on clergymen while only 18 per cent consulted psychiatrists. It was in this atmosphere that the Yorkshire tragedy took place.

Ossett is one of those clustered Yorkshire towns with a population of little over 20,000, a golf course, market days on Tuesday and Friday and not much else visible going on. Christianity, however, was alive there, and as well as the usual churches of different denominations a new Christian Fellowship group had been set up, which gathered worshippers from different chapels and temples for Bible readings, hymn-singing and prayers in private homes. But over this promotion of pure, clear Christian unity hung a feeling of darkness, of conflict to come.

Religion, some friends insisted, did not dominate the lives of the Taylors, but Michael and his wife, Christine, and their children were more than nominal Christians. Indeed, they hosted a meeting of the Fellowship at their terraced council house in Havercroft, Ossett, on Tuesday 24 September 1974.

Former music teacher Marie Robinson, twenty-two years old, single, was there with her guitar. Although not ordained in any ministry, she celebrated a form of holy communion and a form of exorcism. Mrs Barbara Wardman, a neighbour of the Taylors, said that Marie 'thought it would be nice' to introduce the worshippers to a more simple form of faith and to break bread in remembrance of the Last Supper in less formal surroundings. There was some ready-sliced bread, rather than unleavened bread, in the cupboard and some Ribena rather than wine. She said, 'It will be just like holy communion.'

Mrs Wardman added, 'Everyone seemed to enjoy it. Afterwards everyone went home and got fish and chips and seemed quite happy.' Miss Robinson stayed overnight with the Taylors and the next day, the Wednesday, they had a singing and prayer meeting. During the prayers, Michael spoke 'in tongues'.

Speaking in (or with the gift of) tongues is known as glossolalia, a soliloquy of ecstatic spiritual emotion. When a high state of fervour is reached in group worship the result can be a torrent of words expressed in a language unfamiliar to the speakers or the listeners. The Bible acknowledges it in the miracle of Pentecost in the Acts of the Apostles, ii, 4: 'And they were all filled with the Holy Ghost, and began to speak with other tongues, as the Spirit gave them utterance.' Worshippers in the early Church practised it, as did the Irvingites (1829), named after Edward Irving of Annan, the Scottish divine who was later found guilty of heresy and deprived of his ministerial status. 'Speaking in tongues' must be involuntary.

In the Taylor household, Mrs Wardman recalled:

> While Michael was saying prayers he suddenly spoke in tongues. It is the gift of the Holy Spirit. It's rather beautiful. Michael had just received the gift and was rather afraid of it and inclined to speak in a normal voice at first.

No one knew, or if they did, they didn't mention, that a change of voice from normal to deep to gruff to 'belly speaking' is a common mark of demonic possession. As long ago as 1656, Thomas Ady, a controversial theologian, said, 'By this imposture [the young] do make the people believe that they are possessed by the Devil speaking within them.'

At the same fellowship meeting was twenty-five-year-old Mrs Mavis Smith, who lived not far away in Healey View. She was herself in crisis at the time but was alert to what was going on.

> I was disturbed at the time Marie Robinson joined the fellowship and attended their gospel and hymn-singing meetings in people's houses. Marie decided at that meeting that I had an evil spirit and she said she'd exorcise it. Christine [Taylor] was there, with one or two others. Marie said some prayers over me and beckoned the spirit to leave. But a strange sensation came over me. I felt it was getting out of hand. Then I broke into tears. I told her to stop the prayers. She did and I decided to leave.
>
> I felt that if I'd gone any further with the exorcism I might have gone home and done something dreadful – perhaps even to the children. Marie certainly has an influence over people, especially when they're like Michael and me, nervy and depressed.

Mrs Wardman said that Taylor had been upset by Marie's attempt to exorcise evil spirits from Mrs Smith. 'I would not say he was violently upset. When I told him to calm down, he did.' Within days, however, the calm was fatally shattered.

On 29 September Michael Taylor, an unemployed handyman, went to church at St Thomas's, Gawber, to hear Father Peter Vincent, the pastor who had spoken out against *The Exorcist*, preach. Later there was a Christian Fellowship meeting in his own home. Marie Robinson was there, and on this occasion she herself began to shake as if possessed and gibbered and chanted 'in tongues'.

Two days later, Taylor applied for a job, was rejected and became depressed. On Wednesday 2 October he told his mother and his neighbours, Mr and Mrs Wardman, that he had seen the Devil, who had told him to go and kill himself in his car. Later, the guitar-playing would-be priest Marie Robinson called at the Taylor home. Michael, she said, 'kissed me on the lips. It was not a Christian kiss and we bounced off each other, repelling each other.'

The following day Taylor approached neighbours in the street, knelt before them and told them that the world was coming to an end. The same day he went to another meeting of the fellowship, this time in Barnsley, at the home of Ron Smith, choirmaster at St Thomas's Church, and his wife, Margaret. Father Vincent and others were present.

That is when Taylor told the assembled group that he had been seduced by the Devil. The group voted that they should hear him in detail, that he should confess all that had taken place. A prayer of absolution, known as 'the infilling of the Holy Spirit', was recited. The word 'exorcism' was not mentioned. The meeting ended and Taylor went home. His mother-in-law said, 'He looked strained and tired and was afraid to go out in the dark.'

On Friday 4 October Michael told his wife to get rid of all the crosses and all the religious books in the house. She complied. When it was time to go to bed, he left the radio on because, he said, 'I am frightened of the silence of the night.'

On the Saturday, John Eggins, a member of the fellowship who lived in Wakefield, the old woollen centre on the River Calder a few miles to the east, decided to give the Taylor family a rest from their troubles. They would, he thought, benefit from a car ride in the fresh air of the Yorkshire Dales. Wharfedale and similar beauty spots were within an hour's drive.

With John at the wheel, Christine relieved and the children happy, the only disturbance came from a sullen Michael, who suddenly uttered a piercing scream. It was as if all his prayers vociferated in one high-pitched cry full of pent-up blasphemies and curses. The children were instantly frightened. Christine said quietly, 'He desperately needs help.'

John turned the car round and headed back to Gawber and Father Vincent's vicarage. By 7.30 pm, Michael was behaving irrationally, violently and noisily. He picked up the vicarage cat and flung it through the window. When a meal was placed before him to placate him and occupy his mind, he threw it on the floor. His children were put to bed upstairs for their peace and safety.

Sally, the vicar's wife, took the view that there was an enormous force of evil emanating from Taylor and that this was undoubtedly a case of demonic possession. Taylor needed exorcising and that was a task which could take all night. Her husband, the vicar, agreed and both favoured the idea that others experienced in exorcism ought to be there. She telephoned the Reverend Raymond Smith, a Barnsley Methodist minister, and his wife, Margaret, who described themselves as practitioners in exorcism, Donald James, a Methodist lay preacher; and John Eggins, the afternoon driver, to make up a team of six.

They counselled Taylor to prepare him for a night-long exorcism. It was clear from Mrs Taylor's words that she was convinced that Marie Robinson was connected with some Satanic group and had pledged Michael, her husband, to the Devil. Michael's violence of speech and action, his threat to murder someone and the fact that he invoked the power of the moon persuaded the listeners that the exorcism should go ahead. There was only one dissenting voice. Raymond Smith, the Methodist minister, a practitioner in exorcism, believed that Taylor was not in need of Church help but of psychiatric care. Father Vincent indicated the wish of the majority that the exorcism should take place.

The six took Taylor to the vestry at the side of the church, where they laid him on his back on a pile of red and gold hassocks. One by one they stood over him, asking questions, finding answers, putting suggestions, saying prayers and announcing that they were casting out devils one by one.

Taylor later told doctors that he had a striking recollection of what took place that night. Words, he said, had been put into his mouth by the exorcists and he had been led to admit sins he had never committed. They named each devil by its own evil. They included bestiality, lewdness, blasphemy, heresy and masochism. A wooden crucifix given to him by Marie Robinson, which he wore round his neck, was repeatedly put into his mouth as the exorcists prayed for him. As he writhed and thrashed on the floor he was held down forcibly. Every time he puffed out his cheeks and gasped and panted for breath the exorcists claimed another demon had been expelled from his body. (This hyperventilation is often associated with hysteria.)

At 6 am Taylor and the exorcists were exhausted. They claimed that the possessed had been rid of forty demons, although there were, alas, one or two still within him, including violence and murder. The Reverend Smith, the Methodist minister who had at first opposed the exorcism, said that only the spirit of murder remained and that that demon could not be expelled. Margaret, his wife, said:

> I feel that there is a doll somewhere for Michael, like the witchcraft dolls into which people stick pins, and unless this is found and burned we will never cast out the spirit of murder. I have had word from God that if he goes home this morning he will murder his wife and children.

There came a time when Father Vincent was asked: 'When he left you at eight o'clock on the morning of Sunday 6 October 1974, you firmly believed he was going to kill his wife?'

Father Vincent answered: 'Yes.'

But those at the vicarage could not compel him to stay. Preventing a person from leaving a private or public building – including churches and parsonages – constitutes false or unlawful imprisonment. The exorcists did try to contact a medical welfare officer but were hampered by the fact that it was a Sunday. In any case, the law and bureaucracy made it impossible for such a person to visit a home without the permission of the owner or tenant, whatever his or her condition. They called the police but here Mrs Taylor objected. 'Michael will be cross if a doctor is called into this matter.'

At 8.30 am Mr Eggins drove the Taylors home, wisely dropping the children at their grandparents' house. At 9 am, he went home, having done all he could to help. At 9.30 Mrs Taylor told her neighbour, Mrs Wardman, 'My husband needs a doctor. We're going to have a good rest.' She added, 'Don't come near me. There is something in me.' That unexplained 'something' was, in the eyes of her husband, more malevolent than anything she could have imagined.

It was 10 am when Michael Taylor attacked and killed his wife with his bare hands. A policeman called by neighbours found him on his hands and knees with his forehead touching the ground, naked except for his socks and his wife's rings on his hands. His arms, hands and body were bloody. The officer asked, 'Where did all that blood come from?'

Taylor replied, 'It is the blood of Satan.'

Later, at the police station, Detective Inspector Brian Smith invited him to make a statement and began by asking him, 'Did you kill your wife?' Taylor replied:

> No, not her. I loved her. I destroyed the evil within her. It had to be done. I am relaxed. What had to be done has been done.

> The evil in her has been destroyed. Chrissie was good. The evil had been put into her by them. I had to kill it. It came through religion. They primed me for this last night.
>
> We went to church in Barnsley and stayed all night. The people at the church, they will tell you. It was a long night. They danced around me and burned my cross. But they were too late. My cross was tainted with evil.
>
> They tried. Oh, how they tried, but I had to do it. I had to destroy. I am relaxed now. I am at peace. It was terrible. They had me in the church all night. Look at my hands. I was banging them on the floor. The power was in me. I could not get rid of it and neither could they. I was compelled by a force within me which they couldn't get rid of. I felt compelled to destroy everything living within the house. Everything living – including the dog. Everything living – but that was a lesser evil . . .
>
> It is done. It is done. The evil in her has been destroyed. It was in Christine. It used my wife, my love. Oh hell, I loved that woman . . . No, no, not Chrissie, Chrissie, Chrissie, she was good. I loved her. I loved her so.

A society doubtful about the existence of God and the power of Satan could not be satisfied with that explanation. Even though the witnesses upon whom our judicial system relies usually swear 'by Almighty God to tell the truth, the whole truth and nothing but the truth', the great Jehovah has little place in the rest of court business. The influence of the Devil is never accepted as a defence to a crime; blame can never be put on any supernatural agency. A human sacrifice must be found. Police offered Taylor. Taylor, in his defence, offered another: the guitar-playing Marie Robinson.

At his trial on a charge of murdering his wife, Taylor recalled the holy communion of Ribena and ready-sliced bread celebrated by Marie at his council-house home. He said of Robinson:

> The evil came upon me. We had a battle of wits. She seduced me with her eyes. I can still see those eyes. I saw her standing before me and I was naked. She was looking at the sun. She turned and her eyes became slits and I felt the evil within me but I fought it – oh, how I fought it – but it overcame me. I sought knowledge for myself. She tried to give it to me. But this is not the way. They were all wrong. They tried to bring me peace of mind but instead they filled me with the Devil.

Friends and neighbours recalled how Christine, his wife, had seen the situation before she died. She told them:

> Marie had begun to act strangely, looking out of the window at the full moon. There had been a battle of wits between Michael and Marie and then talk about the Bible, and then Marie would again look out of the window at the moon. It had gone on like that until dawn. I was frightened to leave Michael and Marie alone because one would have hurt the other and there was already a handful of my hair in the ashtray. Michael told me that he looked at Marie and although she was fully dressed, he saw her naked and he knew that when she looked at him she saw him naked too.
>
> I saw that their eyes had become narrowed. They were hissing and I was terribly frightened but dare not show it. Michael and I wanted to resume our quiet life and we decided we would not attend any more fellowship meetings, but then we were up all night. As soon as it began to get dark, Michael went to the window and started to stare at the moon and go on about it. We sat downstairs in the sitting room all night making the sign of the cross over each other to keep each other safe.
>
> Marie had gone then, but that ceremony conducted by Marie was all a sad mistake.

The subject of the moon-gazing by both Michael and Marie was never again publicly discussed or analysed. The sun and moon were the first gods worshipped by early man and feature in occult worship. The sun as the life-giver is regarded as the male, while the moon is the female, the mother goddess. This probably stems from the fact that it takes twenty-eight days to complete the phases of the moon, and this is the length of the menstrual cycle. Since witches believe in the forces of nature, their festivals are linked with the movements of the sun and moon, particularly with the solstices and equinoxes and with the full phase of the moon.

Michael's mother, a prematurely white-haired woman of fifty-two, said:

> I believe Mike thought that Marie Robinson had put the Devil in him and he was attacking her for it. That terrible Sunday morning, Mike thought he was destroying her, not his own wife. Before Mike started going to these Christian Fellowship meetings he was a normal, loving family man. He loved Christine. If ordinary folk are told by evangelists and Jesus freaks that they're wicked, they could well start believing it.

Marie Robinson, at twenty-two, was eight years younger than Taylor. She was educated, having left school with nine O-Levels and three A-Levels. She worked as an engineering technician in the West Yorkshire County Council Highways Department at Wakefield, lived with her parents in Wentworth Road, Doncaster, and preached regularly in the Congregational church at Horbury, a few miles from Ossett. A devout Christian, she had worked with a missionary team in France and regularly attended religious conferences. She had met Michael Taylor through Christian Fellowship meetings. She was emphatic in her denial of the accusations that she was in some way to blame for the tragedy.

> People are calling me a witch. They are saying I bewitched a man and led him to kill. I have been labelled a Satanist and a Devil-worshipper. Nothing could be further from the truth. I love Jesus Christ. He is everything to me. I have seen my friends look at me with fear in their eyes but I don't hate them for it. It hurts because I loved the Taylor family.
>
> I believe the accusations against me are based on the demented ramblings of a man possessed by the Devil. That man was my friend, Michael Taylor. When I was introduced to Mike and his wife, Chris, he was searching for a kind of peace. They had heard some tape-recordings of my singing and they wanted to meet me. Mike was very depressed and he had a back complaint and could not work to support the family. Like all men he wanted to be the breadwinner.
>
> Over the weeks, I grew to love them all. I used to sing to the children and they all had their favourite songs. I spent so many happy evenings there I felt I belonged with them. But what I didn't realise until it was too late was that Michael had fallen in love with me. I was completely blind to it. I didn't see it until the night he attacked me, a few days before Chris died.
>
> We were together in the sitting room and he suddenly reached forward and kissed me. I was shocked because it was not a Christian embrace, the sort we use in our fellowship, and I pushed him away. The rebuff made him angry. Within minutes his face seemed to change and I sensed almost at once Mike had been taken over by evil spirits. He tore at my hair and hit me in the face. Chris tried to drag him away but he pushed her out of the way and threw me on to the floor. For a moment I felt the taste of death in my throat.
>
> I kept saying the name of Jesus. Chris joined in too, and it seemed to calm him almost immediately. I believed that saved my life.
>
> I never believed that Mike could possibly care for me in that way. You see, Mike and Chris were so beautiful, completely

entwined like the roots of a tree. But Chris knew of his feelings towards me. They were that close. She even offered to divorce Mike there and then so that he could marry me if it would make him happier. I told him I didn't want him in that way. I loved him as I loved all my friends. Mike must have misunderstood. I had never encouraged him in any way, believe me. Yes, I had kissed him first.

It seemed that Mike was looking for more than that. The trouble was that he put me on a pedestal – he expected so much of me. I tried to help him but I failed miserably. The next day I seemed to keep saying to myself, 'You're useless, Marie, do away with yourself.' I was in a state of shock.

Three days later, a member of the fellowship told me of the killing. I was numbed by the horror of it and I was tormented by self-accusations. I thought I was to blame. But I am convinced now that it was not Mike who brutally killed his wife. It was the Devil.

It has been said that Mike was driven to kill by the exorcism service in church the night before. I cannot say if that is true. In my humble opinion, Mike should not have been exorcised when at least one person present [the Methodist minister] did not agree it should go ahead. I believe a united front is essential to defeat the enemy, but perhaps they felt it was so urgent they had to act quickly. Most important, I believe Mike should not have been left alone if they felt demons were still present within him. He may well have been better off under sedation in hospital. I just don't know.

Some people have said it was my evil influence that drove Mike to kill. But I never tried to influence Mike except to help him. I want people to understand that. Looking back, I believe Mike must have been possessed with an evil spirit before I met him. He could have been dabbling with spiritualism of some kind. I talked over Chris's death with a psychiatrist friend. He reassured me that I could not have influenced Mike in an evil way. I don't blame myself for this tragedy. Why? Because God has reassured me and I have complete peace of mind.

Soon after Chris's death, I was asked to leave the Christian Fellowship. They didn't give me any reasons, except that a bishop and some ministers felt it was unwise for me to stay on. But until the court hearings I didn't even realise they were calling me a Satanist. Why couldn't they have been more honest?

When Michael Taylor was charged with the murder of his wife, a newspaper reporter called to tell Marie that evidence had been given of her demonic influence on Taylor. She said:

> I felt physically sick. People think it strange that I have laid hands on people, spoken in tongues and carried out a service of exorcism at these meetings. But why should that make me a Satanist? I believe these are the gifts Jesus can make available to any devout Christian when He feels it is necessary. I am not a disciple of Satan. However, just as I know there is a God I know there is a Devil and I find worship of him abhorrent.
>
> Too many people are dabbling with ouija boards and the occult. They don't understand the dangers. There have been other aspects of the case which have made me sad. Like the burning of the wooden cross I actually gave to Mike's wife. The clergyman took it from Mike and burned it during the exorcism. They felt it radiated evil. Chris asked me to buy it for her at a Christian choir gathering. It was a simple 85p varnished wooden cross inscribed with the words 'Jesus Lives' and many Christians have bought them. How could such a simple gesture be misinterpreted?
>
> There is gossip that I take occult books to work with me. I have three books on the Christian fight against evil in my bedroom. They were loaned to me and I can't even remember the titles. This tragedy has not made me wary of people, perhaps just wary of myself. I have made mistakes and I have learned from them. As for Mike, I don't think I could ever meet him again. But I will always pray for him and his children.

At his trial, a jury found Michael Taylor not guilty of murdering his wife by reason of insanity. That meant the jury accepted that at the time of her death Taylor suffered from a defect of reason, arising from mental disease, which was severe enough to prevent him from knowing what he was doing or knowing that what he did was wrong.

This principal was established in the McNaghten Rules, formulated by judges after the 1843 trial of Daniel McNaghten. He had killed the Prime Minister's secretary by mistake, having intended to kill the Prime Minister, under the delusion that the government was persecuting him, and he was acquitted on the grounds of insanity.

It was up to Taylor's counsel to show that he was suffering from a defect of reason arising from 'a disease of the mind'. This would include most psychoses, paranoia and schizophrenic diseases, but psychopaths and those suffering from neuroses or subnormality would not normally fall within the parameters of the rules.

Taylor's lawyer also had to show that, as a result of the defect of reason, he did not know the 'nature and quality' of his acts – that is, he did not know what he was doing, or he did not know that his acts were wrong.

Mr Justice Caulfield, the judge who presided at Taylor's trial, ordered that he should be detained at Broadmoor, the secure hospital in Berkshire for the mentally ill. The case once again confirmed that the law recognises God but not the Devil.

13
Everyday Possession

At the end [of the exorcism] he was allowed to go home with the spirit in his heart and no reason in his head, and within minutes he had killed the darling of his life with unspeakable brutality.

Mr Harry Ognall QC, in the case of *Regina v. Michael Taylor*, 1974

In matters of death, coroners have the last word. Their duty is to inquire into and discover, sometimes with the help of a jury, who it is that is dead, when he or she died, by what means he came to his death and, if appropriate, to suggest how such death might be avoided in the future. Mr Philip Gill, the West Yorkshire coroner who opened the inquest on Mrs Christine Taylor, reconvened that inquiry after her husband's trial. With the aid of the criminal trial evidence and findings he recorded a verdict that she died from misadventure, which is an accident resulting from some lawful adventure – something within the law which went wrong.

Underlying the verdict were two important summaries. Mr Harry Ognall QC, now Mr Justice Ognall, who defended Taylor on a charge of murder, said:

> Michael Taylor was a decent, hard-working, public-spirited and well-liked young man. He was described by a friend as cheerful, friendly and in no way a violent man. He was a devoted father and a loving husband for whom marriage was one long courtship. He then encountered the Christian Fellowship, and this particular branch of the fellowship was a group of tormented souls who simply fed neuroses to a neurotic, and in a few short days he was a homicidal maniac.

> In that condition he was the subject of what we submit were grotesque and wicked malpractices posing in the guise of religion. And, in the light of all the evidence, supervised by members of two branches of the Christian Church, he was made to confess sins of which he was wholly innocent, and indeed did not understand, and was subjected to indignities which defy comprehension.
>
> At the end he was allowed to go home with the spirit in his heart and no reason in his head, and within minutes he had killed the darling of his life with unspeakable brutality.
>
> He, Taylor, was a mere cypher. The real guilt, and certainly moral responsibility for the appalling crime, lies elsewhere. The clerics in particular, who purported to minister to Michael Taylor on that night, should be with him now in spirit in this court building and each day he is incarcerated in Broadmoor.

Mr Maurice Shaffner, counsel for the West Yorkshire police, thought the exorcism was the ultimate trigger mechanism that produced the final insanity which led Taylor to kill his wife. The coroner, Mr Gill, spelled out the dangers.

> Nothing like this must ever be allowed to happen again. But it could unless the warnings are heeded and action taken. I am greatly disturbed that these warnings have not been heeded by those concerned before. Exorcism itself – and it is a recognised part of the Church's ministry – can have dangers. Those who dabble in it are playing with fire.
>
> Those who believe in exorcism must always consider also seeking medical advice. Exorcism must be performed only by those trained and properly skilled in the work. There is a danger that novices may be overwhelmed by emotion at such religious gatherings.

The Church inquests continued in secret elsewhere. Father Vincent defended himself in the witness box at Taylor's trial with the words from St Mark's Gospel xvi, 17: 'In my name shall they cast out devils.' And the vicar added, 'I am satisfied that my authority for conducting exorcism is vested in me by the New Testament and the Lord Jesus Christ.' Indeed, St Luke's Gospel ix, 1 confirms: 'Then he called his twelve disciples together, and gave them power and authority over all devils, and to cure diseases.' But he left open the question of whether he knew of or had ignored the findings of Bishop Mortimer's 1963 commission on exorcism.

Exorcism was once a normal, frequent and repeated routine in public worship for all people being admitted to the Christian faith, at least from the end of the second century, and it is still included in some baptismal services on the grounds that, whether the person to be christened is a child or an adult, he or she has been born in sin.

This historic truth, the commission thought, helped to mitigate the current unfortunate emphasis on exorcism as an action concerned exclusively with so-called 'demonic possession'. And it recommended that 'no exorcism of a person may take place without the explicit permission of the diocesan bishop of the place where the exorcism occurs, given for every individual case concerned'.

This was no new invention. It is contained in the canon law of 1604. The commission reported:

> Until the more Christian concept of general exorcism returns to the consciousness of the Church, she is likely to be faced – indeed is being faced – with demands for such 'possession' exorcisms. It cannot be over-stressed that, as it is usually understood, this concept of 'demonic' possession is extremely dubious.
>
> In the first place it should be assumed that the patient's illness has a physical or mental cause, and the case should be referred by his general [medical] practitioner to a competent physician in psychological medicine. The exorcism of a person must not be performed until possible mental or physical illness has been excluded in this way, and furthermore until a thorough investigation has been made of the patient in terms of spiritual values by a duly licensed exorcist. Only in an extreme emergency should either of these safeguards be omitted.

The local bishop, Dr Eric Treacy of Wakefield, admitted:

> I am bound to say that the attempts made at exorcism during the night before the murder were unwise. But I believe that the clergymen involved with it were actuated by good intent and had a sincere desire to help Michael Taylor. Exorcism is a type of ministry which is increasingly practised in Christian churches. There is no order of service for this – it is administered as the situation demands. Clearly it is a form of ministry which must be exercised with the greatest possible care and responsibility. No clergyman in the diocese of Wakefield has my specific authority to practise exorcism, but I am aware that some clergymen will feel that it is a normal part of their pastoral ministry.

Yet Bishop Mortimer, by then retired, had insisted, 'No case should be considered suitable for a service of exorcism until physical or psychiatric disorders have been ruled out. Most bishops have accepted these guidelines.' Bishop Treacy, presumably, had not.

If the 1963 report of the Mortimer commission had been studied and formally adopted and Bishop Treacy had adhered to canon law 72 of 1604, that no exorcism of a person may take place without the explicit permission of the diocesan bishop, would Taylor have still been exorcised? Would he have murdered his wife or would she still be alive? These are the unanswered questions.

But the bishop's reference to 'the normal part of their [the clergy's] pastoral ministry' was picked up by the Archbishop of Canterbury, Dr Donald Coggan, who said:

> We must get this business out of the mumbo-jumbo of magic. I do not see exorcism as something set off against and in opposition to medicine. Far from it. I think there are many cases where the more rash exorcists have by-passed the work of psychiatrists. And some of the cases where exorcisms have been carried out should not have occurred at all. They should have been referred to psychiatrists. But there is no doubt that there are many cases of men and women so within the grip of the power of evil that they need the aid of the Christian Church working in collaboration with the forces of medicine to deliver the person so oppressed. Obviously there was a grave mishandling of that poor creature [Michael Taylor], but we should not condemn the ministry of liberation because there has been a bad case of it in [the diocese of] Wakefield.

Doctors summed up the tragedy. Dr Hugo Milne, the forensic psychiatrist called by the defence at the trial, said he considered that Taylor had been in a trance, a hypnotic or dissociated state which was connected to the exorcism. Taylor's violent hyperventilation during the ritual would have reduced his awareness of reality and his control of his behaviour.

Dr Patrick McGrath, superintendent of Broadmoor Hospital, where Taylor had been held pending his trial and where he was later detained on the orders of the court, said he was convinced that Taylor had been brainwashed. Brainwashing is a systematic indoctrination used to change or undermine someone's beliefs, usually by the use of prolonged stress. Dr McGrath said the case was unique in his experience of more than 1,000 murderers.

The judicial comments were, of course, all made public but the report of the Mortimer commission was for many years kept secret.

The commission's recommendation that each diocese should have someone specially trained in exorcism was acted upon by a number of bishops in the eight years following their receipt of the original report and before it was eventually published in 1972. The secrecy and fear of the subject can be judged by the fact that the Reverend John Richards, a senior research fellow at Queen's College, Birmingham, and secretary of the Mortimer commission, was unable to even borrow the published book until he had first obtained permission from the archbishop.

The report was also mocked and criticised because it 'promoted' exorcism. John Irvin wrote in the *Cambridge Evening News*:

Whoever you are, you'd better start vanishing–
You don't stand a ghost of a chance against me;
I've taken the Church's Diploma in Banishing,
And I exorcise often and regularly.
I'm honoured to be on the Archbishop's list
As a fully qualified exorcist.

You've lost your respect for the curate and vicar,
And even the Bishop has left you unmoved:
You'd better go now – or if possible – quicker
To ensure my professional prowess is proved.
For no decent demon can ever resist
The power of the qualified exorcist.

Of devils and poltergeists, spirits and spectres,
I've studied the habits and customs and vices;
I'm fully equipped with demonic detectors
And all the most modern techniques and devices.
No goblin or ghost should agree to be laid
By a layman untrained in the tricks of the trade–
If you've got any spirit you'll surely insist
On a properly qualified exorcist.

Parodies, according to Reverend Richards, should always prompt us to examine the original. Clergy like Father Vincent knew that Jesus 'gave them power and authority over all devils and to cure diseases, and sent them out to proclaim the Kingdom of God and to heal' (Luke ix, 1–2). The authority to exorcise comes not from bishops but from Christ. 'All authority in heaven and earth has been given to me.'

Christians believe what Christ said, and He took his example of exorcism from the Jews. Long before Christ, Abraham, the traditional founder of the Hebrew people, exorcised the Pharaoh in Egypt. According to the Genesis Apocryphon Abraham reported, 'I prayed for him and I laid hands on his head; and the scourge departed from him, and the evil.' The Qumran community, who resembled the Essenes of the Dead Sea Scrolls, read about systematic exorcism in the Testament of the Twelve Patriarchs. The Testament of Reuben talks about the spirit of deceit sending seven other spirits to bedevil man.

In the New Testament, the Christian St Luke (viii, 2) speaks of 'certain women, which had been healed of evil spirits and infirmities, Mary called Magdalene, out of whom went seven devils.' The seven are also mentioned in St Matthew's Gospel (xii, 45) and are: Lust, Gluttony, Anger, Flattery, Pride, Lying and Grasping at Injustice. Today, the seven deadly or capital sins remain very similar: pride, wrath, envy, lust, gluttony, avarice and sloth.

Further evidence that exorcism was known, authorised and carried out can be found in Acts (x, 38), with Jesus 'healing all that were possessed of the devil'. Elsewhere there are many undeniable hints, clues and reports.

But how men and the clergy in particular have interpreted that authority and put it into practice remains an agonising dilemma in the late twentieth century. Who should carry it out, how, when and in what circumstances are matters of fierce debate. For many years, the media would invariably turn to the Reverend J. Christopher Neil-Smith. While most people deemed in need of such religious treatment, like Michael Taylor, are from working-class backgrounds, this cleric conducted exorcisms almost daily in the affluent suburb of Hampstead in north-west London. He presided over 2,200 in four years, although he hastened to point out that not all exorcisms were, by any stretch of the imagination, major cases of demonic possession.

In minor cases, he placed his hands over the head of the person concerned and tried to break the link with the Devil. But, the clergyman added:

> In a major case, you must command in the name of the Father, the Son and the Holy Ghost that the spirit depart. Sometimes then there are eruptions and you have to hold the person down, but it would normally be over in a quarter of an hour.

The Reverend Dr Henry Cooper, who was chaplain to the Archbishop of Canterbury, normally carried out exorcisms, like his brother clergymen, face to face, wearing his robes, bearing himself in the calm, dignified manner of the Church. But night calls were emergencies, and for the nocturnally distressed he ran an exorcism hot-line from University College, London. The telephone rang at all hours of the night.

Callers would blurt out their stories. They were often frightened and could not return home because evil spirits were stopping them, diverting them to debauchery or some other form of evil. Dr Cooper placated them in this manner:

'Calm yourself, don't be afraid. God will help you. Please answer these questions.

'Do you believe in God?

'Do you believe that He is stronger than any spirit?

'Do you believe He can control any spirit you think is in your home?

'Do you believe He cares enough to do so?

'Do you commit yourself in his Love and power?'

If the caller answered 'yes' to every question, Dr Cooper said firmly, 'It is God's will that you should be free to love and serve Him without fear, for you are His child and He loves you and gave His son to die and rise for you and now sends His Holy Spirit to be with you. I bid all that is evil depart from you. And go to its own place. To harm nobody. To remain here. And never to return to trouble you, the child of God. In the name of the Father, and of the Son and of the Holy Spirit. Amen.

'Will you now say with me, together, the Lord's Prayer . . .

'Now go home to bed. There's nothing to be afraid of.'

And Dr Cooper would then wait for the next night caller.

The Reverend Thomas Dearing was vicar of St Paul's, a light industrial working-class parish east of London, almost at the extremity of the London underground system and just north of the London–Southend road. He estimated that in one four-yearly period he had driven literally thousands of demons from the bodies of his followers.

> I don't go to them offering them exorcism. They come to me asking for it. They come and say, 'I hear strange voices,' or 'I see frightening things,' or 'I feel I am being taken over by an evil spirit.'

He cited the case of Margaret, a fifteen-year-old girl brought up as an orphan who was emotionally disturbed. She had been in the care of psychiatrists. They could do nothing for her. She came to St Paul's Church one Tuesday evening with a friend. Suddenly, amid the crowded congregation, she began screaming. She was possessed by hate, fear and anger. Helped by two colleagues and their wives,

Reverend Dearing carried the girl to the vestry. She went berserk, smashing furniture and glasses, attacking them, trying to climb walls, shouting and screaming at the vicar, 'You have no power over me. I am stronger than you. Jesus died for you, but he didn't die for spirits like me.'

Dearing said that they 'had to hold the girl down while I commanded the spirit, "In the name of Jesus, go. Leave this girl." '

He recalled:

> We had a trying and violent few hours. Eventually, at midnight, Margaret calmed down and we were able to take her home. In the following two weeks we had two more desperate fights with her in the vestry before the battle was won. But it was finally over. Margaret, for the first time, was free of the voices and strange happenings in her mind. She is now quite happy, quite normal. A happy, pleasant girl and a regular church attender.

There is more than a suspicion that the people most vulnerable to this so-called 'possession' are young girls reaching puberty. This, of course, is the period during which the sexual organs change from the infantile to the adult form, the secondary sexual characteristics develop and the body assumes adult proportions. Puberty usually occurs between the ages of ten and fifteen and is often associated with emotional upsets as the individual comes to terms with her new-found sexuality. Demonic possession is also often diagnosed among older females in a sexual context.

The same vicar, Thomas Dearing, quoted the case of Marlene, a young, attractive married woman, a good wife and mother for several years – until she was possessed by the spirit of seduction or lust. She just couldn't help herself. The evil spirit drove her to try to seduce almost every man she saw, anywhere, even in the street.

> I don't mean that she had sex in the street, but she just used to pick up men in the street and go with them or take them back to her house when the family were out. All the time she was tormented by feelings of guilt and remorse, but she couldn't overcome the demon that drove her on.
>
> A friend brought her to our church. As soon as she saw me she cried, 'There's something in you that frightens me. I am Seduction . . . I am Seduction . . . I am Seduction.' You see, I then knew what I was dealing with. I commanded the spirit of seduction to go, repeating the order firmly over and over again, until the woman seemed calm and peaceful. She came back

> two or three times before I finally drove the spirit of seduction from her body. Now she is once more a faithful wife and mother, no longer tempted by seduction.

Another woman, who became possessed by witchcraft, was possessed, according to Dearing, by twelve demons. From memory he could recall Desecration, Doubt, Fear, Death, Despair, an enchanting spirit, an animal spirit and some others. She came to one of the regular services of praise and healing at St Paul's and during the service cried out for help. One by one, over the next twelve weeks or so, all the evil spirits identified themselves, speaking through her – 'I am Despair', 'I am Death' – and so on until, Dearing said, he cast them out.

The woman also suffered from back trouble, of which she was cured instantly during the course of one of the services of exorcism.

When the woman's name appeared quite innocuously in a church publication she was hounded by a member of the evil Devil-worshipping group to which she had once belonged. Her own testimony was:

> I became violent and destructive. Usually I would make for our family Bible and tear it up, not page by page, but straight across the covers. I had tremendous strength. Over the years we bought fifteen new Bibles to replace the ones I had torn up. A hymn book my mother had given me also went this way.
>
> I heard stories about the vicar's healing powers. I heard that people were getting rid of backaches and other pains and that he was getting rid of people's depressions.
>
> I went to his church and as the evil spirits came out I began screaming. Since then, I've found peace. My health is now good. I am more tolerant of people. I am generally a happy person. And I feel strong enough to deal with the Devil should he ever try to take me over again.

While the Anglicans could speak with apparent authority and record such apparent success in the matter of driving out demons from the possessed, how did their Roman Catholic brethren fare? In traditional respect for privacy and confidentiality, they have tended, at least in Britain, not to advertise such matters. In the United States of America, they had considered that the public would benefit from the televising of the case of Gina, which is described elsewhere. Other countries have different experiences.

Since the Roman Catholic exorcism is more tightly controlled, the Rituale Romanum of 1614 is more strictly observed than its

Anglican counterpart, although it is not necessarily followed to the absolute letter. Exorcists have considerable freedom in what to say and how to behave during the service. In the light of this it is surprising that two Roman Catholic priests found themselves in the criminal court charged with unlawfully killing a twenty-three-year-old university student during an exorcism. Her parents were similarly charged. But then, errors of human nature have become an unfortunate feature of the failures of exorcism.

14

Satan And The Student

Exorcism was the most inappropriate means of bringing Anneliese out of her psychosis.

Counsel prosecuting two priests and parents of Anneliese Michel for causing her death.

If the death of Michael Taylor's wife, caused by a well-intentioned but irresponsible exorcism, was a tragedy, what term can be used to describe the end of Anneliese? She was surrounded by superstition, even before her birth, and intense faith in Roman Catholicism until she reached university and met her death during exorcism.

In the Harz mountain range of Saxony, Germany, a pagan legend used in rituals, art, music, poetry and other literature was one explanation or excuse offered for her death – and in the latter quarter of the twentieth century at that. Some blamed the influence of witch-worshippers of the Brocken Spectre.

Brocken, popularly called Blocksberg, is a 3,745-foot-high mountain in the Harz range, the most northern highlands of Germany, situated between the Weser (famous for the legend of, and Browning poem, *The Pied Piper of Hamelin*) and the Elbe. Because it is the first range to be struck by the northerly winds after they cross the north German plain, the climate on the summit of the Harz is generally raw and damp, even in summer. Long before the introduction of Christianity, traditional pagan rites were enacted there. Witches joined their chief, the Devil, in revelry on the eve of May Day, 1 May, the witches' sabbat.

Even after the arrival of Christianity, when 1 May became the feast of St Walpurgis, the English nun, missionary and abbess of Heidenheim who died around AD 788, witches continued the earlier pagan festival, now calling it Walpurgis. An important part of the witchcraft is the folkloric Spectre of Brocken, Brocken Bow or Brocken Glory. When the sun is below the mountain peak, the shadow of an observer, greatly magnified, is projected on the mists around the summit of the mountain opposite. It gives the eerie impression of the Devil or, if the image so projected is a crowd of people, witches. The spectre is often observed from aircraft.

Thomas de Quincey, in his *Confessions of an Opium Eater*, gives a powerful description of the eerie illusion in one of his dreams. As the legend grew observers saw many evils, including the Devil waiting for them in the clouds. The spectre also became a bogeyman for children. Goethe chose the Brocken for the climactic scene in *Faust* and called on both Greek and German gods as evidence of the mountainous evil: 'From Harz to Hellas always cousins.' All this added to its macabre popularity and to this day the curious (including Satanists) climb the mountain to see it for themselves. In summer the mountain railway from Wernigerode delivers them but in winter snowfalls of several feet make the ascent difficult.

A combination of such folklore, superstition and legend was woven around Anneliese Michel before she was born in 1953 to Anna, the wife of Josef Michel, a wealthy sawmill owner. When Mrs Michel was pregnant with Anneliese she passed a broken-down cottage in the woods below Brocken where an ugly old woman with only one eye stared and pointed at her swollen stomach and said, 'That one will be seized by the Devil.' Anna Michel ran, stumbling and crying, to her husband. When Josef went to the woods he could find no woman and no broken-down cottage.

Anneliese seemed to build her life round an old-fashioned kind of Roman Catholic devotion. Long before she went to the University of Würzburg, she showed signs of irrational behaviour. Before she was sixteen she suffered convulsive attacks and was treated by a neurologist.

In her dormitory room at the university, the pretty, pious young student covered her walls with pictures of saints, kept near the door holy water in a font, which she had brought back from a pilgrimage to the Vatican, and regularly prayed the Rosary. Timid and intense, she seemed somehow afraid of life, of the worldly atmosphere beyond her own four walls. She was then diagnosed as an epileptic.

Even in her scholastic thesis, which she finished in 1976, she seemed to focus all her thoughts on the phenomenon of fear. She had developed some signs of abnormal behaviour, refusing to eat, flying into violent rages, screaming and trying to attack those around her. Her parents and friends were deeply concerned. They refused to believe that the medical diagnosis was the sole cause of her behaviour. No one suggested that she was mentally unbalanced

– she knew her own mind. Anneliese herself declared: 'The only conclusion for my suffering is that for reasons beyond my control and comprehension, the Devil is trying to possess my soul.' In the local priest's opinion, she was possessed by demons. He recommended ritual exorcism.

There was no haste, no sudden decision to exorcise, as in the case of Michael Taylor at Barnsley. As Roman Catholic procedure requires, the case was first investigated by a leading authority on demonic powers, possession and exorcism. That authority was Father Adolf Rodewyk, an eighty-two-year-old internationally known Jesuit Satanologist from Frankfurt and Germany's foremost practitioner of exorcism. He agreed with the priest's diagnosis of Anneliese Michel and on his recommendation the regional bishop, Dr Josef Stangl, gave permission for the exorcism to take place. From the list of trained and experienced exorcists, he chose for the task Father Arnold Renz, a Salvatorian and former missionary in China, and Father Erns Alt, the pastor in a nearby community.

Anneliese's case was well documented but there seems now to have been doubt as to how much attention was paid to the fact that she suffered from anorexia – loss of appetite, especially as a result of disease – not to mention the possibility that she might well have been suffering from anorexia nervosa, the serious disorder of perception which causes the sufferer, almost always a female, to believe she is too fat when in fact she may be dangerously thin. Food intake is drastically reduced and emaciation occurs as a result. Treatment is difficult and the best efforts of those trying to help are often frustrated by the determination of the sufferer to avoid eating. Hospital care is usually necessary as there is a real risk of a fatal outcome.

The question of whether to treat Anneliese first for anorexia or for possession must have occurred to those in charge of the case. For ten months, beginning on 14 September 1975, and continuing until not long before her death, the two priests conducted an intermittent series of exorcisms at her home in Klingenberg, thirty miles west of Würzburg, to rid the young woman of six demons they believed possessed her. The efforts were to no avail. Her convulsions returned with renewed ferocity and eventually she began to refuse food and drink.

The rites were scenes of ecclesiastical bedlam, with flickering candles, a large statue of St Michael the Archangel, a modern gory picture of the crucifixion, and chanting priests resplendent in purple vestments. Anneliese foamed at the mouth and writhed on the bed, uttering obscenities as her parents watched in silent horror. The rites were repeated seventy-two times over the ten months. The priests dutifully recorded the process on forty-three cassette tapes.

According to Father Renz, the six evil spirits attacking her included Lucifer, Judas, Cain, Nero, the Roman emperor, and Adolf Hitler, who used to shout '*Heil*' through the voice of the girl on the bed. The other demons used her voice in pitches ranging from a high tenor to a low bass, and in languages of different ages not known to Anneliese. Nero spoke an archaic form of Latin which is known to very few scholars.

Lucifer himself spat at the crucifix, howled when sprinkled with holy water and occasionally invited the exorcists to engage in sexual intercourse with their charge. Nero was very interested in sex and went into lengthy discussions of its most extreme forms in between shrieks of 'Take that holy water away!' Cain, the first murderer in creation, seemed more interested in violence, and described in exaggerated detail the torments awaiting the girl, her parents, the two priests and all their friends and relatives when they were consigned to hell. He imitated the voices of persons long since dead, identifying the owners, certifying that they were already in the nether regions, roasting in torment, and promising that those present would join them soon.

Judas Iscariot, the betrayer of Christ, was not heard very often and when he did speak he confined his remarks to complaining that the thirty pieces of silver he had been paid for his treachery were not enough and he would require further recompense. Despite his reticence, it was in his presence that the girl had her worst physical convulsions as her voice took on the low bass of the disgraced apostle.

Another demon who spoke through Anneliese's mouth, this time in a high falsetto, was Father Helgar Fleischmann, a priest who killed his mistress in 1563 and who was subsequently unfrocked, excommunicated and hung, drawn and quartered. This experience had not diminished his interest in the fairer sex and both his language and the subjects of his conversation were filthy and sordid beyond belief. He spoke in a long outdated form of German unknown to anyone except linguistic scholars and historians, and certainly beyond the comprehension of the twenty-three-year-old student.

Anneliese's condition worsened. The convulsive attacks became more frequent and more violent. The language grew ever more obscene and blasphemy was piled on blasphemy. The priests were violently cursed. Her sexual expressions became even coarser and would have been accompanied by sexual actions if she had not been tied to the bed. Throughout this time Father Alt and her parents reported seeing the stigmata, the marks of Christ's wounds, appear on the girl's hands and feet.

Sometimes she gasped into the microphone of the tape-recorder, 'I can't go on any more! I can't go on any more!' Then, when not actually in the grip of one of her seizures, she spoke rationally and prayed for God's guidance, seeking his help and deliverance from the devils that were tormenting her.

She probably believed that God had deserted her as time passed and no help came. The sight of a crucifix threw her into a spate of spitting and cursing in such violent language that it was afterwards impossible for those who were not present but knew her well and later heard the recordings to understand that the words had come from her mouth. The voices of the demons grew louder and more dominant as the cries of the shy, deeply religious girl from a respectable, conservative family background weakened.

The priests concluded that the demons were fighting for possession of her body and soul, and each convulsion became more and more frightening. The exorcists feared they were losing the battle. It was on 16 April – Good Friday, the anniversary of Our Lord's Crucifixion – that Anneliese began to refuse food and had to be helped to take liquid nourishment. The violence of the attacks continued, but her body became weaker and weaker.

Her head and body were bruised and her front teeth broken as a result of epileptic seizures. At length, following a particularly gruelling session, Anneliese fell back into an exhausted, peaceful sleep, the first for months. The next morning, 1 July, the Michels found her dead. They rejoiced: Anneliese had at last found salvation.

According to them, she had starved herself into atonement. The exorcists, when informed of her death, claimed she had shown all the characteristic signs of demonic possession – she had spoken in tongues, had predicted her own death, and, surprisingly, had performed 500 deep knee-bends shortly before she expired. For her parents, this was proof enough that she had been possessed.

They summoned Dr Kehler, who knew Anneliese and had tended her in the past. He was shocked by her appearance. The doctor later reported that the young woman of 23 years of age was five feet three inches tall, and weighed only sixty-two pounds (four stone, six pounds). At the time, he turned to the parents and asked, 'What happened to her? How did she get into that condition?'

'She has eaten nothing since Good Friday,' her father replied.

'Heavens, that was weeks ago! It is now 1 July!' Anneliese had not eaten for seventy-six days.

'She was possessed by the Devil,' said Herr Michel.

'Evil was in her,' his wife sobbed. 'The Devil had her in his claws.

Death has released her. Now she is in heaven.'

'Perhaps so,' said the shaken doctor. 'But you must realise that I cannot issue a death certificate for a corpse in such a condition.'

'Then you may go,' the father retorted. 'We will call in another doctor.'

'No other doctor will issue a death certificate, either, and moreover I shall have to report this to the police. There is certainly going to be an investigation into the circumstances of this girl's death.'

With that Dr Kehler returned to his practice in Aschaffenberg, eighteen miles north of Klintberg, the administrative centre of the district, where he reported his visit to the police. A team of detectives accompanied by a police doctor found Josef and Anna Michel still weeping in their living room. They glanced at the picture of Anneliese on the mantelshelf. The experienced officers, used to the sight of shot, strangled, mangled and mutilated bodies, went into the bedroom and gasped. They saw that only the hair spread over the pillow bore any similarity to the good-looking girl whose photograph they had just admired.

There were injuries to her genital organs, her face had been reduced to a parchment-covered skull and her eyes were so sunken in their sockets that no one could tell whether they were open or closed.

'Cause of death?' asked a policeman with his notebook open.

'Without a post-mortem, I'd say extreme malnutrition and dehydration amounting to inanition,' said the police doctor.

> In your language that's a state of exhaustion or a bodily disorder arising from lack of any of the nutritional elements such as calories, proteins, vitamins, minerals or water. She starved to death.
>
> Death was some time last night. There are wounds on the body, particularly on the genitals, but not serious. I suspect they may have been self-inflicted. She was a virgin. There are also marks on the wrists and the ankles where she'd been tied. This was probably to prevent her from injuring herself, from what I can gather.

When the public prosecutor, Karl Stenger, saw the report, he concluded that the two priests and parents had stood passively by while the girl starved to death. It was murder by negligence. After all, the law does not recognise demonic possession and expects one human being to go to the aid of another, particularly when those who could help are close relatives; particularly when it must be obvious that the person is dying. Nor does the law accept that prayer, even if permitted and approved by competent church authorities, is a defence in such circumstances.

The priests, answering the prosecutor's questions, replayed the tapes. A typical exchange ran:

Priest: 'I beseech you to leave this girl and never return.'
Anneliese: 'You damned pig. Keep your mouth shut. I am not leaving.'
Priest: 'Why are you here?'
Anneliese: 'I am the Father of Lies.'
Priest: 'Why have you gone into Anneliese?'
Anneliese: 'Because she is damned.'

The prosecutor said that Miss Michel's death could have been prevented if she had received medical help. Charges of homicide by neglect were, therefore, brought against the parents and the two priests. All four pleaded not guilty. Bishop Stangl and Father Rodewyk, who were also under investigation, were not indicted because they had no direct contact with Miss Michel during the exorcism and did not know she was not receiving medical treatment.

The trial lasted a month, and more than 300 witnesses, including experts, were called upon to testify for the prosecution and the defence. The defendants claimed that they were within their rights to treat the girl as their religious beliefs dictated. Father Renz went on the attack and declared: 'The demons which possessed her were unusually articulate in voicing sympathy for church modernists – those who discount demonic possession.'

Prominent physicians gave evidence that the girl had suffered from epilepsy and that exorcism had worsened the condition. But they had to admit, under cross-examination, that they had not seen the girl while she was alive. Equally well-qualified doctors testified that her symptoms did not resemble epilepsy, but they, too, had to confess that they had never examined the living Anneliese.

Prosecution medical experts said that 'Exorcism was the most inappropriate means of bringing Anneliese out of her psychosis.' (Psychosis is the name for a group of mental disorders including schizophrenia.) A specialist in nervous disorders thought that the young woman had suffered from an emotional conflict resulting from guilt feelings about a sexual interest in Jesus Christ. Asked to substantiate that opinion, he said it was due to his faith in modern psychology, surely an answer to match those of the priests who testified to their faith in the existence of demons which were able to take possession of human souls.

Another neurologist told the court: 'No demons spoke out of Anneliese. The girl spoke to the exorcists with a psycho-hysterical transposed voice.' A psychiatrist held that 'The girl suffered from paranoiac hallucinatory psychosis in which demons were nothing more than manifestations of a deeper spiritual conflict.'

Paranoiacs have delusions, usually involving persecution, in which intelligence and reasoning capacity remain intact. Hallucinations or other mental disturbances do not occur. Less commonly, there may be delusions of grandeur, of the love of some notable person, like Christ; of grounds for sexual jealousy; or of bodily deformity, odour or parasitosis. Many theories have been put forward to explain paranoia, but the cause is still unknown and treatment is very difficult.

Eventually, the court ruled that the priests and parents were guilty of negligent homicide and sentenced them to six months' imprisonment, suspended for three years' probation in each case. The maximum penalty for such an offence in Germany is five years in jail.

Catholic theologians were disturbed by the implications of the death and trial. Anneliese's own tutor, theologian Ernst Veth, said:

> She was an extraordinary, sweet girl, but very fearful. She told me she had realised that fear was part of our daily existence, but she just couldn't handle that realisation.
>
> Now is the time for our church to reflect very seriously on the role the Devil should still be allowed to play. Anneliese's exorcism was a basic mistake. Possession is a question of belief, not an empirical fact. They should have called the doctor.

Among those who disagreed were her parents. 'The worst thing,' said her mother, 'is that despite what has happened, still no one wants to believe in the Devil.'

Since his daughter's death, Josef Michel has reported that his house is haunted by swarms of huge, fat flies and big, strong white mice. At night, the house is lit up by strange flashes of light which cannot be explained by natural or man-made illumination. Two years after Annaliese was buried, Sister Ursula, a local nun, suffered epileptic seizures. She predicted that if the girl's body was exhumed it would be found undecayed, but when the coffin was opened, this was not the case.

Herr Michel's maintained: 'The guilty are the forces of darkness. You cannot put the Master of Gloom in the dock.'

15

Highgate Vampire Hunt

[Highgate Cemetery] has now become a haven for the black magician who requires ancient relics for use in his rituals . . . Coffin handles and ornaments are the most common targets, but sometimes cremation urns or even skulls are removed.

David Farrant, *Hornsey Journal*, 1971

Whatever the current state of Satanism in Britain, the most common consternation is caused by devilment in cemeteries. The vampire hunt in Highgate Cemetery in fashionable north London is an outstanding example. It began with a reader's question in a newspaper about apparitions in the cemetery in 1970 and ended four years later in an Old Bailey trial in which the same reader, an alleged Devil-worshipper, was convicted of grave desecration.

London's most famous burial ground, where more than 100,000 people have been interred since 1839, was created to cater for the dead for whom space could no longer be found in parish churchyards. It boasts the graves of many famous people: scientist Michael Faraday and poet Christina Rossetti in the older part, on one side of appropriately named Swains Lane; and, in the newer section across the steep street, novelist George Eliot and her husband George Henry Lewes, novelist Mrs Henry Wood, philosopher Herbert Spencer, bare-knuckle boxing champion Tom Sayers and economist Karl Marx.

As in most metropolitan cemeteries, the monuments have been crumbling and the vegetation overgrowing since the First World War. In the Second World War bombs fell on many tombs, which were simply left as they were, blown open, and covered by tarpaulins which in time rotted away.

American Anglophile author Richard D. Altick visited the necropolis, toured the first-class pseudo-Egyptian crypts and the working-class regimented rows of graves, and reported:

> Highgate Cemetery, by its very nature, is warranted to convert what begins as a mere visit into an Adventure. [It] represents what would result if the accumulated monuments of Westminster Abbey were transferred in their full marmoreal extravagance to the Amazonian rainforest. Although the guide maintains that the lush growth is systematically eliminated during the winter by the use of billhooks and wholesale burning, one cannot believe it has been curbed for years. Thick 'cuckoo grass' rises to a height of four or five feet. Trees, saplings, wild shrubs, weeds, all the rank vegetation that a weeping English climate can bring forth, swallow up every tombstone that does not front directly on to the path. To reach [one grave] requires plunging from the path through the brambles and burrs and hip-high undergrowth and tough, ground-clinging vines that constantly trip up the explorer fresh from the London pavements. A machete is not ordinarily part of one's travelling equipment in England, but it would come in handy here.

In the 1960s the neighbourhood and the cemetery itself suffered social disturbances like any other district, usually from the self-styled mods and rockers. Police and clergy were more interested in or alarmed by the quantity of cannabis in circulation and the children left abandoned and neglected by working mothers and abusive parents. Teenagers no longer bothered to approach the cemetery via Swains Lane: by 1970, the gates and railings surrounding it had been broken down and the adolescents went directly through the gaps into the graveyard for their nocturnal activities.

Tramps and schoolboys, according to the groundsman, climbed and danced on graves 'for a dare', damaging the monuments and making it difficult to keep the place in reasonable repair. One elderly woman, visiting a relative's grave in the dense undergrowth, complained that she felt uncomfortable. On at least five occasions she had been 'molested' by groups of strange visitors who followed her and stood silently behind her without speaking.

According to *The Times*, she concluded, 'This may well be part of . . . strange ceremonies and I feel that sooner or later someone will be murdered there.' One group of youths who visited the cemetery at night were interested in the supernatural, and formed the British Occult Society. However, according to the wife of one of them, David Farrant, they set up the society 'mainly for a laugh and a joke. We would wander about, frighten ourselves to death and come out again.'

Farrant, a former public schoolboy at Highgate, was described variously as an author, tobacconist and high priest or president of the society. Much later he admitted conducting rites in the cemetery but insisted that he worshipped God and that these ceremonies were nothing whatsoever to do with Satanism. Farrant claimed that the society members saw no signs of major damage during their first visits, but when he returned early in 1969 he found that:

> Vaults had been broken open and coffins literally smashed apart. One vault near the top gate was wide open and one could see the remains of a skeleton where it had been wrenched from a coffin. Another vault on the main pathway had been thus entered and one of the coffins inside set alight.

Another visitor reported seeing gangs of thirteen- or fourteen-year-olds smashing monuments and setting fire to coffins. Later he found corpses which had been pulled out of already opened vaults and left on the path. No one could be certain, but the general view was that most of the damage was caused by teenage gangs rebelling against normal adult authority or by others doing it 'for a giggle', for a dare or deliberately to make people believe that Satanists were at work. Whoever was to blame, the damage was becoming a major problem for the police.

The British Occult Society always seemed to know first about the night-time activities. Two specific accounts came from different people who had been walking in the burial ground and who had met on different dates a 'tall, dark spectre' which temporarily hypnotised or paralysed them.

Farrant, said to be intrigued by these stories and concerned about escalating vandalism, decided to spend a night in Highgate Cemetery. He chose December 1969, the winter solstice. As well as being the time when the sun reaches the northernmost point from the celestial equator and appears to stand still this is generally regarded by gardeners and others as the regular turning point in the weather. He got the shock of his life.

According to Farrant, he arrived at the top gate before midnight, but before climbing it he saw what appeared at first to be a tall person wandering further up the sloping cemetery. Then he realised that at this distance the figure must have been more than seven feet tall. He saw 'two eyes meeting my gaze at the top of the shape which was not human, rather reflecting some alive presence. I was under psychic attack. I tore my eyes away and the figure vanished.'

According to folklorists, such encounters seem to fit a pattern shared by many cultures. Witnesses often talk about meeting an 'old hag', a 'bedroom intruder' and, among researchers into unidentified flying objects (UFOs), a 'man in black'. Farrant took the apparition seriously and wrote to his local paper, the *Hampstead and Highgate Express.* His letter was published on 6 February 1970.

> Some nights I walk past the gates of Highgate Cemetery.
>
> On three occasions I have seen what appeared to be a ghost-like figure inside the gates at the top of Swains Lane. The first occasion was on Christmas Eve. I saw a grey figure for a few seconds before it disappeared into the darkness. The second sighting, a week later, was also brief.
>
> Last week, the figure appeared, only a few yards inside the gates. This time it was there long enough for me to see it much more clearly, and now I can think of no other explanation than this apparition being supernatural.
>
> I have no knowledge in this field and I would be interested to hear if any other readers have seen anything of this nature.

The letter touched off a sequence of events which brought forth a wealth of stories and beliefs. They formed an unusually detailed picture of Highgate's place in urban folk culture, but at first provided little in the way of demonology. The following week, the paper printed four responses to Farrant's request which confirmed that there was a local tradition of a Highgate 'ghost'. One said that the spectre had been appearing for several years, showing itself nightly for about a week at monthly intervals. Another noted that:

> Many tales are told about a tall man in a hat who walks across Swains Lane and just disappears through a wall into the cemetery. Local superstition also has it that the bells in the old disused chapel inside the cemetery toll mysteriously whenever he walks.

A third correspondent added that he had seen the ghost cross a cemetery path while he and his fiancée were walking there, admitting, 'I am glad someone else has spotted it. I was convinced it was not my imagination.'

The following week, the *Ham and High*, as the paper is known affectionately in the locality, published a front-page comment and drew attention to five more letters inside under the headline, SPOOKS. Two of them talked about a mysterious form seen moving about just inside the cemetery gates, behind the headstones; others described a figure on a bicycle which chased women down Swains Lane. The week after that a local pub-crawler told how he had collected from bars different names for the phantom, including 'The Wild Eggman', 'Mad Arthur' and 'The White Ghost'.

Six more readers added to the range of paranormal experiences reported in the area. One claimed to have seen a figure wade into a pond, motioning for the witness to follow. Curiously, the figure made no ripples or splash as it entered the water but uttered a 'terrible cry'. Two others described a woman in white who went through a locked gate and a mysterious voice that called 'Hugo!' from deep in the cemetery. Finally, David Farrant wrote to express his thanks and relief that his ghostly experience had been corroborated by others.

Many further letters were openly sceptical about the apparitions. Academics analysed the correspondence and pointed to many parallels both in Britain and overseas. Yet hardly two informants gave the same story about Highgate. Most were young and had not gone to the cemetery alone but in couples or single-sex groups.

Of course, every generation hears of ghostly cyclists, the twentieth-century successor to the 'headless horseman' of previous ages; of white ladies who appear to drown in ponds and of 'white witches'. And those about to sit examinations often 'hear' ghosts shouting names of entrants, often those they know will fail, or some name from a set paper with which the examinees know they will be confronted.

In America the stories often arise as a result of witnesses deliberately visiting particular sites in the conscious or subconscious anticipation of such an experience. They are, at the outset, expecting 'something to happen'. American adolescents call such adventures 'legend trips'. Europeans tend to think that they are one-off experiences and not sufficiently constant or repetitive to constitute legends. Professor Bill Ellis, of Hazleton Campus, Pennsylvania State University, the principal behind this 'vampire hunt' analysis, argues that any story, as long as it produces a willingness to suspend disbelief, can be used to justify a trip to any site and insists that variations are the essence of all legends.

I asked Paul Smith, of Sheffield University and head of folklore at Memorial University, Newfoundland, a great collector of legends, for his view. He thought that British teenagers were too sensible or wary to intentionally go on legend-hunting trips in the hope of being scared by something.

Before the Highgate Cemetery affair had died down, teenagers at Saltwood, near Hythe, Kent, reported a similar ghost. It was visible only to those under the age of twenty-one, mostly young couples out for a twilight walk. Again the appearances were amorphous. One correspondent saw 'this eerie, bat-like figure', another a 'red light, like a red ball of fire' that suddenly changed into a figure with 'webbed feet and no head . . . carrying a red lantern'.

By then, both the Highgate community and locals in Hythe had come to the conclusion that it all had something to do with 'black magic cults'. That meant the Devil, or whoever was behind the spectres had to be demonically possessed.

Dr Jacqueline Simpson, the current president of the Folklore Society, surveyed a similar collection of experiences associated with the Chanctonbury Ring, a prehistoric hill fort in Sussex, which involved ritual actions said to invoke a Druid, a ghost, a lady on a white horse, flying saucers, Satanists and the Devil himself. This is one of the sites where teenagers know 'for certain' that they will have some experience or other.

David Farrant wrote an article for the *Hornsey Journal* entitled 'The "Black History" of Highgate', in which he warned:

> [The] menace of Satanism is very real indeed. The countless reports of desecration in Highgate Cemetery have also caused much concern lately. Although the cemetery has been used occasionally for the purpose of conducting ceremonies, it has now become a haven for the black magician who requires ancient relics for use in his rituals. These vary according to the purpose for which they are needed. Coffin handles and ornaments are the most common target, but sometimes cremation urns or even skulls are removed.

Satanists, priests and adherents, he said, practised the black mass with its sexual abuses. Farrant was himself photographed examining the remains of a recent Satanic mass in the cemetery. The contents of a coffin had been removed and were scattered on the floor of the vault.

While Farrant claimed that he worshipped God he said that black magic covens used the same ceremonies to worship the supreme evil force.

> This is a complete contrast to worshipping God and they use the power derived from their ritual to harm people. I have known victims of their curses to be driven to the point of suicide and others to have ended up in mental hospitals.

> Unlike our coven they shun all publicity and work in great secrecy. They are evil men, and after I crossed their path once I received several threatening communications.

The vicar of St Augustine's Church, Highgate, responded:

> This is just whitewashed black magic. Christianity is the only answer to evil.
>
> When we hear about this sort of thing we tend to dismiss it as the work of cranks. But anyone who has dealt with evil knows it is very real. There has been a renewed interest in Devil-worship and young people who go just out of interest initially become more deeply involved. The Devil seeks them as disciples.

At the time Farrant was engaged in a battle via the local newspapers with Sean Manchester about which of them was president of the British Occult Society. Manchester avowed 'a certain amount of reluctance as most forms of publicity put investigations of this kind at considerable risk'. He was concerned, he said, about the numbers of carcases of foxes and other large animals that were showing up with 'lacerations around the throat and completely drained of blood'. His amazing conclusion was that there was a vampire at work. The *Ham and High* headlined the revelation, DOES A WAMPYR WALK IN HIGHGATE?

A vampire is a reanimated male or female corpse supposed to seek nourishment or do harm by sucking the blood of sleeping people. This malignant and loathsome Slav creature has been popularised as a subject of fiction, particularly by Bram Stoker (1847–1912). He revived the Gothic horror romance with *Dracula* (1897), a story based on traditional European folklore. Through the eyes of an English gentleman narrator, it introduces a chilling arch-fiend in the mysterious Count Dracula, whose seat is a lonely castle in Transylvania in Romania, a region that by tradition is particularly infested with vampires. The vampires can be killed only by a stake through the heart, which prevents them from benefiting from the blood of others.

Sean Manchester warned residents of Highgate that the spirit which had taken up residence in their cemetery was far worse than had been thought: he speculated that it was a king vampire from Wallachia, a district of Romania, which had been brought to England in a coffin by its supporters at the start of the eighteenth century, the time the Magyar word *vampir* crept into the English language.

The king vampire, according to Manchester, was installed in a fine house in London's West End (he later upgraded it to a castle) and this site became the traditional focus of England's vampire plagues. (Vampires thus became demons, or evil spirits, which are responsible for demonic possession.) The vampires then took over Highgate Cemetery. Manchester said in the *Ham and High*:

> Now that there is so much desecration of graves by Satanism, I'm convinced that this has been happening in Highgate Cemetery in an attempt by a body of Satanists to resurrect the king vampire. We would like to exorcise the vampire in the traditional and approved manner – drive a stake through his heart with one blow just after dawn between Friday and Saturday, chop off his head with a gravedigger's shovel and burn what remains. This is what the clergy did centuries ago. But we'd be breaking the law [if we did that] today.

Years later, Manchester recalled with some satisfaction that he awoke on the morning this item was published and found himself 'famous'. Among the experts consulted was the Reverend Christopher Neil-Smith of Hampstead, one of several Church of England priests involved in exorcism and other forms of parapsychological research. Even he called Manchester's vampire theory 'a novelistic embellishment'. Another sceptic ironically applauded the British Occult Society's 'last-ditch battle on behalf of the romantics' but concluded, 'Alas, regretfully, it is too late, by at least three generations.'

Manchester was not deterred. He gave detailed accounts in which he claimed to have personally confronted and destroyed two dangerous vampires in the area while investigating the unusual loss of blood and neck wounds of one, Elizabeth Wojdyla, and the unusual demonic possession of another woman, identified only as Lusia. Much of what he later said and did was not actually based on the folk tradition of vampires but was derived from the international pop culture descended from Bram Stoker's *Dracula* and the major films based on the novel, which numbered twenty-seven at the last count.

Manchester's scenario was itself committed to film by Hammer Studios as *Dracula AD 1972*. A group of rebellious teenagers desecrate a disused London church to hold a black mass and succeed in raising a Satanic vampire (Christopher Lee) from the graveyard outside. *The Satanic Rites of Dracula* was a variation on a similar theme, in which a vampire (Lee again) presides over a coven of intelligent, influential Satanists planning to destroy the world with a genetically engineered disease.

Although few people took the idea of a vampire being raised by occultists literally, it did provide an explanation for both the paranormal events and the very obvious physical signs of intrusion and vandalism, and Manchester focused discussion of the happenings at Highgate Cemetery on his theory. While the concept of a king vampire of Wallachia might have been too camp for most, many people were quite willing to believe that occultists were using the grounds for weird rituals. Manchester's description of how to 'lay' the vampire, again indebted to the numerous vampire films then in production, also suggested to many that a cemetery hunt might not be a bad move. At worst, a spooky good time could be had by all; at best, one might get a front-row seat at a black magic ritual.

Manchester's rival, David Farrant, when contacted in March 1970, preferred to say that if the being he had seen in Highgate Cemetery turned out to be a vampire, 'I for one am prepared to pursue it, taking whatever means might be necessary so that we can all rest.' Questioned later, he said that this remark had been intended to humour some 'over-zealous reporter'.

Friday 13 March was too auspicious a day for television to miss. They posed Manchester and Farrant outside the gates of Highgate Cemetery to be interviewed. Farrant claimed to have received 'threatening letters with black magic symbols on them' warning him to stay away from things he could not understand. Manchester repeated his description of how to destroy a vampire and warned Farrant indirectly.

> He goes against our explicit wish for his own safety. We feel he does not possess sufficient knowledge to exorcise successfully something as powerful or evil as this vampire, and may well fall victim as a result.

The programme also aired a series of ghost sightings by a group of children who lived nearby, one of whom asserted: 'I actually saw its face and it looked like it had been dead for a long time.' The child did not say how many dead people he had seen, either soon or longer after death.

The programme was screened at 6 pm. Two hours later, Swains Lane was packed with a crowd of would-be vampire-hunters who arrived by foot, car, van and bus. By ten o'clock, a witness said, the onlookers resembled a football crowd, and several squads of police tried unsuccessfully to control the mob that shook the cemetery gates and scaled the walls. One who managed to attract attention was the aptly named Alan Blood, a twenty-five-year-old history teacher who had come forty miles from Chelmsford, Essex, with several students in tow to participate. He commented: 'I have taken an interest in the black arts since boyhood.'

About a hundred spectators managed to get into the old part of the cemetery before being rooted out by the police with searchlights. Manchester, who claimed to have been present at the vampire hunt, told a reporter:

> It was like the end of a Frankenstein film when the monster was chased. People had weapons and looked as if they could have turned nasty if they had seen a tall lean person in dark clothing.

The police, of course, could not be certain whether the hunters would be the very young, the young or adult, nor whether they were on the excursion for a lark or in the serious belief that they had a mission and duty to slay a vampire.

The mob scene on the Friday night in Highgate was followed by smaller incidents. On the Saturday night five youths were found inside the cemetery and ejected by the police. 'We were hoping to see an occult ceremony and got lost,' one explained. Others took it more seriously. The London *Evening News* stressed the cult connection in their version of the story, which was entitled SATAN RIDDLE OF OPEN TOMB and carried the opinion that 'the vampire must be Satan-like in character'.

Manchester was still being quoted at length. He spoke about the 'abominable desecration' he found.

> It is too much to be merely the work of vandals. There are black magic signs and symbols, limbs and even entire bodies missing from graves. It all points to something very evil.

Police vigils were beginning to have some effect. Two youths were caught on 24 July 1970 with a sharpened stave and a rucksack containing sandwiches and coffee. Although the police wanted them to be committed for trial at the Old Bailey, the magistrate dismissed the case after hearing from one lad's father. He said he was quite aware of his son's activities, and they were innocent – in fact, he had been invited to accompany them. 'We often go on expeditions. He has a sense of atmosphere and I have encouraged it.'

Manchester, responding to police appeals to stay away from the cemetery, warned that such activities impeded the 'serious research' carried out by his wing of the British Occult Society. He also admitted that there were strained relations even between the psychic researchers like himself and the police.

The same night as the two youths were arrested in the cemetery police came across Farrant and his girlfriend, Martine de Stacy. They were suspected of being in possession of cannabis, an illegal drug, and taken in for questioning. They were released when the substance seized turned out to be camomile, a strong-smelling garden herb used in the exorcisms conducted by British Occult Society members.

Farrant claimed that while in the cemetery the group had found evidence that black witches had broken into a mausoleum and painted a pentagram on the floor, decorating it with black magic symbols representing Jupiter, Mars and the moon. A bust of the deceased had been placed at the head of the pentagram, and burned-out candles sugested that a ritual had been performed, perhaps to summon the dead man's body. 'There was no doubt it was not the work of amateurs,' Farrant concluded. 'In fact, I know who was responsible for that desecration.'

He and de Stacy explained that eight society members had entered the cemetery after midnight with a Bible, crucifix, holy water and herbs. Entering the already opened mausoleum, they joined hands, and the girls removed their clothes 'as a symbol of purity'. After reading from the Bible and 'spells taken from ancient books', the group felt the icy-cold atmosphere of the crypt warm up – a sign, they believed, that the evil had been dispersed – and so they prepared to leave.

Farrant remained to take a few photographs. He wanted them for documentary purposes, he said, to keep as a record of the exorcism, and he intended to show them to the police. One of the pictures showed de Stacy, still naked, in the vault. 'It must have been the flash that gave us away,' she commented. The photograph, which was to become known as the 'Nude Rites' picture, later resurfaced to cause Farrant more problems.

The Highgate vampire was back in the news on Friday 1 August, when three adolescent girls visiting the cemetery found the headless and charred remains of a woman's corpse lying outside a broken vault. Police took the incident seriously, noting that similar desecrations had occurred south of the River Thames in Southwark, just five miles away. A spokesperson commented: 'We are working on the theory that this may be connected with black magic. The body could well have been used for that reason.'

Manchester accused:

These same Satanists that desecrate Highgate Cemetery are

disciples of the Evil One, the vampire, and intend to spread the cult in the hope of corrupting the world.

Stealing a human skull, Manchester warned, was a step towards resurrecting the king vampire with the help of the powers of darkness and increasing the number of the cult with his aid. Although a cemetery employee insisted that he had seen no signs of black magic, both police and caretakers promised they would intensify patrols in the cemetery.

On 17 August one of those caught up in the police patrols in St Michael's Churchyard, which adjoins the north end of the cemetery, was David Farrant. The police found paraphernalia which they described as a crucifix and a sharp wooden stake. Scotland Yard released a lengthy statement they attributed to Farrant, explaining that he had gone to Highgate Cemetery to watch a vampire rising from its grave: 'I would have entered the catacombs in my search and upon finding the supernatural [being] I would have driven my stake through its heart and then run away.'

Farrant later said that the statement had been fabricated by the police. He had in fact been in the graveyard with other members of his society to conduct a seance intended to establish a psychic link with the dark spectre he had seen. Farrant was reluctant to name the other members or to give details of the seance. The 'stake', he said, had not been brought to be put through a vampire's heart but was to have been attached to a piece of string to cast a circle in the seance.

When he appeared in the magistrates' court, he chose not to deny his statement, but his solicitor said that hunting a vampire in itself was no crime – it was akin to the widely publicised searches for the Loch Ness Monster. The magistrate dismissed charges of behaviour likely to cause a breach of the peace. Outside the court, Farrant promised to continue his efforts to exorcise the earthbound spirit conjured up by the 'evil practices that have taken place at the cemetery among black magic followers'.

But that was by no means the end of the tale . . .

16

The Vampire Nailed

I placed the point of the stake between the seventh and eighth rib on the left [of the corpse] . . . [one of my assistants] pleaded with me to desist . . . If what lies before us is an undead, I replied, it would be an act of healing.

Sean Manchester, President, British Occult Society

When David Farrant was acquitted of any offence, his supporters in the British Occult Society returned to Highgate Cemetery. They stood on watch every night for the 'evil master who must be stalked'. Farrant announced that he hoped to spot and photograph the evil spirit, which he described as 'Not exactly a ghost, but something like a vampire that has taken on human form.'

Before long he announced that he had found one body removed from a coffin and placed 'in the middle of a black pentagram drawn on the floor of a vault'. Remains of candles indicated that the body had been the focal point of a black mass. Farrant expressed the hope that the efforts of the British Occult Society would help the police catch the black magic circle 'red-handed'.

The media were anxious for him to repeat his discoveries and soon afterwards Farrant took a reporter from the London *Evening News* to Highgate for an all-night vigil. They chose a night of the full moon. They found more damage, graves opened, skulls stolen, vaults defaced with strange scrawls. Farrant continued to keep watch.

Within a month, his rival, Sean Manchester, was back in the cemetery, at the Columbarium, the complex of ornate crypts in pseudo-Egyptian styles reserved for the wealthy, where police had found another decapitated corpse. Had the heart of the body been staked and the head removed with a shovel in the ritual fashion of killing a vampire, as Manchester had described? The police wondered.

Manchester burned incense, sprinkling 'four cups of holy water from the Roman Catholic Church', and read an exorcism service which he said was in Greek, Latin, Hebrew and English. This ceremony was, however, conducted outside the vaults in the middle of the afternoon at a time when visitors were few. Like Farrant he asserted that a coven of Devil-worshippers was using the cemetery and told reporters that *his* British Occult Society also held exorcisms in places where black magic meetings had taken place. As for Farrant, Manchester said: 'He was lucky the police got to him first. Had he met with the Satanists first, I feel we would not have heard anything more of him.'

The BBC programme *Twenty-Four Hours* brought a film crew to Highgate to record a 'documentary reconstruction' of the exorcism. When it was screened it was introduced with the following words:

> Tonight we have a film report of a secret and Satanic ritual being practised in Britain in October 1970. *Twenty-Four Hours* is building up a case history of the occult. We've heard of ghost-hunters, psychic researchers, covens of witches dancing naked around bonfires in the middle of winter and even the odd black mass. Sometimes the fascination with the black arts leads its adherents to more sinister rituals.

The programme proceeded to show 'evidence of a vampire cult in which diabolists work to raise the undead to contaminate a society whose Christian values they despise'. Manchester obliged by revealing more details about his exorcism: he had followed Lusia, the mysterious London girl, who was alleged to be demonically possessed. She entered the vaults. Going into the crypt behind her, he had discovered an extra coffin with no nameplate, and had opened it to reveal 'a body which appeared neither dead nor alive'. According to his own account:

> I placed the point [of his stake] between the seventh and eighth rib on the left. Grabbing my arm . . . [one of my assistants] pleaded with me to desist, saying that it would be sacrilege. If what lies before us is an undead, I replied, it would be an act of healing. Consternation grew among the group in the vault and the consensus of opinion was that the stake remained unsoiled until, at least, proper permission had been obtained from the correct quarter.

Precisely which authority would have given permission for an exorcism to be carried out by an unqualified non-priest on an unidentified body which was 'neither dead nor alive' was not exactly explained. So Manchester contented himself with sprinkling salt, holy water and garlic in the vault and reading the exorcism while the sun came dramatically closer and closer to setting and 'deep, voluminous booming sounds began vibrating through the tombs'.

All this was so much like the standard vampire film sequences of light and sound that no one could accuse the BBC or Manchester of having disturbed graves or dabbled in worse than the popular culture of vampire lore.

Sean Manchester's next step was to exorcise evil from a vandalised church. Four months after his mock-exorcism in the vaults of Highgate, a church in neighbouring Islington was vandalised and the reserved sacrament taken from the altar. The priest condemned the sacrilege, saying, 'I immediately connected the incident with the body-snatching at Highgate Cemetery. I believe those concerned took the blessed sacrament to use in their Devil-worship.'

Ever willing to help, Sean Manchester contacted the priest and offered to hold a special service to exorcise the evil from the desecrated objects. The priest agreed. The ensuing ceremony included Bible readings, after which Manchester 'uttered a number of incantations over the objects. Then he threw a handful of powder into a tiny flame burning in a small bowl and flames shot in the air.'

The local bishop, understandably upset that the priest had allowed the service to take place without asking his permission or checking Manchester's credentials, ordered an inquiry, the results of which were never published.

Many curious explanations have been offered for such behaviour by amateurs in the field of exorcism. They may be dabblers, who cannot understand why they should go through training for the priesthood before they can drive out evil spirits; frauds, who sell details of their escapades or invented stories to newspapers or television; even people possessed by good or evil.

Folklorists use another name for it: ostension, literally, the act of showing, exhibiting or manifesting and, in church language, the action of the priest holding up the Eucharistic elements, the wafer and the wine, to the people. Whether in religious or secular matters, folklore ostension is acting out the features of a legend. Manchester and Farrant, from the start, having seen an apparition in the cemetery, seemed eager to bring their legend to life by acting it. The stories they had heard encouraged ostensive activities in other youngsters, in the same way that American legends about Satanism have encouraged quasi-improvised rituals in more recent times.

The events at St Mary's on Deadman's Hill, Clophill, Bedfordshire, covered in Chapter 10, were apparently based on ostensive visits encouraged by publicity, and other cases of supposed black masses emerged, clearly derived from media warnings. Manchester, like many vampire 'practitioners', chose ostensive behaviour that looked more like harmlessly acting out a film plot than illegal trespass or any unlawful behaviour. Farrant, on the other hand, continued to focus his activities on late-night watches in the cemetery. There he had to compete – for privacy or attention – with less savoury visitors and the special police 'ghost squad' formed to combat the vandalism. Cleverly, Manchester took no risks. Farrant, on the other hand, was a ready-made suspect.

Eric Maple, the popular witchcraft writer, who probably accurately evaluated the Clophill vandalism, now turned his attention to Highgate. He noted that Farrant's visits were being imitated by 'groups of youths searching frantically for clues among the graves'. The headless corpse, he felt sure, had almost certainly been used for a 'sacrifical rite' of necromancy and he thought that the increasing examples of graffiti was 'voodoo inscriptions', probably little known in Britain.

Despite immigration from Africa and the West Indies, it is not thought that many migrants would know enough about voodoo to go to a cemetery and daub a tomb with voodoo symbols, nor is it likely that even if they did they would choose the tomb of a totally unconnected person. Maple thought that one particular sign suggested homage to Aida Wegg, a voodoo goddess, a fact which could be learned from a good library. He added darkly that he believed that 'more sinister happenings have occurred in the cemetery after bodies have been tampered with by black magic covens'.

The Highgate affair disappeared temporarily from the news until 31 October, the last day of the old Celtic calendar, when all witches and warlocks are supposed to be abroad. It remains an ungodly feast despite having been replaced in diaries by the Christian All Hallows Eve or Hallowe'en. On that night, pilgrimages to the Highgate unresting place had become an annual event. Books on ghosts and hauntings had drawn attention to the expeditions and the media used the forthcoming occasion to speculate anew about secret covens, open coffins and Satan-worship.

Farrant used the opportunity to warn that:

> The people concerned are youngsters 'out for kicks' but genuine Satanists take part in bizarre rites and include sexual practices as part of their worship. It would be wrong to mistake their rites for harmless orgies. They are, on the contrary, using this tremendous sexual power – generated by many people – to direct and help them in the practice of their magic. Although

> the motive is not clear, their main aim seems to be invoking certain spirits to establish contact with the Devil.
>
> The young, with their tendency to think they are invulnerable, are the most prone to the evil influences of Satanism. Many young people, attracted by sexual promise or a daredevil instinct, are quite unaware of the hidden dangers. Consequently they dabble on the surface and are soon dragged down to become hopelessly entangled in a web of corruption from which there is virtually no escape. Yet surprisingly enough, the majority of the general public still live in complete ignorance of this dangerous religion.

Farrant's campaign against the vampire and his Satanic followers was less cautious than Manchester's, and as he became more involved with the new Highgate traditions, his own activities increasingly imitated those of the necromancers he claimed he was observing and exorcising. If, as he said, the British public was at the time ignorant of the dangers of Satanism, Farrant's next series of adventures educated them.

Relations between the two psychic investigators had grown more and more hostile after Farrant had first been arrested in the cemetery. Manchester had then become involved in a public dispute with the man who had stood bail for Farrant. It was reported that Manchester had even telephoned the man's wife and warned her that 'odd things will happen to you and your children. I believe in black magic. Do you? I am an occultist.'

Hearing of the call, Farrant's supporters went to Manchester's flat, where a scuffle occurred and Manchester was admitted to hospital with minor injuries. In the ensuing court case, Manchester's attacker was found technically guilty of assault but discharged without penalty while Manchester was bound over in the sum of £200 to keep the peace.

During 1972, Manchester had publicly challenged Farrant to a 'magical duel'. Farrant at first regarded this as a publicity stunt staged by his rival to win personal support and approbation for his rival group of occultists. When Manchester persisted, Farrant agreed to take part, provided that the 'duel' – which weapons were to be used was never revealed – would be private, with only the duellists and their seconds present. The contest was fixed for Friday 13 April 1973, on Parliament Hill in nearby Hampstead.

Early in 1973, posters using the words 'blood sacrifice' and 'naked virgins' began to appear on hoardings and in north London underground stations. While Manchester was referred to as a 'white magician', his opponent was described as 'the black magic practitioner David Farrant'. The bad publicity and the fear that he would be lynched persuaded Farrant to stay away. Manchester was content to perform an exorcism, allegedly to banish the evil powers of Farrant's magic, for the benefit of the reporters and photographers he had invited to the duel in spite of Farrant's condition that it should be private.

In August 1973, Highgate Cemetery was closed to all but the relatives of those buried there while caretakers evaluated the increasing damage caused by intruders. The evil-minded moved to a nearby park, Highgate Woods, where keepers discovered an elaborate occult symbol painted on the pavement, three burned candles, a bloodstained knife and stockings and a pool of blood.

The local *Hornsey Journal* at once blamed the coven led by David Farrant and described the ritual in detail. A stray cat had been caught, anaesthetised and sacrificed to celebrate the 'Festival of the Black Moon'. The ritual had been conducted with the help of a naked high priestess and after each member of the coven had been smeared in the cat's fresh blood, an orgy followed. Farrant was quoted as saying:

> Hundreds of years ago a naked virgin would have been sacrificed but obviously we couldn't do this now so we had to have an animal for the important ritual. We rarely sacrifice animals at rituals, but this sacrifice was essential to our belief that we derive power from blood. The power we gain is used for good against evil.

Farrant, described as the 'evil high priest', was also alleged to have said:

> I do not see animal sacrifice as drastic as people have made it to be. Thousands of cats are used annually for medical research. The very livestock we eat have their throats cut.

His girlfriend, Martine de Stacy, now estranged from him, gave a lurid description of the orgy to the *News of the World*.

Farrant claimed that the whole affair was based on hostile rumours and misquotations. The mundane truth was that a local rock musician, Long John Baldry, had a cat which had gone missing. Baldry accused Farrant of having taken it for a sacrifice. In the heat of the moment, Farrant's explanations to reporters and callers to radio programmes were misinterpreted on the air and garbled in print. The body of the 'sacrificed' moggie was never found. A few weeks later, John Baldry's cat wandered home, none the worse for whatever adventures it had experienced.

The police never brought any charges in connection with the incident. Manchester limited himself to saying that Farrant had claimed 'responsibility for [unspecified] blood sacrifices'. It seemed that rumour-mongers using more fancy than fact were having malicious fun at the expense of the publicity-seekers and there the matter might have rested but for the fact that Farrant continued to press his case to be regarded as a serious occultist.

Within a matter of days he was distributing photographs showing himself looking at a corpse in a partly opened coffin. When an inspector from the Royal Society for the Prevention of Cruelty to Animals and his wife called for Farrant to be prosecuted, the 'high priest' sent them black boxes containing voodoo dolls with pins stuck in their heads – the black magic practice used to injure people. The dolls were accompanied by a rhyming threat:

Once this gift has passed your hand
Your power to us you'll understand
And be it understood by you
We thus control all that you do
LEAVE US ALONE – BEFORE WE MAKE YOU DO SO

The notes bore a voodoo seal and Farrant's signature in red ink. When the BBC TV *Nationwide* programme interviewed the two voodoo victims, Farrant pleaded that he intended them no supernatural harm, only to turn their malice against themselves.

Two miniature coffins were sent to Long John Baldry, the owner of the errant cat. The rock musician was sufficiently worried to ask for some form of exorcism. He called in Graham Bond of the heavy-metal rock group Cream to 'neutralise' the spell. Bond, who had a keen interest in magic, performed a protective ritual at Baldry's house. The following year, Bond fell in front of an underground train in mysterious circumstances and was killed. Baldry claimed that this was a direct result of Farrant's 'curse'.

Media attacks on Farrant as a 'black magician' did not deter him from continuing his occult investigations. By December 1973, he had agreed to help John Pope, a labourer from Barnet, north of London. Pope had fallen foul of the law and claimed he had been roughly handled by the police during questioning. Farrant agreed to send out two more dolls to the detectives involved to prevent them from doing any more harm and warning them, in a note, 'Your evil will be returned to you/before another month is through.'

Pope was rewarded for his interest and faith in the occult by being invited to take part in some of the British Occult Society's new projects. On 7 December, evidence of witchcraft ceremonies and a Star of David inscribed on the floor were found in a dilapidated house in Crouch End, to the east of Highgate. Schoolchildren told scary tales about goings-on there and dared each other to go alone into the house after dark.

The police suspected that adults were using the house for more sinister purposes and kept watch. On 13 December they raided the premises and found Farrant and Pope, both naked, kneeling beside a plate of glowing embers. No owner of the house could be found to prefer a charge of breaking and entering. The police charged the pair with arson.

On 11 March 1974, at their trial, Farrant explained that he and other society members had been conducting a Wiccan ceremony to try to contact the spirit that was haunting the house. They needed the element of fire as well as air, water and earth to do so. The judge warned them that they were 'clearly asking for trouble', but the jury acquitted them.

Continued complaints about vandalism alarmed the police. They were convinced that Farrant was responsible. On 12 January, only days before Farrant and Pope were acquitted of the arson charges, an architect who lived in Swains Lane, the hill that divides the old and new parts of Highgate Cemetery, woke to find propped up in his car what he thought was a log of wood. It turned out to be the remains of an embalmed, headless corpse. Police called on Farrant, the usual suspect, who admitted holding monthly meetings with the British Occult Society in Highgate Cemetery 'if the weather is fine'.

The police searched his home and uncovered a mass of photographs showing desecrated vaults, 'necromantic' symbols on tombs and the flashlight picture of Martine de Stacy standing naked in the vault. With this evidence, Farrant was charged with a range of offences from body-snatching to using voodoo dolls to threaten a witness who may have given evidence at a criminal trial.

When he appeared at the Old Bailey on 10 June, Farrant chose to conduct his own defence. He described himself as a persecuted Wiccan who had never carried out any necromantic ceremonies. He conceded that he and his followers had entered the cemetery many times, but insisted that all the physical damage and body-snatching had been carried out by Satanic cults.

Secrecy, he said, was essential because whenever one of their meetings was publicised 'hundreds of people turned up and this causes a lot of work for the police'. He denied that his work had anything to do with vampires and declared:

> Our beliefs have nothing to do with dead bodies. Our beliefs

> are pure. We do not desecrate coffins. That is done by Satanic cults. When people don't understand, they fear, and automatically condemn.

Farrant's credibility was seriously damaged by the photographs. He claimed that they were documentary evidence taken for police and newspapers, but some of them had been taken as long ago as 1971 without ever finding their way into the hands of police or media, and it was now June 1974. Martine de Stacy, his former girlfriend, could not be found to give evidence about what had happened in the cemetery on the night she was photographed. 'It is a full-frontal nude,' the judge told the jury, 'showing everything she has got, with her eyes raised towards the heavens.'

The prosecution called Francis King, the author of a popular work on ritual magic, to interpret the graffiti shown in the photographs. One pattern, King told the jury, was obviously

> part of a necromantic ceremony, the object of which would be to bring life temporarily back to a body so that it can tell the future or find hidden treasure, or to send the body on an evil mission.

The jury verdicts were a partial victory for Farrant, who was acquitted of the most serious charges. A self-confessed robber came forward and admitted the body-snatching. He and five others, including three girls, had gone into Highgate Cemetery that night and found the body lying beside a smashed coffin. After leaving it in the architect's car 'for a laugh', he took the head home and kept it on his mantelpiece as a trophy 'until it began to smell a bit'. The man also recalled seeing a friend pull another corpse from an opened coffin and dance with it. He and his friends had no interest in necromancy, the thief testified. They were just 'playing the fool'.

In the end, the jury found Farrant guilty of damaging memorials at Highgate and threatening detectives with voodoo dolls, along with other minor offences. A psychiatrist called to evaluate his mental health judged him sane but in need of 'guidance because there is a possibility of his beliefs taking him into a condition of mental disorder'.

After touring the Highgate Golgotha, the judge sent Farrant to jail for four years and eight months, a sentence that even some of his most vehement critics thought harsh.

Farrant appealed against the conviction for grave-tampering and eventually 'found' de Stacy to confirm that the vaults were already damaged, but the appeal was dismissed. He was released with remission for good behaviour after two years and four months. He won a libel action against one newspaper but lost a defamation suit against another. The European Commission of Human Rights declared that his rights had been infringed because his letters from prison had been vetted (as are all letters written by British prisoners) and he had been refused permission to practise Wicca in jail.

The Highgate vampire hunt did not end with Farrant's conviction and other court appearances. There were rumours that John Pope, his last client, was going to sacrifice a cockerel there on Hallowe'en 1974, and 'spread its blood on naked coven members'. Once again revellers travelled to the north London suburb for the annual occasion. A group of rockers in a flashy Ford Zephyr 6 parked outside the gates with the car radio blaring. 'We've come down from Bracknell [Berkshire],' they said, 'but it's a bit dead and we're going now.' A blonde girl from Notting Hill Gate dressed in black with a crucifix 'I borrowed from Granny' round her neck was among the crowd. When an advance party tried to scale the gates, they were ejected by the police. But many teenagers stayed on the street, disturbing the residents.

As late as September 1978, the Wessex Association for the Study of Unexplained Phenomena announced that they were to hold a dusk vigil at Highgate Cemetery outside a tomb suspected of holding a vampire. 'What happens then is anybody's guess,' said a spokesman ominously. Soon afterwards a group of adolescents were arrested inside the cemetery, charged and fined by the local magistrate for 'riotous and indecent behaviour'. The police learned that they had read an earlier article about the vampire hunt and decided to join in. They found the teenagers banging on tombstones with pointed stakes and shouting, 'Come out, vampire, or we're coming in to get you.'

After fifteen years of fund-raising and restoration work, the Friends of Highgate Cemetery were able to reopen the Victorian monuments to the public in 1990. An entrance fee is now charged, and tours of the place are guided, but the coffins are back in their vaults, no more persons, living or dead, have lost their heads and the jungle has been beaten back.

David Farrant is now head of the British Psychic and Occult Society and continues to receive and investigate accounts of supernatural phenomena. Sean Manchester announced that he had been ordained a bishop of the Old Catholic Church and was devoting his efforts to organising the Apostolic Church of the Holy Grail. Their animosity continued.

Many of the participants in the Highgate Cemetery vampire hunt mocked the religious exorcism ceremony, committed sacrilege, damaged tombs, defiled, decapitated and stole corpses. Could they be anything but demonically possessed?

17

Raising Money For The Devil

Clergymen are always being approached with hard-luck stories . . . where fighting Satanism is concerned, the mention of money is always a danger sign.

Canon Dominic Walker, Joint Chairman Christian Exorcism Study Group

Despite considerable evidence that Devil-worship is rife amidst the south downs of Sussex, one man there threw the whole concept of Satanism into disbelief. He was an evil trickster who played on the good but gullible.

When Derry Mainwaring Knight, at forty-six an unprepossessing, balding, six-foot-tall, twenty-stone 'cowboy' in £300 purple suede boots, arrived in the Sussex village of Newick, he delivered leaflets door to door inviting the neighbours to Bible study meetings in a barn. No one came. When he persuaded the rector that he was a Satanist seeking to return to Christ and to destroy the Devil-worshipping community, the clergyman unlocked the coffers of the local rich, influential and titled committed Christians to the extent of £216,000 to help him in his battle against the forces of evil.

Only the artless would deny that there is and has been for ages in Sussex by the sea a flourishing undercover adoration of the Supreme Maleficent Spirit. Unfortunately, the criminal trial of Derry Mainwaring Knight for fraud resulted in many people believing that Satanic worship was either non-existent or that it was grossly exaggerated.

Knight moved into the village, between Haywards Heath and Uckfield, with his third wife, Gwendoline, and told anyone who would listen that he had been a disciple of the Devil ever since his grandmother, Ethel, had put a curse on him at birth and a demonic apparition at the foot of his bed had told him, 'You are born for destruction.'

He was, he said, grand archdeacon in a Devil-worship order and if he could get 'good, clean Christian cash' to buy his way to the top of the Satanic ladder, he could destroy all who stood upon its rungs and save thousands of souls. One of the many methods he suggested was to buy the Satanists' regalia to turn himself and other members back to the path of righteousness.

Knight spent the money thus raised on his mistress and on pampering prostitutes, giving one £900 for a blue fox fur and spending £100 four times a week for the favours of another. For himself there was an £800 coyote jacket. Watches, clocks and jewellery were all bought for cash, never on credit, and given to girls.

While the faithful were praying for the success of his mission he had a room set aside at the Chequers Hotel, Forest Row, which he used for after-dinner sex with one of his many girls. He paid £300 to a long-standing musician friend to entertain a £3,000 champagne Thames river-boat party from Richmond to Shepperton. Knight had difficulty making up the numbers but he did invite band-leader Geoff Love and disc jockeys Alan Freeman and David Hamilton.

Knight, who had a fondness for silk shirts and fashionable blousons, was mad about luxury cars. He always wanted them in white, 'to match my image'. Viscount Hampden spent £37,500 on a Rolls-Royce, complete with telephone, for Knight to keep track of Satanists. Knight also bought a jeep for a girlfriend, one Lincoln Continental for £3,000, another for £7,000, and at various times was seen driving a Cadillac, a Land Rover, a Porsche and several Lotuses, one of which he wrote off in an accident.

The names of his victims read like a society guest list. Viscount Hampden, the donor of the Rolls-Royce, former chairman of the Sussex County Landowners' Association, owns the tourist attraction Glynde Place, near Lewes, home of the famous Glyndebourne opera. Viscount Brentford, head of his family firm of solicitors and chairman of the group set up at Knight's suggestion to fight Satanism, gave Knight £6,000 even though he had never met him. The Earl of March, who has since succeeded to the title of the Duke of Richmond and Gordon, is Chancellor of Sussex University, a member of the Church of England synod and owns Goodwood racecourse. He gave £1,000.

Michael Warren – justice of the peace, farmer and former high sheriff of East Sussex, former chairman of the County Magistrates' Association, local director of the Country Gentlemen's Association, former president of Sussex Rural Community Council – lost about £55,000. He thinks that the police should not have been called into the matter and that there should not have been a prosecution because it would encourage people to believe Satan did not exist. Mrs Susan Sainsbury, whose family gave nearly £80,000, is the wife of Timothy Sainsbury, the Conservative MP for Hove, Sussex, who holds office in John Major's government. The Sainsburys, of supermarket fame are listed among the wealthiest families in the land. The warm-hearted Susan Sainsbury organises prayer meetings at the House of Commons and is a fervent opponent of today's values whereby divorce, abortion and couples living together outside marriage are treated as normal.

Knight first sprang the 'Satan Sting' when he met the kindly, caring Reverend John Patrick Baker, the Oxford-educated rector of St Mary's, Newick, the Norman village church, parts of which date back to 1081. Baker, who was married with five children aged between fourteen and twenty-two, was a member of the International Brotherhood of Magicians and used to entertain his congregation with card tricks in aid of charity. He had been at Newick for thirteen years.

Knight used this charming and innocent man to his own ends and spun him a web of deception. He tricked the rector into paying off 'debts' of something in the region of £20,000 before persuading him to help raise big money to fight Satan. Knight also convinced a couple in the village that he was a Christian down on his luck and they paid other alleged 'debts' amounting to £6,000 while he planned his battle against the Devil and tried to build up his ailing painting and decorating business.

Eventually, a group of Church experts on Satanism urged the clergyman to drop his support for Knight, but Baker continued to believe the trickster's tales. For six months, the con-man lived in the attic of the rambling Victorian rectory. Baker himself said:

> Up there he went into trances, ripped up Bibles in frenzy and spoke in demonic tongues. I became convinced he was so deeply involved that a straightforward exorcism would not have worked. We needed to obtain and destroy the regalia and articles of Satanism on which he had taken vows.

Reverend Baker had previously held posts at Bristol, Cheltenham and Gillingham, Kent, and had been personally involved in exorcising people. He believed that Knight was genuine but he did not believe that exorcism was suitable in his case. His work 'could have helped quite a lot of people get free of Satan. It would have also dealt a pretty severe blow to the organisation itself.' But the clergyman would not reveal the name of the Satanic organisation to which Knight claimed he belonged, nor specify the off-shore funds in which Knight said the money was held. Revelation, he said, might put Knight at risk.

Challenged by Church of England experts on the subject, Reverend Baker was summoned to a meeting at the House of Lords called by the Bishop of Chichester, the Right Reverend Eric Kemp. One of the questioners was Canon Dominic Walker, vicar of Brighton and joint chairman of the Christian Exorcism Study Group who, with another priest and two psychiatrists, is now responsible for training all Anglican priests who undertake exorcism.

When Canon Walker first met Baker, the rector told him that a peer and a peeress were contemplating handing over £1,000 for a Satanic throne which was kept in a Mayfair flat, surrounded by water. He wanted a letter of support from the bishop to show to other potential donors like them. 'It was an unbelievable story,' said Walker.

> I remember remarking, 'After the throne, what next?' Paul Sturgess [secretary of the Christian Exorcism Study Group] and I were both convinced that Knight was a fraud.
>
> The few Satanists I have helped – about seven altogether – wanted to become Christians unconditionally. There were no strings attached. Clergymen are always being approached with hard-luck stories but for me, where fighting Satanism is concerned, the mention of money is always a danger sign. The demands made by Knight were ridiculous – he demanded £10,000 just to get into the same room as a Satanic throne. We were clear that no more money should be paid to him. It was a confidence trick.
>
> In my opinion John Baker was not equipped to deal with this con-man. He has never been a priest in a big city where it is commonplace to be exposed to frauds like this. The Reverend John Baker is too nice for his own good.

Derry Mainwaring Knight's real name was Roderick Taylor Knight. His late father had been a lay preacher in Methodist and Congregational churches in Essex and Suffolk. His mother, Margaret, a born-again Christian, believes her son is the Devil's disciple. Knight flunked school, was selfish and immature, could not hold down a normal job, and pretended he was a success and had held managerial positions with The Rolling Stones, Pink Floyd and Wham!. He joined the Coldstream Guards and was dishonourably discharged after only eighteen months.

Between his three marriages he had served prison sentences for embezzlement and for raping two prostitutes. He told listeners that while in Hull Prison – where he claimed to have taken part in the notorious 1967 riot, although he was never disciplined – he heard the voice of God tell him, 'Go to your cell and pick up the Bible.'

After two divorces, he met his third wife, Gwendoline, at a church meeting and they were married at a Congregational church. Even though he had continued to go with prostitutes and had moved into the home of his mistress, Angela, a barmaid whose father had left her a luxurious country house, his attractive red-headed wife still said, after his trial for fraud, that she would stand by him. Even while Knight was on trial, the Reverend Baker said: 'I'm sure there are people who think we are nutters, but we believe we have been doing God's work and will continue to do so.'

When Knight was found guilty of fraud and sentenced to seven years' imprisonment, the one person who refused to forgive him was his sixty-four-year-old mother, Mrs Margaret Knight. She had lost her smart bungalow home as a result of paying off some of her son's debts and was forced to live in a tiny council flat. She described herself as a committed Christian. 'I am not bitter but I do not want to see him again,' she said. 'I think he should be locked away in Broadmoor or some similar institution for the sake of the nation as well as himself.'

Despite such frauds it is easy to see why the wealthy Christians who had been fleeced in the Sussex scam were against the prosecution of Knight. They feared that because in this case a Satanic cult had been invented for financial gain, the attendant publicity would influence people to view all such cults and practices as fictitious.

Around the same time, the ten-foot-high Easter cross in Dursley, a Cotswold market town, was chopped in half. A black magic cult which worshipped nearby was held responsible. Dursley, incidentally, is the home of an ancient folk legend about a traveller on horseback who was forced by snowdrifts to spend a night at the inn there. When he reached his destination in Stroud, his friends were amazed. 'There is no inn at Dursley,' they declared, and when they challenged him to show them the hostelry, they found no building, only two guineas in the snow, the money he had left for his lodgings. Mine host, it was said, had been the Devil.

France also had a travelling Satanist fraudsman at the time of the Sussex scandal. He offered to exorcise houses for the equivalent of £250 a time. Since he selected the rich houses of the French Riviera the police inevitably caught up with him and asked to see his equipment. When they opened his exorcism box they found it contained a load of junk.

Yet there were plenty of examples of real sinister practices. In Rishton, a village near Blackburn, Lancashire, two young men beheaded a family's pet goat, sawed off its horns and collected its blood for drinking in a black magic sacrifice. On other occasions they tortured and killed cats. Such Satanic rituals are not in themselves criminal offences, so the police prosecuted the youths for causing criminal damage to a goat and causing unnecessary suffering, and for cruelty to animals. The first charge related to the destruction of the goat by torturing, terrifying, beating, stabbing and decapitating it. The cruelty to animals charges were brought for the torturing and skinning of cats.

David Hughes, a twenty-one-year-old former Royal Artillery bombardier, was jailed for four months and Derek Barnes, aged twenty, for three.

It was just after midnight when the two men crept into allotments near their homes where Billy, the pet goat, was tethered. The eight-year-old goat, a favourite with the village children, was chosen because his horns reminded Hughes of the picture of a devil-woman with cloven feet, goat's head and long, curling horns in a black magic book. With Barnes' help, he attacked the animal, hacking at it with a kitchen knife he had taken from his home. By mistake, he severed the goat's collar and the animal ran off down a nearby embankment. The two men chased and caught it and Hughes stabbed it repeatedly in the neck before beheading it. The goat's owner found the decapitated carcase the next day. The goat's pen was spattered with blood.

When the police went to Hughes' home they found the goat's horns under his bed and its head at the bottom of his back garden. In his bedroom were three books, Aleister Crowley's works *Magick* and *The Sorcerer's Handbook* and another work entitled *Black Art*. Hughes said in his statement that he had become interested in witchcraft after parting from the woman with whom he lived and his children. He had left the army for health reasons with an exemplary discharge. He took a job as a slaughterman and drank the blood of sheep and cows because he had heard it was beneficial to health. He had collected the goat's blood too, in a decanter, but he had not enjoyed the taste.

Hughes had also snatched two cats from village back alleys. He tied up the paws of the first one with shoelaces, strung it up on a barbed-wire fence and kicked it unconscious. He then skinned it alive before beheading it. The second animal was nailed to a cross which was then strung from a tree. Hughes again skinned the animal while it was alive and then cut its throat. The prosecuting counsel said, 'It was a sacrifice for the worship of the Devil.'

Hughes, the self-confessed ringleader, had borne the brunt of public outrage, and had received many anonymous letters. His widowed mother, Mrs Doris Hughes, said of her son, 'David deserved what he got. This terrible affair has aged me ten years. We have had obscene telephone calls and threatening letters. Things are so bad we are leaving the area.'

Attention then switched to Devon. At Honiton, the Devil is supposed to have left a souvenir of his clash with local inhabitants in the form of the Devil's Stone, which lies by the roadside on Church Hill. At Hemyock, nearby, lived a twenty-one-year-old woman whose jealous husband had attacked her lover with a chain-saw. She was expecting her lover's baby and complained that she lived in fear of the bizarre sect her husband had joined. Followers of the Charismatic Community Church told her, 'You are carrying the Devil's child.'

Denise Padfield claimed that she had received the chilling warning that her child would be born dead, but that if for some reason it was alive she must give it away. Members of the sect had burned an E.T. doll, a toy based on the character in Steven Spielberg's popular film, as a symbolic gesture because one member thought the unborn child was interfering with family life. They also burned heavy-rock albums because it was believed that some of the lyrics referred to witchcraft.

Denise went into hiding from the sect members, whom she said had caused her to have nightmares.

> They drove me to the verge of a nervous breakdown. Even when I went into hospital for a few days' rest, they turned up and frightened me by rocking to and fro as they prayed by my bed. I was scared of them.

Her husband, a twenty-four-year-old draughtsman, was jailed for five years for causing grievous bodily harm to his wife's lover, twenty-eight-year-old Mark Taylor. Padfield had joined the sect when his wife left him with their young son. Armed with a chain-saw, he hacked through the front door of their house and slashed at Mark, cutting his thigh, arms and wrists to the bone. Taylor required a hundred stitches in a three-hour operation. 'There is no doubt in my mind he was trying to castrate me,' he said.

A Charismatic Community Church elder said he thought Denise had misunderstood the people who wanted to help and comfort her, and that to say her baby belonged to the Devil was not very Christian. Denise, however was not mollified. The protagonists all went their own way in troubled peace.

At West Wycombe in Buckinghamshire, attention was drawn, not for the first time, to the caves which had been the meeting place of the eighteenth-century orgy-loving aristocrats known as the Hellfire Club. Around 1755, the notorious Sir Francis Dashwood, afterwards Baron Le Despencer, and thirteen other members conducted their profanities at Medmenham Abbey and the nearby caves which formed part of the Dashwood property. Among the 'Monks of Medmenham' were John Wilkes, the politician; Paul Whitehead, the satirist, who was secretary and steward; Charles Churchill and the Earl of Sandwich, the gambler who is credited with the invention of the snack which was named after him.

Pastor Frank Mathews of the local Christian Fellowship called for the famous caves, a well-known tourist attraction, to be closed, but no one seemed to be listening. The club had 'released a power of evil', he said, and was attracting Devil-worshippers.

These cases represent just a sample of the organised demonic wickedness which existed then and continues today, fought by an army of committed opponents but as yet without any sign of victory. In Sussex, the fight goes on. Devil-worshippers there still exist in large numbers and are organised within numerous groups and covens. They claim that they 'see' a figure that is half-goat and half-human, with horns and staring eyes. He is a dark greenish-brown in colour. This image comes from a famous German print showing the tenth-century German bishop Saint Wolfgang of Regensburg confronting the Devil, who by then was widely believed to have the power to interfere in daily life. Even now he is believed to sometimes carry a pitchfork, the traditional instrument for ensuring that his victims do not escape the flames of hell.

Like Christians, the Satanists are schismatic and worship in sects, but they wear black robes devised as a diguise. A few sects worship naked at all times but most strip to the buff only on special occasions.

They have their own form of 'consecrations'. One of their most precious objects is a human skull. Obtaining skulls, except by corrupting medical students to sell them for cash, is no easy task and so they have been obliged to rifle dilapidated graves, as in the case of the Highgate Cemetery desecrations.

Human blood is also used in ceremonies. It is collected from members of the sect, stored in bottles, then smeared on the bodies of worshippers during rites. In a few sects members cut each other to draw blood during the ceremonies themselves. For this purpose they use a black-handled ritual knife, the Athame, an essential tool of magicians and witches alike. During its consecration they trace the circumference of the magic circle with it to control and banish 'offensive' spirits.

Black candles are also consecrated and used at all ceremonies. The rituals promise their devotees success in business and sex. The most common rite, apart from regular worship, is the one which asks the Devil to harm someone, even sometimes to kill him or her. These gatherings are all held on the night of the full moon. Two special ceremonies are held on 30 April, which is celebrated as the Devil's birthday, and 31 October, Hallowe'en, when the Devil is supposed to cavort with all his demons and witches.

During Satanist ceremonies, the cross, symbol of Christianity, is held upside down. All participants take the oath of secrecy until death. When they join they deposit with the master nail clippings and cuttings of hair. If they break their vow, these are destroyed and so, Satanists believe, are their owners.

It was strange that many of these matters came to light during the trial of the Sussex con-man, an indication that Satanism was common, if not rife, in the county. But the Reverend Christopher Neil-Smith, of Hampstead, London, the best-known exorcist in Britain because of his record number of 5,000 exorcisms conducted, put it in perspective.

> Most cases of Devil possession are in the imagination of the victim. In thirty years as an exorcist I have encountered only twenty or so cases of genuine possession. And most of these were evil spirits, not the Devil himself.
>
> The most difficult case of possession I ever came across was of a high priestess of a coven who was seduced into the Satanic cult after discovering her skills at chanting. She was possessed. The power of the spirit inside her caused me to have palpitations as I exorcised it. I carried out the usual exorcism of 'binding' prayers: 'I bind this spirit by the true God, the living God, the holy God, that it does not hurt or harm anyone.' Successful, yes, but a doctor told me that I might not have been here if I had been older.

Reverend Neil-Smith can also recall a Hell's Angel who was high on his list of demonised people.

> There was a hectic interlude in the prison chapel. I placed my hands on the man's head to demand that the evil spirits depart and must have fallen deeply unconscious, as if I had been struck. When I came round, this man – with long, greasy hair and covered in tattoos – was standing over me, shouting, 'It's gone. It's gone.' And he immediately asked for a Bible.

At the same time as the Sussex fraud trial came yet another public opinion poll. Professor Jan Kerkhofs of Louvain University, Belgium, commissioned research terms to interview 2,000 people in each of nine Western countries about their moral values and beliefs. In Britain, one in three people believed in the Devil, one in four in hell, but three out of four people believed in God.

How many people involved in Devil-worship are actually possessed is difficult to fathom, but some of their practices suggest an abnormal number. Sex during Satanic ceremonies, for instance, is ritually performed 'by the Devil', but 'the Devil' is probably only a minor demon who assumes the form of the master of the sect. One girl is chosen as the 'maiden', and is expected to behave like a virgin even if she is not one. Every male member of the sect is permitted to have sex with her. If a Satanist wants to have sex with a certain person, he or she needs an item of clothing belonging to the object of desire before he can cast the necessary spell as a prelude to the sexual act. On rare occasions, during Devil-worship sadistic sex is practised, usually with whips, which symbolise black magic power.

Satanists use hallucinatory substances to invoke the image of the Devil and his work. This is achieved more often with hallucinogenic mushrooms, which grow wild, rather than synthetic drugs such as LSD which are controlled and are therefore more likely to attract the attention of the police.

18

Moon Killer

I remember the moon, I know Mrs Aston, the widow, I know her house. I don't know what came over me . . .
Allan Whitcomb Dennis, Birmingham 'moon killer'

Allan Whitcomb Dennis worshipped the moon. There is nothing new about that: regarded by pagans as a god, the moon is to this day still venerated by witchcraft cults. What made Whitcomb Dennis an unusual devotee was that when the moon was full he became a murderer. Over a seventeen-year period he killed three times before he was caught. In the meantime, he had confessed to the first murder, that of his own baby niece, but no one had believed him. Nobody close to him, neighbours or the religious community of Brookfields, Birmingham, seemed to have asked for help before or afterwards to lure him away from the great moon goddess, by any definition another demon.

On Friday 10 March 1933, when he was seventeen, Whitcomb Dennis's baby niece was found dead at the family home in Hingeston Street. His sister, the child's mother, accused him of causing the baby's death. The police agreed that he was strange, perhaps even psychopathic, but felt that did not make him a killer. Besides, Professor James Webster, the famous pathologist, said that the baby had died from a lymphatic disorder, possibly coinciding with an epileptic fit.

The strange loner, who did not smoke or drink, who took up countless jobs only to quit almost immediately – indeed, he got married and the following day walked out on his wife. Ten years later – when he was in the army in custody in a guard room for some military offence, he asked to see a civil policeman. He wanted, he said, to confess to a murder. This is what he said:

> On 10 March 1933, I was in my bedroom at 1/120 Hingeston Street, Brookfields, Birmingham. My sister's child, Doreen Bradley, aged two years and nine months, was asleep in the bed in the room. I went to her and put the bedclothes over her head and pressed them down. I felt ill at the time, and I don't know what made me do it. I kept the clothes over her face for some time – I don't know how long – and then I think I fell asleep.
>
> Later in the afternoon I took the blankets off the little girl's face. She lay on the bed without moving, her dummy still in her mouth. I crept out of the house and went to my aunt's. We were told that the cause of death was something stopping up the baby's neck, but I knew it was due to what I had done.

When Professor Webster was told about the statement, he said that even after a ten-year lapse an exhumation of the child's body might reveal some new information. But there was no exhumation, and despite Whitcomb Dennis's confession he was not believed and therefore never charged with any offence. He was transferred to a mental hospital at Talgarth, south Wales, and after three months he was discharged from the army as a psychopathic personality – that is to say a person whose behaviour, consisting of anti-social and sometimes violent acts, suggests indifference to the rights and feelings of others.

Five years passed, and on Sunday 26 September 1948, as the church bells were calling Christians to prayer, a woman and her husband called to take her mother, Mrs Harriet Mills, an elderly widow, for a drive in their car. The address was 2/110 Hingeston Street, five alleyways along from Whitcomb Dennis's address.

There was no reply to their knocking but the door was open and, after a brief search, they found the old lady lying across a bloodstained bed. She had injuries to her head and throat and had been dead for at least twelve hours. Professor Webster was again called and said that she had died from manual constriction of the throat, which bore a bruise the size of a thumbprint. She also had a head injury which could have been caused by a blunt instrument or a fall against a like object.

The local coroner, because the case was 'most puzzling', sat with a jury to establish the cause of death. He said: 'The circumstances have given us some anxiety for some time . . . There is no evidence of a break-in, a struggle or robbery.' The jury returned a verdict of accidental death.

Eighteen months later, on Thursday 30 March, Mrs Ivy Watkins of 1/162 Hingeston Street, wondered why her mother, Mrs Elsie Aston, who lived at number 108, had not called in as she usually did. She went to her mother's home, let herself in with a spare key and found her mother lying dead in bed with a pillow over her head. Blood had dried on her face, her arms were flung back, palms uppermost, and the bedclothes had been vigorously disturbed.

Professor Webster was once again called. He noted a pressure mark on Mrs Aston's throat and a bite mark on one of the fingers, and took away with the body a bloodstained sheet and a hammer found nearby. Police found that the intruder had entered the house via the coal cellar and left by the front door.

During routine inquiries, Allan Whitcomb Dennis, now a baker's roundsman, was asked about his movements and how he had sustained scratches on his face. When he said he had cut himself shaving, the officer pointed out that he hadn't shaved. He was taken to the police station, where his arms were found to bear scratches caused by a woman's fingernails. Then he confessed:

> Sometimes I can't sleep and I feel I must get up and walk around. Last night I felt like that. I got up and went out. The moon was shining but it was dark. I must have walked down Hingeston Street. I remember the moon. I know Mrs Aston, the widow. I know her house. I don't know what came over me. I don't even know why I was in the street.
>
> For a time I felt tired, as though I was going off . . . in a funny feeling. When I came to in Mrs Aston's cellar, I either lifted it [the flap] up or fell down. I can't remember. I went upstairs.
>
> Something came over me and I must have gone for Mrs Aston, using up all my strength quickly. She was lying in bed asleep. I went for her throat. In the struggle I remember biting something hard. I put a pillow over her face, then I went off into a faint.
>
> I came round and found I was lying on her bed. I realised I'd done something wrong when I saw her lying there, dead. I got up and went downstairs. I opened the front door. I had to pull the catch back to open it. It was daylight and a bus was going by. I slammed the door. It made a noise behind me as I had to bang it.
>
> When I got back home I couldn't get in. I must have dropped the catch on the door when I went out. I rattled the door and my mother came and let me in. It was about half-past seven. She didn't know where I'd been.
>
> I'm sorry I told lies now about cutting my face shaving. Mrs

> Aston did it in the struggle. She clawed me when I was killing her. I don't know what made me do it. I had no intention of stealing from her. I have got no hatred towards her. I just don't know what came over me.

Detectives on the street discovered that Mrs Aston had actually suspected that a male neighbour, whom she did not name, had been responsible eighteen months previously for killing Mrs Mills. Every time she saw this man she would cross the street, refusing to walk on the same side of the road, and she was so scared of him that sometimes she would rush into her house and bolt the door.

Whitcomb Dennis's sister, Mrs Ethel Bradley, whose baby he had confessed to murdering back in 1933, gave evidence at his subsequent trial for the Aston murder. She said that she had never thought him normal. 'He often told me that the moon did strange things to him.' Dr Albert Arthur Huse, holder of a diploma in psychological medicine, when asked about the adverse effect of the moon on people, said: 'I do not know of any scientific reason for it, but I know it occurs from time to time.'

The jury could not for a long time make up their minds whether Whitcomb Dennis was sane or not. They returned to ask Mr Justice Lynskey to explain the law and eventually gave a verdict of guilty but insane. Whitcomb Dennis was sent to Broadmoor.

No policeman had bothered to look up the phases of the moon on the dates of the three deaths in Hingeston Street; no relative had questioned the murderer closely about what he thought about the power, influence and strength of the moon and what it actually did to him. No priest was called to ask whether the moonstruck loner was a Christian and accepted or rejected Christian teaching. Presumably, by church rules he was not possessed and therefore not eligible for deliverance from evil or exorcism to drive the moon goddess from his mind. In modern sociological terms, he fell through the net.

No one would expect the many different Christian churches to have the same rules. Yet Whitcomb Dennis lived in a Christian Anglican community, and still he was not helped. It seems that those who believe in exorcism or deliverance do not go out and seek those who may be possessed of the Devil and his demons. Many of them are well known, even notorious, yet the mainstream churches retreat from them.

Perhaps careful monitoring of the foundation and growth of new cults would produce more cases of genuine demonic possession than the established churches. Such observation would have revealed the activities of Krishna Venta, who proclaimed himself the reincarnation of Jesus Christ. He persuaded his followers that he was ageless, had arrived on planet earth in the spaceship *Neophrates* in 1932 and had then been teleported from the Valley of the Masters below Mount Everest in Nepal. He recruited many, took their money and seduced their wives – until 10 December 1958, when he emerged in flowing yellow robes from the administration building of the twenty-six-acre Fountain of the World headquarters in Box Canyon, forty-five miles from Los Angeles, where he ruled his kingdom with twelve disciples. There he was confronted by Ralph Müller and Peter Kamenoff, two followers, who accused him of being possessed.

According to witnesses, Krishna shouted at them, 'You are instruments of the Devil. You were sent by the Evil One to disrupt our organisation and sway us from the paths of righteousness. You deserve to die.'

Müller shouted back, 'And you are going to die.'

Kamenoff screamed, 'You are an evil Christ who takes our money and our wives.'

Krishna Venta's voice could hardly be heard claiming, 'You can't kill me. I am Christ himself.' At that moment, Kamenoff pulled out a cigarette lighter and ignited a box of high explosives, destroying the building and killing the new 'Christ' together with the two accusers themselves and seven other followers.

It would not have taken much investigation to discover that Krishna Venta had once undertaken a mission to heathen Britain, staying in the best hotels and recruiting beautiful women, and had been given a very cool reception. But he combined his free-love activities (sometimes conducted in the back of his stationwagon) with social good deeds to divert the attention of authority and critics to allow himself to continue his doubtful career unhampered.

Even at the turn of the century London was plagued by odd sects. Frank Dutton Jackson, also known as Theo Horos, and Editha Loleta Jackson, known as the swami (a religious teacher), who posed as his mother, persuaded applicants to Jackson's cult of the Theocratic Unity that he was Jesus Christ, the son of God, returned to earth, and that, if sperm, egg and Holy Spirit bore fruit, they might each become the new child of God.

Originally the unholy couple were charged with fraud and theft of jewellery and money, but Vera Croysdale, one of the applicants to the sect, claimed that Theo had raped her. A sixteen-year-old, Daisy Pollox Adams, sent by her parents 'to see to my proper religious and worldly education', said the swami held her arms while Theo planted 'the seed of God in me'. Both Theo and the swami were sentenced to long terms of penal servitude.

Possession and exorcism were no more polite or popular subjects of conversation then than they were half a century later when, in 1950, Father Mueller, a Roman Catholic, introduced Sister Greta to his parish in Bremen, Germany. 'She has had a vision from heaven,' he said.

> The message says that in 1953 there will be a series of cataclysms that will destroy the world as we know it. We will be told of a safe place to gather in order to be spared the destruction that will visit the rest of the earth.

This prediction of an apocalypse was a forerunner of the declarations of the Reverend Jones in Guyana and David Koresh in Texas, USA, in later decades.

To prepare for the day Father Mueller promised to build a retreat for his followers. He formed the New Jerusalem Society and the money rolled in. Belatedly, the Church authorities investigated the society and discovered that some of the money was being used to furnish a house for the priest's mistress, Margaret Kuhlman, by whom he had two children, and for the purchase of a Porsche for the priest. He was disciplined and unfrocked, but still the money poured in from his devoted former parishioners.

Eight years went by before the civil authorities, rather than the Church, discovered that Sister Greta, the prophetess, was being held in the mistress's house against her will, for fear she would talk. They also learned that Mueller had founded the Disciplined Society of Love to drive out demons from sinful bodies, especially those of nubile young women. The possessed were flogged. In March 1963, long after the pastor had been deposed, Emil Hinrichsen, a friend of Mueller and an officer of the society, sent his daughter, Karol, to the disgraced priest to be exorcised. Mueller and Kuhlman ordered her to be flogged. No one knew whether or not the lengthy ritual was successful because Karol was found dead from her injuries in bed at home the next morning. The couple were brought to trial and jailed.

Surely, at some stage long before the fraud and the tragedy, the carefully tried process of dealing properly with demons must have been offered to the wayward father of the Church? Perhaps not. But if not all priests are eligible, what chance is there for the laymen and women?

Daniel Rakowitz, the twenty-eight-year-old son of a deputy sheriff from Edna, Texas, was believed to be possessed but was never treated. He proclaimed himself the new lord and sold marijuana and amphetamines on the streets of New York. He founded a new religion, and explained that Satan had changed since Biblical times and that the mark of the beast, 666, had been altered – his was the Church of the 966. His girlfriend, Monika Beerle, a Swiss student of the famous Martha Graham School of Contemporary Dance, grew weary of Daniel's den, bizarre preaching and the screeching of his prophet, a noisy cockerel. On 19 August 1989, he punched her as hard as he could in the throat, killing her. He dismembered her body, boiled the flesh and kept her skull and bones in a fire bucket as a souvenir of their relationship. When the police took him to court, he asked the judge for a jury composed entirely of marijuana-smokers so that he would get 'a fair trial'.

Many demoniac beliefs have their origins in esoteric studies. Marty Hughes, a middle-aged Scottish carpenter originally from Paisley, was a Celtic scholar who had taught the language known to the ancients of Ireland and the Scottish highlands. He was also a musician and an historian. As a young man he moved first to Boston, Massachusetts, the American parish closest in culture to the United Kingdom, and later to Virginia Beach, Virginia.

He had a job on a building site and was a good worker but he suffered from porphyria, an inherited disease with numerous side-effects of which baldness, from which he suffered, and over-sensitivity to sunlight and garlic are the most common. The disease can cause the gums to recede, making the sufferer look as if he has fangs. Such symptoms mirror those of the fabulous vampires, the ghosts of heretics and criminals who are supposed to return from the grave in the disguise of giant human bats to suck the blood of sleeping or dead people who then become vampires themselves.

When Hughes vanished from his workplace and local haunts, the police obtained a search warrant and entered his flat, where they were repelled by the stench of rotting dismembered flesh, bone and viscera. Eventually, a local man, Dean Bolan, who was five feet four inches tall and weighed less than nine stone, admitted killing Hughes, a strapping fourteen-stoner, in self-defence.

Hughes was the kind of man described in the Highgate Cemetery 'vampire hunt'. He seemed affable enough to his workmates but his Celtic studies had encouraged him to perform occult rituals to summon spirits from the dead. In April 1986, after Hughes and Bolan had shared a meal of pizza and beer, Hughes stood up and began dancing in a circle, chanting, 'I am a vampire. I am evil. I am a vampire.'

To Bolan he said, 'You can have your pick of any one of three evil spirits. I will allow you to make contact with the spirit of Billy the Kid, Adolf Hitler or Jack the Ripper. Tell me quick, which one do you want?'

Bolan chose Jack the Ripper. Hughes pulled from the shelf a volume on the occult and began reading what Bolan took to be Gaelic phrases which sounded eerie and ominous. Louder and louder, Hughes began to shout that he had become possessed. 'I am evil. I am evil. I am evil,' he cried.

At last he said, 'The evil spirit is communicating with me. I am awaiting his orders.' Then: 'The evil spirit commands that I must kill you.'

By this time, Hughes had a knife in his hand and was approaching his intended victim ready to strike. According to Bolan, in the struggle his attacker fell on his own knife and died. There was no way Bolan could dispose of the body, so he cut it up. But his clothes were saturated in blood and before the police knew anything about the body, he told everybody he knew how he had had to kill the demonically possessed Hughes. Since he did not try to hide the facts from them, they believed him. One of the listeners went to the police.

Alas, the jury at his trial in January 1987, after retiring for six hours, found him guilty of second-degree murder and sentenced him to twenty years' imprisonment.

19

Serial Killers In The USA

It was the most frightening experience I've encountered. I knew the cases of each victim and Mr Watts was reading them back. We were digging up a body and it didn't bother him. He wanted a hamburger. So when we were done we took him to a hamburger joint and bought him one.

Jack Frels, prosecuting attorney,
on serial killer Coral Eugene Watts

Coral Eugene Watts did not rob; he did not rape; he did not even know his victims. He chose them at random, stalked them and killed them, strangling, stabbing and even drowning them. He always took an article of clothing from the women he had murdered, 'to rid the world of their evil spirits', and then burned it. And he was careful to make sure they were women, even if they wore trousers, by choosing only those with shoulder-length hair. Women, he believed, were evil. They were deceitful, unfaithful and parasitic and relationships with them were potentially harmful. He fastened his intentions particularly on the successful women of the future: university students.

Even the fact that he limited almost all his crimes to the sabbath and became known as the 'Sunday Morning Slasher' did not suggest to anyone that he might be possessed – not even the pastor of his own church. The Reverend Paul Ellis was seventy-five years of age and thought Watts was ordinary; a bus mechanic and a loner.

A twenty-one-year-old woman who was in love with Watts said they had met in church on Easter Sunday 1981.

> I wouldn't describe him as a Christian, but he did attend church regularly. The man was sweet, very intelligent. He would pull out chairs for me, open doors, everything a

gentleman would do. Lots of times we would sit and read the Bible together. That's why it's hard to believe what the police say he did. There must've been a side to him I didn't know about.

Even though Watts, who was twenty-eight, had certainly killed thirteen women, he was never prosecuted for murder – juries don't believe that people kill for no reason. He was charged only with burglary and given sixty years' imprisonment.

He first came to the notice of the police in 1974 in Michigan, where the body of Gloria Steele was found with thirty-three knife wounds. She had been slashed to death near Western Michigan University. He was released, then re-arrested for an attack on a fellow student just prior to the Steele murder and jailed for a year.

Although Hallowe'en was not a Sunday but a hangover festival from pagan days, this was the day in 1979 when Mrs Jeanne Clyne, aged thirty-five, a former *Detroit News* reporter, was stabbed to death in Grosse Poine Farms, a Detroit suburb, as she walked home from a consultation with her doctor. The body was found by a man who had come outside his house because he was worried about children out on their 'trick or treat' rounds.

Watts fitted the description of a black jogger seen in the area at the time of the murder. The police kept him under surveillance from patrol cars, on foot and from helicopters, and even had a court order permitting them to install a surreptitious homing radio device in his car so that they could check his whereabouts. They could not detect any wrongdoing.

In 1980, while Watts was still living in Ann Arbor, three women were stabbed to death on Sunday mornings in April, July and September. There was no direct evidence to connect him with the murders, but so intense was police interest in him that Watts moved himself and his belongings to Houston, Texas.

Watts had been born in Texas, and as many blue-collar workers in Michigan were being laid off due to an economic slump it was quite natural that he should return. Nevertheless, when the Michigan police heard of his move they informed the Texas authorities of their suspicions. And Sundays became death days in Texas for several women.

There were eleven murders between Sunday 29 March 1981 and Sunday 23 May 1982. Before dawn on 29 March 1981, thirty-four-year-old Edith Ledet, a married woman, who had the previous day completed her fourth year as a medical student, was killed while jogging on the campus of Texas University Medical School. Her body was found at 5 am, about eleven blocks from her apartment, by a newspaper carrier. The only clue was a bloodstained hooded sweatshirt it was believed her attacker had been wearing and had discarded. The police were shocked. She was the daughter of Judge James K. Allan, of Dallas, Texas, a former state district criminal judge and before that the senior district attorney.

Elizabeth Montgomery, aged twenty-five, had taken her dog for a walk just before midnight on Saturday 12 September and returned after the chimes struck twelve o'clock. Her fiancé said, 'I heard her scream when she neared the courtyard area and I ran out there. She finished up bleeding to death in my arms.' A man had plunged a knife into her chest.

At 2 am the same morning, Susan Wolfe was carrying home groceries from the all-night supermarket where she worked. As she left her car and reached the door of her home, someone stabbed her six times. She too died from considerable loss of blood. There was a strange coincidence: Wolfe and four other girls had moved from Bay City, Michigan, to Houston, Texas, at about the same time as Watts had moved from Ann Arbor, Michigan, to the same city.

After a four-month interval, Phyllis Ellen Tamm, a twenty-seven-year-old married advertising art director, was found hanging from a tree on Rice University Campus at 7.30 on a January morning in 1982. She had been suspended in a sitting position about two inches off the ground. Initially, no other wounds were found other than markings on her neck from the knitted fabric that had been used to hang her. She was wearing jogging clothes.

Margaret Everson Fissi, an architectural student at Rice, was planning to settle in Houston once her boyfriend graduated from law school at Harvard University, Massachusetts. She had been to visit him and was due back on the morning of Sunday 17 January. When she did not return, her brother-in-law became worried and went out to investigate. He found her car 150 yards from her house. The police broke into the boot and found her body. She had been beaten and strangled somewhere between the university car park and her home.

On Sunday 7 February, Elena Semander, a beautiful Houston University physical education student, headed home from a night-club at 2 am. Even though she was described as strong and athletic she was strangled with her own blouse and dumped in a large rubbish bin on a housing complex only a few blocks from where she lived. Not one of the victims had been sexually assaulted.

March saw another killing which was attributed to Watts. Emily LaQua was fourteen and had disappeared from home. She was never seen alive again. Although they did not vanish on a Sunday, the disappearance of two more girls in April was also linked with

Watts. Carrie Mae Jefferson, aged thirty-four, a post office clerk, failed to return home after her night shift ended at 2 am. Blonde Suzanne Searles, twenty-five, was last seen leaving a party early one Sunday morning. The police were called on the Monday when she did not arrive for work. They found her car and the signs of a struggle, a pair of broken spectacles and the contents of her handbag.

Within twenty-four hours of the disappearance of Carrie Jefferson and Suzanne Searles, Yolanda Garcia was found dead with multiple stab wounds a few blocks from her home. Police Lieutenant Mason, in answer to anxious questions, said, 'Whoever this sadistic killer is, somebody's got to know him. He is ritualistic and he may have killed people in other states. Ritualistic killers do not kill once. They have to repeat the ritual.'

Relatives of the dead girls were angry. It seemed that nothing was being done to stop the serial killer. Detectives were frustrated, but what could they do when there was no discernible motive, no witnesses? Whoever the killer was, he just picked his victims and slaughtered them for no apparent reason.

Watts frequently changed addresses and disappeared for weeks at a time before he was seen again and his trail could be picked up. Police complained that he was always living with friends, or out in his car. It was physically difficult to keep up with him or to do anything without violating his civil rights.

Psychological profiles on the killer, prepared by the FBI in Washington, local police forces and private agencies, all came to the conclusion that the guilty man was obsessed with a passion to kill women, an inherent pattern in many mass murderers. The profiles predicted that he would continue until he was caught.

Sunday 23 May was Michelle Marie Maday's twentieth birthday. She did not live to celebrate it. At 6 am her mother found her nude body twisted on its side in the bathtub. A doctor certified that she had been strangled but not sexually assaulted. The police noted that there was no sign of forced entry to their home, no sign of a struggle and nothing had been stolen.

An hour after Michelle's body was discovered, two patrolmen were sent to investigate a disturbance at an apartment shared by Lori Lister and Melinda Aguilar. When they arrived at the building they heard the sound of a door being kicked in an upstairs apartment. Suddenly they spotted a black man running from the flat.

What they didn't know at the time was that the man had sneaked up behind Lori outside her apartment building, wrapped his arms round her neck, choked her unconscious and left her lying on the pavement. Using her key, he had unlocked her front door and found her flatmate at home, which he hadn't bargained for. He promptly tied up Melinda and left her kneeling by her bed. Then he went back for his first victim. He bound her hands behind her back with a coat-hanger and dragged her back into the apartment, where he beat her and left her for dead in a bathtub of water.

Melinda said:

> I had been sleeping badly because my room-mate had been away for the night. Early in the morning I thought I heard someone scream. Then I heard a key rattle in the door and called out Lori's name. The door was opened by a black man wearing a red sweatshirt and faded jeans. He rushed at me, yanked me from the bed and started choking me. He dragged me into the bedroom and tied my hands behind me with a wire coat-hanger and a belt.

When Melinda heard the sound of bathwater being run, she knew 'he was going to kill me too'. That is when she hurried to the balcony and, despite her bonds, flung herself over the four foot railing. Fortunately, she flipped over as she went and landed on her knees, thirteen feet below on the grass. From there she ran 200 yards to raise the alarm. 'Please help me!' she cried. 'Someone's trying to kill me!' It was a neighbour kicking the door to try to get into the flat whom the police heard as they arrived. The neighbour dragged Lori from the bath and saved her life.

The officers, guns drawn, chased and captured the runaway assailant as he fled into a dead-end area. Watts was not at all helpful upon his arrest. He maintained his right to silence. Lieutenant Mason had already posed the question, 'What can we do when we don't have a tiny drop of physical evidence? What we seem to have is a murderer without reason.' Or the Devil?

Psychiatrists confirmed that Watts hated women but had been sane when the offences were committed. The defence psychiatrist said he was a paranoid schizophrenic.

Relatives of the dead girls protested about the delay in bringing the killer to justice. It was bad enough to lose a loved one, but not to know, in some cases, what had happened to the body brought distress and anger. Some demanded the death penalty. But capital punishment in Texas is limited to murder during a rape, a robbery or a felony. Watts had not killed anyone in those circumstances, and he knew the rules.

When Watts was brought to trial, his counsel sought a plea bargain. Watts would plead guilty to burglary in exchange for a fifty-year prison sentence and in return would tell authorities about the murders of women in Houston and Michigan of which he was suspected, providing he was given immunity from prosecution for these crimes. There were thirty-three murders under investigation.

The prosecution feared that in the absence of a motive a jury would not believe the story and would record a verdict of insanity. But a fifty-year prison sentence was not acceptable. The prosecution wanted sixty years to ensure that it would be a minimum of twenty years – one third of the sentence – before Watts became eligible for parole. Watts agreed.

Describing the death of Edith Ledet, the judge's daughter, he recalled, 'There was another woman with her. I jumped on her back but my grip slipped because I had blood on my hands from killing the first woman.' He also admitted killing Montgomery, Wolfe, Tamm, Fissi, Semander, Garcia and Maday. When it came to those whose bodies had never been found, Watts led lawyers and police to different sites, where he verbally reconstructed the killings as officers checked them against the records and searched for bodies.

Prosecuting attorney Jack Frels recalled:

> It was the most frightening experience I've encountered. I knew the cases of each victim and Mr Watts was reading them back. We were digging up a body and it didn't bother him. He wanted a hamburger. So when we were done we took him to a hamburger joint and bought him one.

Frels described Watts' ability to remember details about his crimes as 'frightening, phenomenal and uncanny. The man could remember the time, the date, locations, clothing worn by his victims and the makes of their cars.'

Watts told the police that he used to drive around all night. Once he spotted a victim to whom he was attracted he would follow her until he could make contact. 'They were all done quickly, like a signature. I would run up behind them and just kill them and flee from the scene.'

Later he changed his *modus operandi*, taking a shovel with him in the car and burying some of the victims rather than leaving them to be discovered.

Watts took the police to a bayou where a body was discovered in the weeds. It was identified by dental charts as that of Carrie Mae Jefferson. In a giant waste pipe they found the decomposed body of fourteen-year-old Emily LaQua. A locket containing a portrait of her mother, brother and sister was picked up nearby.

There were more horrific surprises to come. Watts confessed to two other assaults on women in Galveston, Texas. Both had been slashed or stabbed, but had survived. In one of the cases, the stabbing of a nineteen-year-old waitress on 30 January 1982, another man had been arrested and given a life sentence. Watts' confession to the attack resulted in the man being released.

A week after the plea bargain had been agreed, Watts admitted to the killing of a twenty-two-year-old Texas University student in Austin, the state capital, on 5 September 1981. Linda Katherine Tilley had been found drowned in a housing-complex swimming pool but the police had ruled out foul play. Linda Tilley had been very unlucky. Watts had been following a different woman for the 158 miles from Houston to Austin. His intended quarry must have turned off the highway unnoticed by Watts, and when he saw Tilley returning from a date in a similar vehicle, he mistook her for the woman he had been stalking. He tried to drag Linda behind a wooden fence but she struggled and they both fell into the pool, only fifteen feet from the safety of her apartment. Watts held her under the water but medical experts who examined her injuries thought they had been sustained when she tripped accidentally into the water.

Watts, as part of the plea bargain, cleared up unresolved assaults and murders from Ann Arbor, Kalamazoo, Detroit, Michigan, and nearby Windsor, Ontario, which he had committed before his departure for Texas. Judge Shaver sentenced him to sixty years in jail, regretting that in his case:

> The death penalty is not available. The sixty-year sentence recommended [for burglary] is the exact equivalent of the maximum sentence allowed under the law. Sad to say, it is the only crime that the state of Texas has evidence on. It is not what I believe is an appropriate sentence for you. I hope they put you so deep in the penitentiary that they'll have to pipe the sunlight into you. I hope no one will ever be so foolish as to let you walk the streets again.

Prosecuting attorney John B. Holmes said that he thought Watts should be taken behind the court house and shot dead, 'but we don't do that sort of thing in a free country'.

No one, but no one, asked whether or not the Devil still existed, had taken advantage of a lonely, disadvantaged churchgoer, possessed and controlled him and then vented his evil on women who went out alone – and on Sundays, too.

20

Satanised Son Of Sam

The demons wanted girls. Sugar and spice and all things nice.
'Son of Sam', David Berkowitz, New York serial killer

Born-again Christians, like many other religious people, have an excellent record in converting the most evil of twentieth-century law-breakers, the serial killers. We shall come to examples of such conversions, Henry Lee Lucas and Myra Hindley, in Chapters 21 and 22. The usual pattern is that such a murderer has been sentenced to life imprisonment with little or no hope of parole, or has been condemned to death row for a long wait until execution or reprieve. When there is no hope, the clergy are quickly there to offer him salvation. It is unfortunate that in many cases the clergy did not manage to reach the potential convert before he embarked on his catalogue of slaughter. For it is reasonable to suppose that serial killers as a type would include a very high proportion of people who must have shown some of the symptoms of demonic possession before starting to commit their offences.

Prosecutors – police, lawyers and politicians, more interested in guilty verdicts than in justice – tend to sneer at any defence which suggests that the accused was not responsible for his acts. They took that view over Joseph Kallinger, who claimed to be God's executioner. He was very eccentric, lived in a twenty-foot-deep pit in the cellar of his house and wore wedges in his shoes so that he could, as he moved about (he said), balance his feet with his unbalanced brain.

Kallinger claimed that he was the chosen one and God wanted him to destroy mankind. He too would have thought it a very strange thing to do, he declared, had he not received directions from the Almighty and from the Devil. On 7 July 1974, he abducted a child from a Philadelphia playground, and killed and sexually mutilated him. He insured the life of one of his sons, and then on 28 July drowned him to claim $70,000 (£46,000). Then he hired his younger son, who was twelve, as his assistant.

For three years, from 1973, he burgled, mutilated and murdered many victims before he was caught in 1975. In the dock, Kallinger, who claimed he had been directed by a demon called Charlie, foamed at the mouth and spoke in tongues, but the court declared that he was able to distinguish right from wrong and he was sentenced to a minimum of forty-two years' imprisonment. The doctors decided afterwards that he was mentally deranged and most of that sentence has so far been spent in the Fairview Hospital for the Criminally Insane in Pennsylvania.

Critics of the judicial system in Britain are no less prejudiced when it comes to deciding the state of mind of criminals brought before the courts. Peter Sutcliffe, the 'Yorkshire Ripper', claimed that he received a message from God to clean the streets of prostitutes. He did just that, from 29 October 1975 until 2 January 1981, bludgeoning, stabbing and mutilating a total of twenty women, thirteen of whom died from their injuries. The victims were aged between sixteen and forty-six and not all of them were prostitutes. They included a girl who happened to live six doors away from a prostitute, two separate cases of university students returning home after studies, a civil servant and a doctor from Singapore.

Sutcliffe had an arsenal of more than thirty weapons, which included seven ball-peen hammers, a claw hammer and a metal-framed hacksaw, several carving knives, eight assorted screwdrivers, a wooden-handled cobbler's knife and a length of rope used to strangle his intended victims. In one case, that of Josephine Whitaker, a respectable nineteen-year-old building society clerk, he plunged a sharpened screwdriver point into his victim's eye.

Sutcliffe had worked in Bingley Cemetery, where he developed a macabre sense of humour. He used to hide in graves and jump out to frighten the other grave-diggers when they came by. He would lie down on a marble slab with a shroud over him and make eerie, moaning noises when his workmates approached. He once fled with another young worker from a grave they were digging at twilight when they heard a ghostly wind. On another occasion, in a nearby mortuary, he was washing down a young woman who had been killed in a car accident when her mother suddenly appeared and started hitting him because she thought he was assaulting her daughter.

Of course, all this could have been a natural way to play down the gruesome nature of his work, but it was too much for the tastes of his colleagues.

Sutcliffe also boasted about prising open graves and stealing jewellery from corpses and washing himself with powerful disinfectant to get rid of the stench of the dead.

No one knew whether he spoke the truth. They never understood him, they said later. Because he had a dark beard, they called him 'Jesus'. And they tended to avoid him.

At his subsequent trial, he claimed that it was while working in this cemetery that he had heard God speaking to him. While digging a grave, he heard a voice coming from the top of the hill. He had traced the echoing and mumbling to a cross-shaped headstone above the grave of a Polish man. The voice, he said, told him that he was a 'street-cleaner' and that his mission was to go out and kill all harlots. Sutcliffe's bad timekeeping earned him dismissal from his job in 1967 but it was not for several years that he went out and followed these instructions – and then, of course, he killed others, too.

He later confessed, 'They are all in my brain reminding me of the beast I am. Just thinking of them reminds me what a monster I am.' But monster or man? Bad or mad?

Could he have harboured the secret voices from the graveyard for eight years before carrying out what he said were the Almighty's orders? Or was it that he was sexually impotent and his violence merely revenge on women, whom he could not satisfy?

The answer lies in his state of mind at the time he carried out the attacks. When he came up for trial on 5 May 1981, Sutcliffe pleaded guilty on the grounds of diminished responsibility to the charge of thirteen murders and seven attempted murders. James Chadwin, QC, his counsel, maintained that Sutcliffe was suffering from paranoid schizophrenia. Three psychiatrists who had interviewed him agreed with this diagnosis. But it was, as is often the case, based on Sutcliffe's claim that since the age of twenty he had been following instructions from God. God had even helped him evade the police. And he admitted that he had been about to do the Lord's work on Olivia Reivers, his last pick-up, when he was arrested.

Attorney-General Sir Michael Havers insisted that Sutcliffe's 'divine mission' was a lie and that he was a clever, callous murder who may have deliberately faked schizophrenia. His ability to do so might have been helped by the fact that he had at least one personal experience of the illness. In 1972, his wife, Sonia, had suffered a nervous breakdown while studying in London. She had talked of being the second Christ and had claimed pain in her hands from being nailed to the cross.

The Attorney-General told the court that Sutcliffe had at first behaved perfectly normally, laughing at the suggestion that he might be mentally abnormal, and had introduced the talk of the voice or voices from God fairly late in his statements to the police. That, alas, is all too often the line taken by prosecuting counsel when this kind of defence is produced. Demonic possession, demonic control and the like are no defences in law. The accused must plead sanity or insanity or diminished responsibility.

A prison warder claimed he had overheard Sutcliffe tell his wife, Sonia, that if he could convince the jury that he was mad, he would only have to spend ten years in a mental asylum. Of course, prison walls have mouths as well as ears, and eavesdroppers are not always believed by the courts. In any case, there was no guarantee that ten years would be the minimum time he would spend in compulsory mental care if found insane.

The jury did not believe Sutcliffe was really suffering from paranoid schizophrenia, which is an illness that affects the thought processes of the brain so that the sufferer is unable to think logically. Hallucinations, which may be in the form of voices, visions or the sense of being touched (somatic hallucination), are symptoms, and Sutcliffe spoke of a hand gripping his heart. Delusions, wildly fantastic beliefs and a sense of persecution are included in the syndrome. And on top of all this the subject may be totally unaware that there is anything wrong with his or her behaviour.

The jury believed the case for the prosecution that there had been evidence of sexual sadism in at least six of the fourteen attacks. The psychiatrists conceded that if they were wrong about paranoid schizophrenia then there was only one likely alternative explanation, which was that Peter Sutcliffe was a man who enjoyed killing women, a cold-blooded murderer.

Sutcliffe's plea that he was mentally ill failed. He was found guilty of thirteen murders and seven attempted murders. Mr Justice Boreham sentenced him to life imprisonment with a recommendation that he not be released for thirty years. But he became mentally ill, even if he was faking it before the trial, and was transferred from prison to Broadmoor, where he was said to be often totally incoherent.

It was much later reported that Sutcliffe, a lapsed Catholic, had undergone a series of exorcisms by a Roman Catholic priest while in Armley Jail, Leeds, awaiting trial. His cell was supposed to have been converted into a Roman Catholic chapel. Day after day, the Ripper knelt before a makeshift altar, according to the story of a fellow prisoner, who claimed:

> The Ripper was accompanied by two warders at all times, except when the priest paid a visit. I wandered about the

> block quite freely and one day I was surprised by chanting and wailing coming from the Ripper's room. It used to be part of the prison hospital observation ward and had two slits you could look through. I stole a look the first time I heard the noises, the chanting, almost screaming, and saw Sutcliffe kneeling before the priest.

The priest visited Sutcliffe daily and the prisoner, who served them meals, added, 'Sometimes, when Sutcliffe was shrieking, I heard him cry, "I accept. I accept." The meeting seemed to reach a peak, then the noises began to get quieter and quieter.'

Was Sutcliffe exorcised or not? Only a week before this service was reported, Sutcliffe, wearing a silver cross round his neck, gave evidence against a fellow prisoner who had attacked him. At that time, Sutcliffe claimed that what was wrong with the world today was 'greed, immorality and depravity. There's no moral values at all.' But the Catholic chaplain to the prison, Father Anthony Lawn, a Jesuit, denied that he had 'driven out the Devil' from Sutcliffe.

The Matthew Trust, a Christian-based health lobby group which helps criminals and their victims, never discuss the cases of individuals they help, but Peter Thompson, the honorary director of the trust, said that he believed prisoners like Sutcliffe could be released after exorcism. If this had occurred, then 'Peter Sutcliffe today is not the Peter Sutcliffe that committed those dastardly crimes against thirteen women.' Mr Thompson explained:

> We give advice when required. Out of the prison patient population of 2,100 people in four special hospitals, such as Broadmoor and Rampton, there is a small group of patients who do not respond to traditional treatments and who have committed unexplicable acts of violence. The trust believes that it is possible that such inexplicable acts of violence might have been caused as a result of spiritual malaise.
>
> The trust seeks no more than that the DHSS, through its medical and nursing services and the established churches, with us, form a consultative committee to examine the appropriateness or not of the Christian service of deliverance, which embraces exorcism, for those who might benefit from it. The trust only recommends such a service, in this instance, in a security situation with attendant disciplines as well as spiritual advice, providing always that permission has been obtained not only from the patient but his or her relatives or guardians as well as psychiatric and nursing services and appropriate priest and bishop.

When Sam Berkowitz, the self-styled 'Son of Sam', was arrested after a twelve-month reign of terror during which he killed six young people with his .44 calibre revolver as they went about their social life in New York, he was asked his name. He replied, 'My name is Legion, for we are many.' St Mark's Gospel v, 9 says that when Christ came across the man in the tombs who was possessed, 'He asked him, what is thy name? And he answered, saying, My name is Legion: for we are many.' And in St Luke's Gospel viii, 30: 'Jesus asked him, saying, What is thy name? And he said, Legion: because many devils were entered into him.'

It was strange that a man of traditional orthodox Jewish upbringing like Berkowitz should produce such answers from the Christian scriptures of the New Testament. He was arrested and charged with shooting dead six people and wounding seven others between 1976 and 1977. He saved the taxpayers' money by pleading guilty and was sentenced to 365 years' imprisonment. He continued talking and talking. He also left society with one very great problem: was he or was he not Satanically possessed?

Police checked again the amazing demonic letters, signed with colourful pseudonyms, which he had sent to them and to newspapers while on his murderous spree. He was the Duke of Death, the Chubby Monster, Joquin the Joker, the Wicked King Wicker, the Twenty-Two Disciples of Hell, John Wheaties – Rapist and Suffocator of Young Girls. The last was a lie. On the walls of his home he had scrawled messages such as: 'In this hole lives the wicked king', 'Kill for my master' and 'I turn children into killers'. And he used black magic signs in his drawings – circles and pentagrams, just as Aleister Crowley had done many years previously.

Did Sam, intentionally or accidentally, misspell the word Wicca, the old-English name for a witch, when he called himself the Wicked King Wicker? His own words before and after his arrest suggested that he had links with Satanism. In a letter to his father, a month before the first killing, he wrote, 'Dad, the world is getting darker now. I can feel it more and more.' He spent days before his first murder 'looking for a victim, waiting for a signal'. He claimed he was tormented by 'demon voices' instructing him to kill. But he also had a complex about the opposite sex and added: 'The girls call me ugly and they bother me the most.' After he murdered his first victim, eighteen-year-old Donna Lauria, with two bullets in the neck, and injured her friend Jody Valente, nineteen, who was sitting in the same car, he said, 'I never thought I could kill her. I couldn't believe it. I just fired the gun, you know, at the car, at the windshield. I never knew she was shot.'

He didn't like horror movies but he liked visiting cemeteries and

The pub is shut, the lights dimmed. There are no customers as an Anglican clergyman sprinkles salt in holy water over the darkened bar of the demonically possessed tavern in Devon. He then calls on the principles of his faith to banish the evil spirits from the four corners of the room. *Credit: Mirror Syndication International.*

The Anglican clergyman prepares to drive away devils whose evil influence has been affecting the inn and its inhabitants. Here he drops salt into holy water to form the sign of the cross. *Credit: Mirror Syndication International.*

After the exorcism the Anglican priest pours the consecrated holy salted water on to the grounds of the tavern to ensure the evil spirits are banished. *Credit: Mirror Syndication International.*

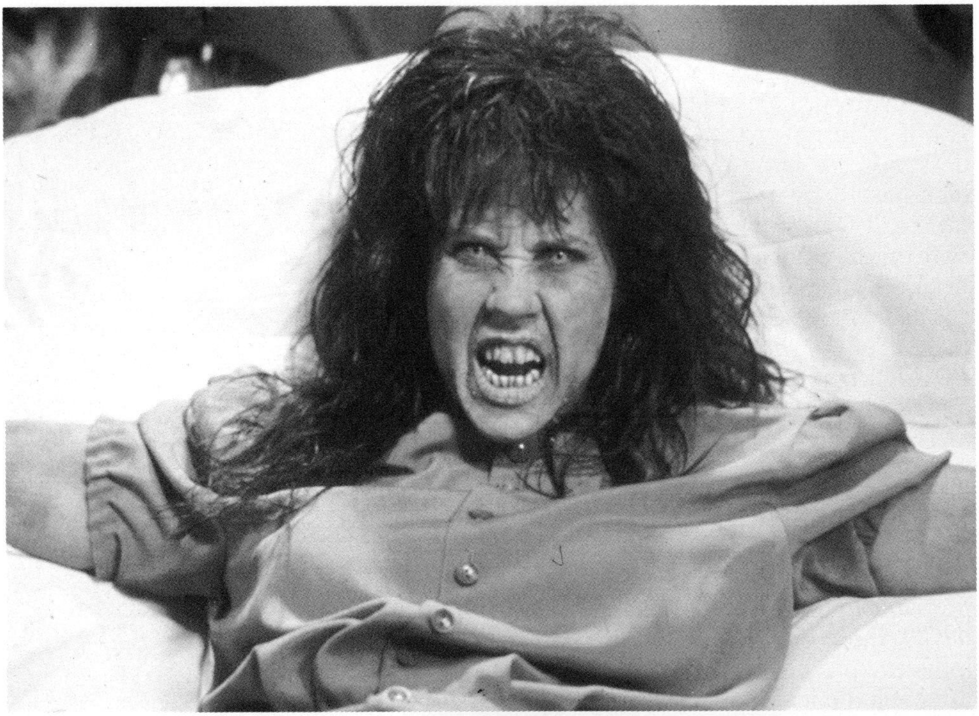

Linda Blair, the American juvenile actress, who made a spectacular start to her screen career as a possessed child in *The Exorcist*. Here, as a suburban housewife in the *Repossessed*, her teeth and hair encrusted with green gunk, she is again possessed by the Devil. See Chapters 11 and 12. *Credit: The Kobal Collection.*

Linda Blair, doesn't know which way to turn in the sequel, *Exorcist II: The Heretic* which is about transcendental spiritualism. *Credit: The Kobal Collection.*

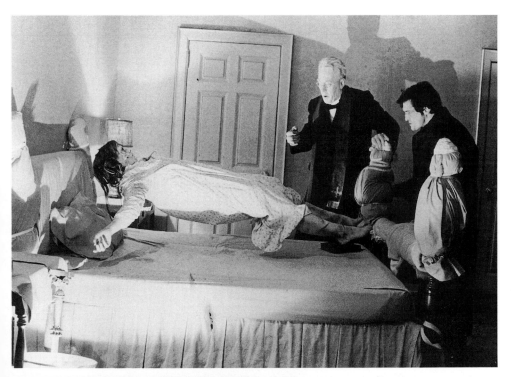

The demonically possessed Regan McNeil, played by Linda Blair in the 1973 film, *The Exorcist*, levitates from the bed – an act of supernatural defiance of gravity – as Max Von Sydow, the exorcist, centre, and the psychiatrist–Jesuit (played by Jason Miller), right, look on. *Credit: The Kobal Collection.*

Ozzy Osbourne, one of many heavy metal pop-stars with a big following in Satanic music, Satanic lyrics, Satanic album covers, Satanic dress and ornaments. Their works, particularly Osbourne's 'Suicide Solution', were condemned by New York's Roman Catholic Cardinal O'Connor. Osbourne was also accused in courts by parents who claimed he had caused their children to commit suicide. See Chapters 21 and 22. *Credit: Mirror Syndication International.*

Noisy and destructive demons often possess homes. The owner of this house at Dodleston, Chester, claimed to be receiving computer messages from a man living in the 16th century when his furniture was upended and small items thrown around in May, 1985. *Credit: Fortean Picture Library.*

Anneliese Michel (inset) pretty 23-year-old German university student, died from starvation while undergoing a ten-month long exorcism at the hands of two Roman Catholic priests. She had not eaten for 76 days. Her parents, Josef and Anna Michel (main picture) and the two priests were found guilty of negligent homicide (second degree manslaughter) and sentenced to six months imprisonment suspended for three years probation in each case. See Chapter 14. *Credit: Keystone.*

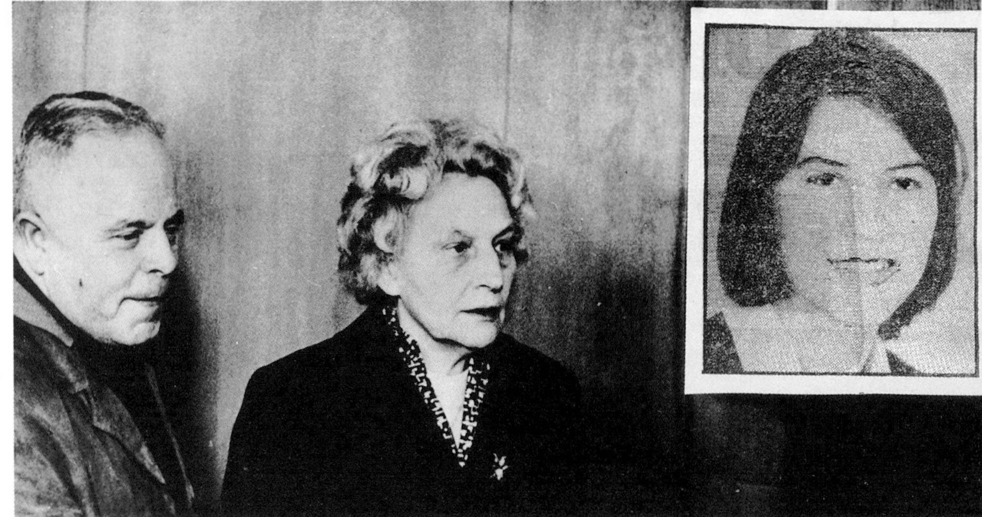

spent much time by the tombstones of girls he had killed. The army had taught him how to use a gun, the post office how to use the mail to send falsely postmarked letters to hide his whereabouts, and a nightwatchman's job showed him boredom. The demons, he said, instructed him in something else.

He taunted the police and the press with his letters, goading them to catch him out with messages like 'Hello from the gutters of New York city, which are filled with dog manure, vomit, stale wine, urine and blood' and 'Sam's a thirsty lad and he won't let me stop killing until he gets his fill of blood.'

After being jailed, he said: 'After the shootings, I thought I might weep for some of the people killed. But I couldn't. It was all puzzling, you know.' Later, he wrote, 'At this [another] point I imagine I didn't care much any more, for I had finally convinced myself that it was good to do it . . . and that the public wanted me to do it.'

In his prison diary he added, 'Yes, the demons are real. I saw them. I felt their presence, and I heard them.' Yet uppermost in his mind was his hatred for women. Another diary note said, 'I must slay a woman for revenge purposes to get back at them for all the suffering they caused me.' And: 'The demons wanted girls. Sugar and spice and all things nice . . . The demons were protecting me. I had nothing to fear from the police.'

Berkowitz, who had obviously kept abreast of events through the newspapers, confessed to having acted alone but the evidence was full of contradictions. There was a suggestion that two killers had been involved and that the murders were linked to groups practising witchcraft across America. Several witnesses to the shootings saw a hippy with fair stringy hair, while Son of Sam was dark-haired and neatly groomed. Another puzzling factor was that some of the murders had been carried out with precision – Berkowitz had been a marksman in the army – while others had been wild, random shootings.

Berkowitz had a neighbour, Sam Carr, for whom he had developed an irrational dislike, probably because Carr kept noisy German Shepherd dogs with which Berkowitz was obsessed. One of Berkowitz's pseudonymous signatures had been 'John Wheaties'. It emerged that Wheat was a family name of the Carrs. Sam's daughter was called Wheat Carr and one son was John 'Wheaties' Carr, who shared his birthday, 26 October, with Aleister Crowley and took a great deal of interest in witchcraft. Young Carr was a fair, stringy-haired hippy and Berkowitz knew him. Furthermore, while the killings went on, Berkowitz adopted the name Son of Sam.

There was evidence that in the year before the murders John had invited David to the Twenty-Two Disciples of Hell witchcraft coven, of which he was a member. During the period when the killings occurred, eighty-five German Shepherds and Dobermanns were found killed and skinned in Walden, New York, about an hour's drive from Berkowitz's home in Yonkers. More dogs had been found in Untermeyer Park, Yonkers, where police had been told that a Devil-worshipping group held rituals.

Just before the murders began, Berkowitz had applied for a job in a dog pound. The pay was low but, he said, 'There was another way in which I could get paid. Somebody needed dogs.' That seemed a clear reference to witchcraft groups in search of animals for their blood.

By the time the police located the real John 'Wheaties' Carr in October 1978, Berkowitz was in jail and had confessed to all the killings and Carr was dead, in far-off North Dakota, apparently shot in the mouth with a rifle found by his side. The number 666, the Biblical mark of the Satanic beast, was found daubed on his hand, and on the skirting of the walls, 'SSNYC' – Son of Sam, New York City.

When the police examined photographs of Carr they found that he fitted the wanted picture, based on witnesses' statements, that had been circulated during the hunt for Son of Sam. A year later, Sam Carr's other son, Michael, was killed in a car crash and it was suggested that he, too, had been involved in the Son of Sam killings and that the 'accident' had been a murder.

In jail, Berkowitz's communications became more and more rational. He told his captors, 'Call the Santa Clara sheriff's office in California. Please ask them what happened to Arlis.'

On 13 October 1974, the body of Arlis Perry had been found in Stanford University Church. She was naked and spreadeagled in a ritual position with an altar candle in her vagina and another between her breasts. Her arms were folded across her chest. Her jeans were arranged across her legs to form a diamond pattern, a well-known witchcraft 'signature'. She had been beaten, choked and stabbed behind the ear with an ice pick.

Not unnaturally, after Berkowitz's arrest and trial, interest in the Son of Sam and anything connected with Satanism attracted public attention. On Friday 6 January 1978, the body of Robert Hirschmann was found riddled with bullets in Yonkers. His wife, Mary, was also found dead, stabbed and strangled, in Queens. Hirschmann was covered with tattoos, one of which was a swastika, a figure used since pagan times which was adopted by witchcraft cults as well as by the Nazis.

On 16 December 1977 Howard Green, an abstract painter, and his girlfriend, Carol Marron, were found bludgeoned to death in New Jersey. They were clutching in their hands clumps of hair, a Satanic symbol. Both corpses had been drained of blood – presumably for sacrificial drinking – and there was evidence that a veterinary surgeon's hypodermic had been used to remove it. Investigators discovered that Carol had shown an interest a year previously in witchcraft rites, particularly those of the sex-magic-orientated Ordo Templi Orientalis (ODT), although this cult had no connection with the deaths.

Berkowitz wrote to a preacher in California:

> I really don't know how to begin this letter but at one time I was a member of an occult group. Being sworn to secrecy or face death, I cannot reveal the name of this group. [They] . . . contained a mixture of Satanic practices which included the teachings of Aleister Crowley and Eliphaz Lev [*sic*]. It was and still is blood-orientated. These people will stop at nothing, including murder.

Eliphas Levi (1810–75) was the pen-name of Alphonse Louis Constant, a French priest who was thrown out of the Church for his left-wing political writings and because he failed to keep his vow of celibacy. He believed he was in touch with the dead and practised magic, the secrets of which were adopted by the Hermetic Order of the Golden Dawn, founded in London in 1888. Aleister Crowley, who was born in the year Levi died, claimed he was the reincarnation of Levi and became a member of the order in Paris.

The London chapter, which included William Wynn Westcott, the London coroner and Rosicrucian, as well as the poet W. B. Yeats, refused Crowley admission even though he staged a dramatic entrance to their premises wearing a black mask, Highland dress and a gilt dagger. One can only wonder whether the knowledge of such matters exhibited by Berkowitz was gained at first or second hand.

When Berkowitz was attacked by a fellow high-risk prisoner with a razor and needed fifty-six stitches, many to the throat, he refused to name his attacker, but said the attempt had been inspired by an occult organisation which wanted to enforce the vow of silence he had made under the threat of death.

21

Mass Murderer Of Muswell Hill

Detective Chief Inspector Peter Jay:
'Are we talking about one body or two?'
Mass murderer Denis Nilsen:
'Fifteen or sixteen since 1978: three
at [Muswell Hill], and about thirteen at . . . Cricklewood.'
Metropolitan Police interview, 1983

The Yorkshire Ripper and 'Son of Sam' Berkowitz were by no means the only serial killers who claimed or were deemed to be demonically possessed. Because possession has become an ignored or taboo subject, societies which decry violence and crime cannot hope to know or understand the Devil or demons who influence or motivate the perpetrators of such anti-social behaviour.

Since motive is not necessary evidence to convict murderers in law, no one – except perhaps a defence lawyer hoping it will gain leniency for his client – bothers to publicly reveal the beliefs, faith or religion of the killer or whether he believes in God or the Devil.

Before he was executed in 1930, Carl Panzram, of Warren, Minnesota, wrote in his prison diary: 'I have murdered twenty-one humans, I have committed thousands of burglaries, robberies, larcenies, arsons and sodomy on one thousand male human beings.' He had burned down a reform school when he was twelve and was eventually sentenced to twenty-five years for murder. He was then sentenced to death for killing a fellow convict. He wanted to die and took it upon himself to write to President Herbert Hoover, demanding that he should be hanged without delay. 'The only way to reform people is to kill them. I don't believe in Man, God nor Devil. I hate the whole damned human race, including myself.'

Alton Coleman went from being one of the most eligible bachelors in the black community to becoming the most wanted fugitive across several states of America. Police wanted him for seven murders, at least one attempted murder, half a dozen or more sexual assaults and a long list of assault-and-battery crimes, burglaries, robberies and car thefts. Only one person, the mother of one of his victims, provided a clue: 'Whenever she [my daughter] was with him she became some kind of robot.' Rumour had it that his power came from casting voodoo spells and sprinkling pepper over the ground.

When police eventually caught Coleman and his female accomplice, Debra Brown, the pair were sentenced to death and ordered to serve long terms of imprisonment in different trials for different offences committed between 1987 and 1989 in three states, Ohio, Illinois and Indiana. They were last heard appealing against all convictions and sentences, but no one had fathomed whether they were spell-binding voodoo devotees or victims of demonic possession.

In 1968 and 1969, the zodiac killings in California and New York produced evidence of occult influence. A man with a gruff voice telephoned the police department in Vallejo, San Francisco, to report a double murder.

> If you go one mile east on Columbus Parkway to a public park, you will find the kids in a brown car. They have been shot with a 9mm Luger. I also killed those kids last year. Goodbye.

Police went to the spot indicated and found the teenage lovers.

Three newspapers also received letters signed with a cross superimposed on a circle, which is the symbol of the zodiac. The letters contained sufficient detail to exclude anyone but the killer from having written them, and also validated his claim to the previous murders made in his call to the police. He challenged anyone to break a code in one letter which, he alleged, would reveal his identity. In that note his demonic motive was illustrated by the following words:

> I like to kill people because it is so much fun. It is more fun than killing wild game in the forest, because Man is the most dangerous animal of all. To kill something gives me the most thrilling experience. It is even better than [sex]. The best part [will be] when I die. I will be reborn in Paradise, and then all I have killed will become my slaves. I will not give you my name because you will try to slow or stop my collecting of slaves for my afterlife.

The caller phoned the police again and said he had killed another couple. But one of them survived, and the victim's description of his assailant matched that of a survivor of a previous attack. The killer was stockily built with light brown hair, and wore a black mask with slits for the eyes, behind which were spectacles. On the mask, painted in white, was the sign of the zodiac. The last San Francisco police heard of him was in 1974. Thereafter there were no more murders attributable to him, no more telephone calls and no more letters. The crimes remain unsolved.

Suddenly, another publicity-seeking self-styled zodiac killer turned up, this time in New York. Described as black, thirty to thirty-five years old, bearded and moustached, six feet tall, and thirteen stone, he was almost certainly an imitator of the San Francisco killer, rather than the same man. The gunman, who used a .38 or 9mm weapon, claimed to murder not at random but according to his victims' birth signs. He promised bodies of people on their birthdays, one for each sign under which they were born: Aries, Taurus, Gemini, Cancer, Leo, Virgo, Libra, Scorpio, Sagittarius, Capricorn, Aquarius and Pisces. The New York victims were all ageing drifters or dossers who slept rough.

Police believed that these astrology-obsessed killings were based on the Devil-worshipper Aleister Crowley's 1904 *Book of the Law*, in which he advocated 'weeding out the weak' from society. Detectives known as the 'swami team' checked who had borrowed copies of the Crowley book from city libraries. Another lead was a mystery man who offered people airline jobs, always asking for their dates of birth. When officers checked the telephone number given by the airline representative they found it was a public payphone.

This zodiac killer did not complete his target of twelve victims – in fact, he shot only eight and fortunately did not manage to kill all of those.

Astrologers asked to analyse his letters pointed out that he started his shooting spree with a Scorpio victim. Scorpio is a very intense sign, mythologically related to death and sometimes used as the symbol of death and rebirth. He even signed his letters 'Faust' after the famous character who sold his soul to the Devil. He also used the zodiac sign, a cross surmounted on a circle, in letters to newspaper editors, just as his San Francisco counterpart had done. In spite of these clues, albeit very small ones, the identity of this zodiac killer, like that of the first, was never discovered.

Can there be any more accurate description than 'demonic' for Richard Chase, the vampire of Sacramento, California? On 23 January 1978, this tall, scruffy man called at the home of David and Theresa Wallin. David was out. Theresa was expecting their first baby in six months. She opened the door carrying a rubbish bag. They stared at each other for a moment. The intruder fired a .22 pistol, shooting her in the head, the arm and then, fatally, in the temple.

Chase then dragged her body to the master bedroom, fetched a knife from the kitchen and picked up a yoghurt carton from the spilled rubbish. Returning to the body, he pulled up Theresa's clothing, sliced open her abdomen and dipped the yoghurt cup into the spilling blood. This he drank, eagerly replenishing his own blood supply, which he believed was dwindling. He was a vampire, killing others to stay alive.

Chase believed that someone had stolen his pulmonary artery, causing his blood supply to become gradually reduced. To remedy this he practised first on animals, torturing, killing and drinking the blood of cats, dogs and rabbits, and then progressed to humans. He went on to murder others: he killed a mother and her baby, mutilated her and was about to do the same to the baby when he was disturbed. He fled with the infant's corpse, which was later found on waste ground, where he had thrown it. Eventually, in 1979, he was tried, convicted and sentenced to death.

Cannibalism as a natural or unnatural habit has long been argued about by anthropologists and folklorists. Jeffrey Dahmer, the man who cooked and ate his victims, ranks high among the most infamous mass murderers of modern times. The grotesque life and work of the cannibal killer came to light on 24 July 1991, when a terrified teenager, still wearing handcuffs, escaped from Dahmer's apartment in Milwaukee, Wisconsin. Police who raided the apartment were sickened and revolted by what they discovered.

Nine human heads were found – on an altar, in the refrigerator and in pans, where Dahmer was in the process of boiling the flesh off the skulls. Four male bodies were wedged into a barrel and several male genitalia were stored in a pot. Scraps of human skin and bones were everywhere, and the stench was so unbearable that officers and technicians asked for breathing apparatus.

Dahmer had been in the army medical corps, where he was viewed as a bit of a contradictory personality. He could be polite, talkative and intelligent or boorish, hostile and obnoxious. He would spend hours on his bunk, sipping martinis and listening to heavy-metal bands, particularly Black Sabbath, whose leader, Ozzy Osbourne, was notorious for biting off the heads of dead animals during his concert performances. When arrested, Dahmer confessed that he picked up homosexuals, mostly black or Hispanic, in bars and invited them home for sex and a drink or two. He spiked the drinks he offered with stronger alcoholic spirits and sleeping draughts. He drugged, strangled and dismembered seventeen people, some of whom were still alive. Dahmer would often cook the fleshy parts of his victims and have them for dinner. He also took photographs and home videos of his handiwork, mounting the camera so it would look to unsuspecting guests like a security device.

On the shelf were the videotapes of five of his favourite movies, *The Exorcist, The Exorcist II* – which gave him the idea of using yellow contact lenses to make himself look Satanic – *Hellraiser I, Hellraiser II* and *The Hellbound Heart*. Originally based on Clive Barker's novel, *The Hellbound Heart* concerns a dissipated adventurer in the Orient who buys a magical music box which provides undreamed-of pains and pleasures. It causes him to be imprisoned in a temple which turns itself into a torture chamber, where he is torn to shreds.

Dahmer's zombie temple had its own altar, on which were arrayed carefully cleaned and painted skulls, bones and other human souvenirs, guarded at each end by skeletons. He said that by keeping the heads he could retain the true essence of his prey and sustain his relationships with those he had killed.

On 18 February 1992 Dahmer began serving sixteen life sentences for murder. The state of Wisconsin has no capital punishment, but his sentences added up to more than 1,000 years' imprisonment. In fact he served only a fraction of his punishment – in 1994 he was himself killed, by a fellow prisoner.

Dennis Nilsen, the uncivil civil servant of suburban Muswell Hill, north London, was caught because the neighbours, irritated that their lavatories would not flush properly, called in the Dyno-Rod man. He found lumps of rotting flesh, some with hair attached, floating amid the slime.

A policeman asked Nilsen, 'Are we talking about one body or two?'

Nilsen replied, 'Fifteen or sixteen since 1978: three at Cranley Gardens [Muswell Hill] and about thirteen at my previous address at Melrose Avenue, Cricklewood.'

Nilsen, who worked in a job centre in London's Soho area, had plenty of opportunity to pick up out-of-work drifters, sometimes across the counter at his workplace, sometimes in popular gay bars. He would take them home, fill them with laced drinks, and then, as they slept, strangle them with their own shoelaces. He then cut them up or burned the bodies and, at Cranley Gardens, flushed them down the lavatory, which led to his discovery.

Nilsen, brought up in a strict religious Scottish home, gave thirty hours of detailed confession and much more to author Brian

Masters for his book *Killing for Company*. Masters says:

> A personality disorder reveals for them [religious men] that the Devil is at work, and that man imprisoned in fancy has forsaken the world of God to pursue his miserable life in the vivid, seductive, intoxicating world of Satan. From this point of view, psychology has not slain religion, it has on the contrary reaffirmed man's spirituality, previously represented to him in the language of myth, now muddied by the obtuse jargon of doctors.

In his voluminous papers, Nilsen offers some insights. 'We either make very good angels or very bad devils.' 'Man comes apart when he does not listen to his god at the crucial times of his life.' 'I ignored my demons for years, they sprung out and destroyed me.' Talking of his work in the job centre by day and his nocturnal killings, Nilsen added, 'This total principled moral purity in its extremes balanced up all the sickening evil of my private world.'

Mr Ivan Lawrence QC, MP, who defended Nilsen, argued in court that at the time the defendant was suffering from such abnormality of mind that he was incapable of forming the specific intent to murder. The jury, confused by the complexities of the murder and the convincing 'obtuse jargon' of psychiatrists called for both the prosecution and the defence, were not unanimous. They voted 10–2 that Nilsen was both sane and guilty of the six sample counts of murder and two of attempted murder with which he was charged.

Mr Justice Croom-Johnson sentenced him to the mandatory life sentence of imprisonment with a recommendation that he serve not less than twenty-five years. It can only be a matter of speculation what the jury would have decided if demonic possession, so clearly a fact, particularly in cases of strict religious upbringing, had been permitted to be argued in court.

Compare these cases with the events at Matamoros, Mexico, just across the border from the United States, where a police raid in search of illicit drugs uncovered an evil combination of Satanism and murder. Officers were manning a checkpoint when one man tried to escape their roadblock. The ensuing chase led the police to a cattle ranch twenty miles from Matamoros. There they found the grandly named Rancho Santa Elena and uncovered a $200,000-a-week (£133,000) illegal marijuana business. While they were there, they happened to show a caretaker the picture of Mark Kilroy, a missing twenty-one-year-old undergraduate from the University of Texas who had vanished in the area a month previously.

Yes, the janitor remembered, he had seen Kilroy, and he pointed to a rust-coloured shed 400 yards away. There, and in and around a nearby paddock, police made the grim discovery of several makeshift graves. The overpowering stench of decaying flesh led them to dig up the site to find a total of thirteen male corpses, two as young as fourteen years of age. Several victims had been slashed with knives, some bludgeoned, one hanged, another set on fire and at least two were riddled with bullets. The mutilation was horrendous: some victims had obviously been tortured with razor blades or had had their hearts ripped out. Nearly all had lost their ears, nipples and testicles. Eyes had been gouged from one body; another was headless.

Inside the dark 15-by-25-foot shack they found a pot full of dried blood, a charred human brain and a turtle. Other containers held a witch's brew of human hair, a goat's head and pieces of chicken. There were also ritualistic items including a machete and white votive candles in a box bearing the picture of Our Lady of Guadalupe, the patron saint of Mexico.

Mexican police gradually uncovered the story of the 'red-haired devil'. This was the name given to El Padrino (the godfather), also known as Adolfo de Jesús Constanzo, a twenty-six-year-old Cuban American who had grown up in Miami, Florida. He practised Santería, Caribbean voodoo, a religion which evolved when African slaves blended the worship of the gods and spirits of their ancestors with Catholicism.

Santería has as many as 100 million practitioners worldwide, many of them concentrated in the Caribbean and South America. In the United States, the spiritual centre is La Iglesia Lukumi Babalu-Aya, a church in Miami. Although the rites include animal sacrifice, Santería is regarded as a benign religion, but some of Constanzo's relatives had practised it in a vindictive manner, such as settling grudges by leaving headless animals on the doorsteps of their enemies. One woman found a dead goose with its head wrapped in a red handkerchief. Another opened her door to find a decapitated chicken on her stoop.

Constanzo recruited men into the cult to persuade them that orgies of human sacrifice would win Satanic protection, even from police bullets, and sustain the cross-border marijuana-running operation. The killings would, he said, draw around them a protective shield provided by the voodoo gods. It would ingratiate them with the Devil.

More recently, Constanzo had switched his rituals to those of the Palo Macombe, a malevolent Afro-Caribbean cult which experts believe advocates evil for evil's sake. The effective gods are the all-powerful group leaders who, in an increasing number of cases, appear to be drug barons using the occult as a disciplinary tool. Professor Carl Raschke, who occupies the chair in world religions at Denver University, says, 'What we are seeing is a religious ideology that is being used almost like a corporate motivational training programme to bond and enforce absolute obedience among criminal groups.'

One of the 'training aids' used by Constanzo was the 1987 Hollywood film *The Believers* which purported to investigate the Santería and Palo Macombe cults. His partner, Sara Maria Villareal Aldrete, said it was intended to lure men to the cult and ultimately to the killing shack. Experts, armed with police evidence, pointed out that Constanzo had even expanded the rituals of the two cults to include elements of voodoo, satanism and *santismo*, in which the essential ingredients are human sacrifice.

The killers boil the brains and hearts of their victims and make a concoction of leg and arm bones and animal heads, which the participants eat and drink.

Kilroy, the missing undergraduate, had crossed the border for the 1989 Easter break and had been drinking in local *cantinas* in Matamoros, among them Sergeant Pepper's and the London Pub, when he was lured into accepting a lift in a pick-up truck, driven to the ranch, gagged, blindfolded and executed. Police searched for El Padrino's companion, Sara Aldrete, who lived a double life: in Brownsville, Texas, she was a physical training honours student, but over the border in Matamoros she became a high priestess of the drug and occult ring. Found in her home was a blood-splattered altar and children's clothing.

Both Sara and El Padrino had vanished. Searching Constanzo's neat, white, two-storey home outside Mexico City, the police were disturbed to find baby clothes although it was thought that he had no children. Rumours swept through the lower Rio Grande Valley that cultists were planning to kidnap children in revenge for the Matamoros discovery. Panicked parents withdrew their children from school and officials posted security guards around classrooms until the rumours proved to be unfounded.

Meanwhile, the four under arrest included one who removed his shirt from his back to reveal, on his shoulders, chest and back, scars in the shape of an upside-down cross, inflicted with a red-hot knife to indicate that he had been chosen to select whom to kill. Not all the thirteen victims were strangers. Some turned out to be cult members who were judged to have offended and had to be disciplined.

Theodore 'Ted' Bundy, the most unlikely serial killer, never admitted that he had personally killed twenty-plus women in the USA between 1974 and 1978 but was probably responsible for double that figure. He was handsome, witty and intelligent and won a scholarship in Chinese Studies, a BSc in psychology and was admitted to Utah University Law School. His movement from state to state indicated a pattern: when he left one area one set of killings stopped and when he arrived in a new location another began. He raped and killed.

Bundy always talked about the murderer in the third person and defined him as 'an entity'. Describing the first killing with which he was charged, that of a girl who vanished from her bedroom, he told his biographers, Stephen G. Michaud and Hugh Aynesworth, for their book *The Only Living Witness*:

> What happened was this entity inside him was not capable of being controlled any longer, at least not for any considerable period of time. It began to try to justify itself, to create rationalisations for what it was doing. Perhaps to satisfy the rational, normal part of the individual. One element that came into play was anger, hostility. But I don't think that was an overriding emotion when he would go out hunting, or however you want to describe it. On most occasions it was a high degree of anticipation, of excitement, of arousal. It was an adventuristic kind of thing.
>
> He received no pleasure from harming or causing pain to the person he attacked. He received absolutely no gratification. He did everything possible within reason – considering the unreasonableness of the situation – not to torture these individuals, at least not physically. The fantasy that accompanies and generates the anticipation that precedes the crime is always more stimulating than the immediate aftermath of the crime itself. He should have recognised that what really fascinated him was the hunt, the adventure of searching out his victims. And, to a degree, possessing them physically as one would possess a potted plant, a painting or a Porsche. Owning, as it were, this individual.

When his trial came to an end and he was asked if he had anything to say before sentence was passed on him, he replied:

> I will tell the court that I am not really able to accept the verdict because all the verdict found in part was that these crimes had been committed. They erred in finding who committed them. And as a consequence I cannot accept the

> sentence, even though one will be imposed, even though I recognise the lawful way in which the court will impose it, because it is not a sentence on me. It is a sentence to someone else who is not standing here today.

Judge Edward D. Cowart was not impressed by this other entity, which, if it did exist, was not recognised in law. 'Mr Bundy, the court is going to sentence the person found guilty of the offence. Your name, sir, was on the verdict form [handed in by the foreman of the jury].' He then sentenced Bundy to death. He was electrocuted ten years later, in 1989.

At the time of Bundy's execution police were still trying to work out if Henry Lee Lucas could possibly have killed 600 people, as he claimed. It depended on his mood and memory when the question 'How many did you kill?' was asked. He certainly killed some, but once he was in police custody he quickly realised the benefits to be gained from confessing to an increasing number of murders. This realisation came to him, he said, when the police put him in an ice-cold cell, furnished with only a bare steel bed frame, and, although it was still spring, turned on an industrial-strength air-conditioning unit to blast him with freezing air twenty-four hours a day. The police denied this accusation.

From that time onwards, however, Lucas became the master of cant and recant. He always wanted to 'help' the law to 'discover' more corpses and 'solve' more murder mysteries for them. They would treat Lucas, the prisoner, to gifts, comfortable surroundings, appetising meals, take-away food from drive-ins. They allowed him to watch prime-time cable television, to travel first-class to anywhere where there was an unsolved homicide. He was even encouraged to take up oil-painting. 'I keep my weight down by having a strawberry milkshake for every murder I confess,' he boasted.

Lucas, as a result, kept confessing for eight years. As some wit said, 'That's really singing for your supper.' At one stage, officers from twenty-seven states called at an hotel in Louisiana and sat through videotapes of Henry's confessions, which lasted for a total of forty-eight hours.

Some police officers believed him, others did not, and the argument continues to rage. The Texas Rangers, according to Judge Brunson Moore, had been fooled into giving Lucas 'good treatment and perks. You can catch as many flies with a fly-swatter as you can with honey.' They were taken in by him but when their error was discovered they declined to go to other law enforcement authorities and admit it. Some law agencies stopped investigating unsolved murders; others had to start all over again.

Who was Lucas? A small man, the ninth son of nine children, the runt of the litter, he had lost an eye when his brother stabbed him. His mother, a prostitute, forced him to watch her entertain clients and dressed Henry as a girl for the first three years of his life. She even sent him to school with his hair permed. 'I was treated as the dog of the family. I was beaten. I was made to do things that no human being would want to do.'

At thirteen, Lucas claimed his first murder when he killed a teacher who snubbed his advances. At twenty-four he stabbed his mother to death and was jailed. When, six years later, he was due to be released, he told doctors, 'I'm not ready to go.' He was released nonetheless, and went on a seventeen-year killing spree – or so he said.

At one stage he teamed up with Ottis Toole, a six-foot-tall transvestite and arsonist, at a relief mission in Jacksonville, Florida. The Sunday-night prayer meetings, held in what had once been a chicken coop, were frequently interrupted by people speaking in tongues, the gift of the Holy Spirit. With them in this sanctuary of succour were Toole's niece and nephew, Becky and Frank Powell, aged twelve and nine, a pet chihuahua, a cat and some parakeets. They often all lived together in Lucas's broken-down Oldsmobile car. Lucas was so poor that every week or so he sold his blood for $7 to $10 ($4.60–£6.60) a time.

When the car broke down, like hobos of old, he and Toole rode on freight trains, hitch-hiked, sometimes separately, and somehow returned to Florida. On the way (according to Lucas) they would rob, rape and murder, probably two or three times a week, always with the children travelling with them or somewhere nearby. Lucas claimed to have murdered both of the children, but although Becky vanished, Frank was taken into custody to talk about whether or not he actually saw Lucas commit any serious crimes.

One police officer challenged Lucas to write down all the murders he had committed. The con-man listed seventy-three, illustrating them with childish cartoon-like sketches. The following example is typical.

> Junction. Plainview. Date 1979. Death, cut head off, knife. Started strangling, stab back, white female, 20, medium, red hair, lots of make-up, five [feet] two, 135 [lbs], pretty. Picked up, put head in sack, dropped in Arizona, body.

Lucas bragged that the sheriff took one look at his confessions, called a press conference, and said, 'He's killed hundreds.' All

Lucas was doing, however, was using information provided by one officer or officers and passing it on to other officers so that it seemed he knew details of the crimes. Or he made it up: one force wanted to solve the mystery of a murdered unidentified female wearing only orange socks. The moment Lucas heard, he immediately invented a fanciful story about the fate of 'Orange Socks' because he realised that the police knew no more about her than he did.

Police still reckoned he had killed 160, but that didn't include his fantasy that he was responsible for the abduction and death of Jimmy Hoffa, the trade union leader, or his claim that he flew the poison to Guyana so that the Jonestown cult could commit suicide by drinking it.

Eventually, Lucas claimed he had been 'saved', by a spiritual counsellor and platonic sweetheart, Sister Clemmie, a devout religious lay person who ran a jail missionary service in Georgetown. Toole, his companion, he averred, was to blame for his misdeeds – he had recruited Lucas into the Hands of Death, a Devil-worshipping cult. 'The Devil made me do it,' he said. 'I am now a man of faith on a mission from God.' Surprisingly, Toole, who was in custody elsewhere, was reportedly confirming every detail of Lucas's story.

Sister Clemmie appeared on a religious radio chat show to tell how she brought a serial killer to the Lord. Lucas broadcast 'advice to Christian youth on how to avoid the snares of Satanism', telling listeners:

> God himself appeared as a bright, white light in the corner of my cell and spoke to me, urging me to confess all my murders for the sake of the families [of the murder victims]. God told me to tell them where the victims were so they could have a Christian burial.

Even though Lucas was convicted of eleven murders, some of them were based on confessions which he later withdrew. Nevertheless, he remains on death row in Texas, leaving others to ponder what possessed him.

22

Satan's Lovers On The Moors

Please God, help me! . . . Please take your hands off me a minute . . . I can't breathe . . . Don't undress me, will you? . . . I have to get home by eight o'clock.

Tape-recorded voice of a victim of the Moors Murderers

In an age in which crimes have reached proportions of diabolical violence and cruelty, it is surprising that even the churches do not appear to think that the perpetrators may be possessed by the Devil. As we have seen, the law requires witnesses in the courts to take the oath on the Bible or the New Testament, swearing by Almighty God to tell the truth, the whole truth and nothing but the truth, after which the Almighty is quickly forgotten. As more than one court wit has quipped, 'When a man says he is talking to God he is praying. When he says God is talking to him he is schizophrenic.'

Surely, amid the multitudes of experts who go into the witness box during a trial and give their expert opinions, there is a place for the forensic theologian to offer a view, based on his or her experience and careful investigation, on whether the person in the dock was or was not diabolically possessed at the time he or she committed the crime in question. When, in my book *Holy Killers*, I suggested that this might be advantageous, particularly in horrific cases of serial killings, support came from some influential quarters.

George Mandel, author of *Crocodile Blood*, wrote:

> Brian McConnell's three central ideas are incisive, revolutionary and of immense social urgency. To be specific, I mean his forensic theology, its application as a qualified criminological procedure in conjunction with others, and the interchange of

its generated data among police authorities worldwide in the preventative search for a non-human source of savage crime as a presence among us.

Father Jordan Aumann, OP, Professor at the Pontifical University of St Thomas, Rome, says:

> Brian McConnell's thorough investigation of demonic possession and serial killing sounds an alarm that should be heeded particularly at a time at which Satanic cults and worship as well as multiple murders are a plague on our society.

Malachi Martin, the former Jesuit priest and author of *Hostage to the Devil*, which deals with his experiences as an exorcist, declared:

'The presence among human beings of a non-human power could in certain cases be the only adequate explanation of the aberrant behaviour of such criminals.'

Ever since Cain slew Abel, people have murdered for gain, for revenge, for elimination, for lust, out of conviction that killing is right and, more importantly, from the apparently mindless compulsion to kill. Demonic possession, by the clerical definition, must have been involved in the work of many of the more bloodthirsty killers. To many, their crimes beggar any other description. And many murderers and mass-murderers in particular have claimed, when caught, to be possessed by the Devil and have not been believed. How many spoke the truth remains, until they are properly examined, in doubt.

Meanwhile, the only alternative to a finding of guilt is a plea of insanity – that the person did not know what he did or that what he did was wrong as a result of mental disease. Since mental illness often rests on psychiatric evaluation, an interpretative science, someone must wonder why demonic possession is excluded from the list of arguable mental problems.

The 1960s crimes of the notorious Moors Murderers were indicative of the close links between sadism, Nazism, pornography and Satanism. Ian Brady, who was then twenty-eight, a £12-a-week stock clerk, and Myra Hindley, twenty-four, worked in the same office and lived with Hindley's grandmother in Hattersley. They were friendly with Hindley's sister, Maureen, and her seventeen-year-old husband, David Smith.

Brady would show off with his books on sex, sadism and Adolf

Hitler, his hand-guns and his talk of robbing banks and killing. By way of a practical example he picked up a seventeen-year-old, Edward Evans, a homosexual, on 6 October 1965, and took him home. There, with David Smith watching, Brady, wielding an axe, proceeded to smash in Evans' head. 'It's done,' said Brady. 'It's the messiest yet. It normally takes only one blow.'

A terrified Smith fled to the police, who duly found the body but showed much more interest in two left-luggage tickets which, when presented at Manchester Central Station, produced two suitcases containing coshes, wigs, papers, photographs and two tape-recordings. Some of the photos were of Lesley Ann Downey, a ten-year-old who had been missing since she went to a fairground at Hattersley almost a year previously. The child's voice, pleading to be allowed to go home, was on one of the tapes.

> Please God, help me! . . . Can I just tell you summat? . . . I must tell you summat . . . Please take your hands off me a minute, please . . . I can't breathe . . . What are you going to do with me? . . . Don't undress me, will you? . . . It hurts me. I want to see my mummy, honest to God . . . I have to get home by eight o'clock . . . Or I'll get killed if I don't. Honest to God . . . It hurts me neck . . .

John Kilbride, a twelve-year-old also missing from home, featured in some of the recovered notes, which included a plan for murder. His moorland grave was found 400 yards away from Downey's. She had been stripped of her tartan skirt and pink cardigan. His trousers and underpants had been rolled down to the thighs.

At the trial, Attorney-General Sir Elwyn Jones said that 'in association with all these killings there was present not only a sexual element but an abnormal sexual element, a perverted sexual element'. Brady's counsel, Mr Emlyn Hooson QC, MP, read what Brady had written in a notebook. 'People are like maggots, small, blind, worthless, fish-bait. Rape is not a crime. It is a state of mind. Murder is a hobby and a supreme pleasure.'

Brady and Hindley were convicted of murder and sentenced to life imprisonment, but more was to come. Hindley was counselled by Lord Longford, the Roman Catholic prison reformer, and was said to be a reformed character. She had returned to the Roman Catholic Church, in which she had been brought up, and was, said Longford, fit to be paroled. That recommendation was refused, not the least because of rumours that there were more bodies yet to be found on the moors.

In 1986, twenty years after her conviction, Hindley made a

private confession to two more killings, which led to searches for further graves on Saddleworth Moor. The following March, her confession was made public, confirming that she and Brady had killed Keith Bennett, who was twelve, and sixteen-year-old Pauline Reade. The girl's body was found in August 1987, almost quarter of a century after she disappeared from home.

Both prisoners helped police separately in searching the moors and were returned to their different prisons. In January 1988, the Director of Public Prosecutions announced that no further charges would be brought against the couple. All pleas for the release of Myra Hindley have been refused, while Brady says he does not want to be freed. The question of how they could have committed those crimes unless they were dominated or possessed by some supernatural element, like the Devil, remains unanswered.

Mr Justice Fenton Atkinson told the jury at their trial:

> I suppose that hearing and reading about these allegations, the first reaction of kindly, charitable people is to say this is so terrible that anyone doing anything like that might be mentally afflicted. You must put that aside at once. It is a presumption of our law that anyone who comes into the dock is sane. There has not been the smallest suggestion that either of these two are mentally abnormal or not fully and completely responsible for their actions. If, and I underline it, the prosecution is right, you are dealing with two sadistic killers of the utmost depravity.

Satan was not mentioned.

What of the 1985 'Bambi' massacre at Tolleshunt D'Arcy, the Essex village with a maypole and a moated hall? Jeremy Bamber, the twenty-five-year-old killer, was born the illegitimate child of a teenage daughter of the senior chaplain to the Archbishop of Canterbury and a humble curate. He had been adopted as a baby by the well-off Bamber family. Jeremy, a bed-hopping Romeo, coolly told his current girlfriend that he was going to drug and shoot his family and set fire to their eighteenth-century farmhouse. She later confided to a friend, 'He's so evil. He's the Devil incarnate.'

Jeremy went ahead with his plan and killed his adoptive parents, Nevill, a sixty-one-year-old Essex magistrate, and June, his sister, Sheila, also adopted, and her twin six-year-old sons, Nicholas and Daniel. Then he calmly persuaded the police that Sheila, nick-named Bambi, who had a known drug problem, had committed the killings before turning the gun on herself.

The police believed him, even though this would mean that the frail former model had used a high-velocity .22 Anchutz rifle on her family, then committed suicide, reloading three times and using twenty-five rounds in the process. When it was subsequently established that a silencer had been used, which would have made the gun thirty inches long, this seemed doubtful – Sheila was known as Bambi because of her long, colt-like legs, but she would have needed arms a yard long to have killed herself as suggested.

Handsome Jeremy ate a hearty breakfast after the shootings, wept copious tears at the funeral, whispered to his girlfriend that he hoped the television cameras would catch his best profile, and took a holiday in St Tropez. While he was away, his twenty-two-year-old girlfriend, Julie Mugford, upset by his behaviour, went to the police. Jeremy was charged with and convicted of all five murders and sentenced to life imprisonment with a recommendation that he serve not less than twenty-five years.

Was the Devil in Tolleshunt d'Arcy? Bambi, the Crown admitted, was so mentally disturbed she had claimed to be the Virgin Mary and Joan of Arc in late-night telephone calls to her father. Julie said that she had even tried to contact the spirits of the dead. 'I wanted to find out the truth and ask Bambi's advice on what I should do because I believed Jeremy to be the Devil incarnate.'

Might there not have been a need for an exorcist in the case of Bambi? Or Jeremy Bamber?

Consider Charles Manson, the highly publicised leader of the Manson 'Family', whose brutal killings in California seemed to inspire a whole run of serial slaughters.

Manson boasted: 'I am God and the Devil.' He was born the son of a prostitute, spent his early life in and out of reform schools and later served prison sentences for forgery and procuring prostitutes. Released after a ten-year spell in prison in 1954, he set up a commune-based cult, recruiting hippies, drifters and the out of work to his Spahn Ranch, a disused movie lot, near Los Angeles.

He wore his hair long like an old-time prophet, and a red 'X', the mark of an outlaw, on his forehead. His followers, like a religious congregation, regarded him as their saviour. They indulged in free love, pseudo-religious ceremonies and experimental drugs and followed his revolutionary teachings against the Establishment. Their willingness to obey his commandments came to a head on 9 August 1969, when a group of his followers broke into the home of film director Roman Polanski and murdered his eight-months pregnant wife, the actress Sharon Tate, and four others. They were shot, stabbed and clubbed, and slogans such as 'War' and 'Pig' were daubed on the walls in their blood.

It was curious, for revolutionaries, to use a word like 'pig', because they knew that it was slang among the black community for the police. It was chosen in an attempt to shift the blame for the slaughter on to black people. Curious, too, that they selected the home of Polanski to attack the Establishment – he was by no means a conformist figure and had directed a film they might, in their Satanic glee, have enjoyed: *Rosemary's Baby*, in which a woman is drugged to conceive Satan's child.

The following night, the same group of killers repeated their mayhem at the home of Leno and Rosemary La Bianca, killing them both.

Manson, now thirty-three years of age, was the absent leader of this group, but together with three women followers was tried for the seven murders. The prosecution referred to Manson's grudge against society and argued that he masterminded the murders even if he did not actually take part in them.

One defector from the 'Family', Linda Kasabian, gave evidence that when they went to the Tate house one of the killers had pursued a victim with a knife, screaming, 'I'm the Devil. I'm here to do the Devil's work.'

Manson's bizarre defence was that the three girls involved wanted to testify to their guilt and his innocence, but Manson's lawyers refused to question them so that no one could then cross-examine them. Thus there was no evidence. The judge ruled that they were entitled to testify but that he would first remove the jury. This was the signal for Manson to whisper, 'Don't testify.' The women refused to do so. Manson said that the members of his Family were those discarded by society. His hatred was demonstrated in a series of statements such as: 'I have done my best to get along in the world and now you want to kill me. I say to myself, "Ha! I'm already dead, have been all my life. I don't care anything about any of you." '

Chief prosecutor Vincent Bugliosi referred to Manson as 'one of the most evil, Satanic men who ever walked the face of the earth'. All four were found guilty and sentenced to death, which was reduced to life imprisonment. Again, no clergyman ever mentioned freeing them from the possession of the Devil or the demons they admitted.

If ever there was a candidate for exorcism it was Richard Ramirez, known as the 'Valley Intruder', after the limited geographical area near to freeway escape routes in which he operated, as well as the 'Night Stalker' and the 'Night Prowler'. A twenty-eight-year-old drifter from El Paso, Texas, he terrified residents of single-storey homes in suburban Los Angeles with an orgy of thirteen murders as well as the shooting, stabbing and sexual abuse of many other victims, including children. During the torrid summer heat of 1985, many residents of Los Angeles' middle-class suburbs could not sleep safely in their beds.

The self-confessed Satanist was on the loose for longer than a year, breaking into houses and wantonly raping, torturing and mutilating his defenceless victims. He left a 'visiting card' in the form of pentagrams, either on the bodies of victims or on the walls of their homes. The pentagram, the five-pointed star enclosed in a circle, is one of a number of symbols used by Satanists in their rituals. Also known as the witches' star, it represents the Devil's horns and its central point is always directed downwards. The intruder also had a pentagram tattooed on the palm of his left hand.

When Ramirez attacked lawyer Vincent Zazzara and his wife, Maxine, he left her body naked and mutilated. He had gouged out her eyes, of which no trace was found. A police officer said, 'I hope I never live to see anything like it again.'

Some of the victims were dragged from their beds and forced to swear allegiance to Satan before being beaten and raped. In one house he raided, he left behind a telltale clue, a baseball cap bearing the logo of AC/DC, a popular heavy-metal band. This reinforced the widely held belief that aggressive rock 'n' roll and heavy metal are degenerate; the voice of Satan which can inspire fans to torture, murder or suicide.

Ramirez was an avid heavy-metal fan, usually high on drugs, always listening to his Walkman, the music pulsating loudly through the headphones. His favourite bands were Led Zeppelin, Black Sabbath – how's that for a devilish title? – Judas Priest and AC/DC. The last group provided Ramirez with the inspiration to model himself a new image. He admired their album *Highway to Hell*, and in a statement at his trial he referred to 'Night Prowler', one of the tracks, which had provided him with his own preferred alias.

Witnesses at the Ramirez trial were reduced to tears by the violence of the crimes. One juror committed suicide after murdering his girlfriend. The defendant reacted to such news by smirking, giggling and making the sign of the Devil to spectators. When one witness told how she had been raped and beaten while her husband lay dead beside her, Ramirez laughed out loud.

He was found guilty of twelve murders and several attempted murders, rapes and burglaries. In mitigation, his counsel suggested that he may have been possessed, that the Devil made him do it, and that he was the helpless victim of his own sexuality, which drove him to rape. The lawyer pleaded for him to be spared the death penalty. 'Mr Ramirez will die in prison. Life imprisonment without parole means he will never see Disneyland again.'

Julian Ramirez, the killer's father, insisted that the media had turned his son, who was raised to believe in God, into a monster. Asked if he had anything to say before sentence was passed, the drifter replied:

> I have a lot to say, but now is not the time or place. I don't know why I'm wasting my breath. But what the hell? I don't believe in the hypocritical moralistic dogma of this so-called civilised society. You maggots make me sick.

And to the judge he added, 'You don't understand me. You are not expected to. You are not capable of it. I am beyond your experience. I am beyond good and evil.'

The judge pronounced the sentence, death in the gas chamber and twelve times fifty-nine years, plus four months' imprisonment for the lesser crimes. As the Satanist was led away, he told reporters, 'Big deal. Death always went with the territory. I'll see you in Disneyland. I will be avenged. Lucifer dwells within us all.'

Psychiatrists spent many hours pondering the behaviour of the murderous fan and its connection to the lyrics of AC/DC's 'Night Prowler':

> I am your night prowler, I sleep in the day,
> I am your night prowler, get out of my way,
> Too scared to turn your light out, 'cuz there's something on your mind?
> Was that a noise outside the window? Watch that shadow on the blind.
> And you lie there naked like a body in a tomb;
> Suspended animation, as I slip into your room.

Roman Catholics, evangelists and other fundamentalist Christian leaders have all condemned rock and heavy-metal music. The groups all deny any connection with Satanic cults, despite the fact that many of them use demonic imagery on their album sleeves and in their dress: they often wear jewellery with Satanic motifs and sometimes horned headgear. At the same time, they deny any corrupting power or influence in their music or their lyrics.

Just before the Night Stalker killed his first victim in 1984, a seventeen-year-old New Yorker, Rick Kasso, another AC/DC fan, killed a friend by stabbing him seventeen times and plucking out his eyes. Like Ramirez, he also tortured his victim and forced him to proclaim his love for Satan before killing him. Kasso, too, took drugs, said he was a Satanist and listened constantly to heavy metal.

Such bands have been accused of sending out subliminal corrupting messages which are detectable only if you tape the music and play the albums backwards. One group was accused of publishing in this fashion the message, 'Satan! Satan! Satan! He is God!' Judas Priest were sued by relatives of fans who, their families claim, committed suicide during or immediately after listening to their music.

Rock musician Ozzy Osbourne's song 'Suicide Solution' has been cited in several cases. The father of nineteen-year-old Randy Duncan, who shot himself in 1984, sued Osbourne but lost the case. In Georgia, in 1991, law suits were filed in connection with two gunshot victims, Michael Waller, aged sixteen, who died in 1986, and Harold Hamilton, seventeen, who died in 1988. Both committed suicide shortly after listening to 'Suicide Solution', which, the plaintiffs claimed, persuaded them to take their own lives.

There is another bizarre case in the files of a mass shooting which is generally accepted to have been committed as a result of demonic possession. Robert Sartin was a twenty-three-year-old civil servant and a Satanist. His interest first came to light when he wrote an essay on Satanism at school. On being questioned, he told adults that it was just harmless human curiosity. What he did not tell them at the time was that he heard a voice belonging to the mad killer in the *Halloween* films, which told him to kill his parents. He did not do so.

There are five films in the series: *Halloween, Halloween Two, Halloween Three: The Season of the Witch, Halloween Four: The Return of Michael Myers* and *Halloween Five*. Sartin was presumed to have seen them all by the time of his crime. In the first, a young boy sees his sister necking with her boyfriend, dons a Hallowe'en mask, pulls out a butcher's knife and attacks. He is sent to a state hospital whence he escapes and returns to the scene of his original crime, where he finds a trio of babysitting friends. In the second, the masked predator is shot six times only to walk away, zombie-like, to continue his mayhem. The others are imitators of different sorts.

Sartin walked out of his home in Whitley Bay, Tyne and Wear, on the morning of 30 April 1989 and shot seventeen people. One man died. At Newcastle Crown Court a psychiatrist pronounced the killer a schizophrenic. The jury, by a majority of 10–2, found him unfit even to stand trial by virtue of mental illness. Sartin was sent to a mental hospital, but the evidence, hinted at rather than stated, was that he was, at the time of the shooting, not insane but demonically possessed.

23

The Exorcists Speak

Exorcist: 'In the name of the Virgin Mary.'
Demonic voice: 'Madam! Oh Madam!'

Monsignor L. Cristiani,
Satan in the Modern World, 1959

The casebooks of the clergy speak volumes about the backgrounds of those who suffer from demonic control: about their plight, about the strange voices of the possessed, about their actions, about the violence often carried out by their demonic influences. Despite the relatively small number of exorcisms conducted by most individual priests, the records of the Roman Catholic Church, the Church of England and the evangelical churches are full of detailed accounts of the presence of Satan.

Judy Backworth, a shop assistant of Newcastle-upon-Tyne, was a devout Christian, deeply disturbed. When the minister, having established that she was possessed, asked during her exorcism, 'Do you want to live in peace?' a voice replied: 'I don't want her to live because she wants to serve the Lord.'

'Judy,' the minister began again, trying to exclude the demon.

'I am not Judy. I want to kill Judy. You don't believe in Satan, do you?'

'I certainly do not,' said the reverend.

'All right then, I'll prove it to you,' the voice bragged. And he then proceeded to list the most intimate details of the clergyman's private life.

Disruption is another element of the Devil's work. Pastor A. Williams tells a story of a man trying to disturb a prayer meeting in Holland in 1960. It took six or seven other men to bundle the interrupter out of the hall into a vestry. The Dutch clergy present assured Pastor Williams that this apparently normal man had suddenly displayed enormous strength, which is why it had taken so many people to quieten him. He was 'deeply sinful', they said.

When Williams asked what kind of sin, the pastors were embarrassed. 'He goes with the beasts of the field,' one said. 'I shall never forget that man, nor the manifestations of his demonic power,' Pastor Williams declares.

Animal connections sometimes feature in demonisation. A Sheffield University graduate who held a good degree in mathematics had two severe nervous breakdowns. He was taken into a room so that a minister could talk to him and suddenly got down on his hands and knees and began barking. After prayers he seemed to get better, but unless there is aftercare, who knows?

H. A. Maxwell Whyte, a well-known and experienced evangelist of Toronto, Canada, points out that the public often see performances of demonic outbursts and it is up to the minister present to have the afflicted person moved to a quiet place of prayer. Whyte was once addressing a meeting when a man jumped to his feet, shouting, 'He's lying! He's lying!' The man was shaking so hard with anger that his spectacles fell off. Unruffled, Whyte cooled the situation by pointing at him and saying, 'Young man, if you can control yourself, sit down. If you cannot, then go to the prayer room and we'll minister to you later.'

After the disturbed member was taken to the prayer room, Whyte told the rest of his audience, 'What you have witnessed is not unusual in a meeting where the deliverance ministry is being introduced. The truth of deliverance often causes evil spirits to react in some dramatic manner.' This is not because, as many assume, all deliverance gatherings are full of the ecstatic, the hysterical, the hell-roarers and the holy terrors. Those who practise deliverance regularly get more than their share of voluntary sufferers, but the mainstream churches tend to attract only those who belong or who are personally recommended by other members.

Hatred and mockery of Christ and all Christian things and persons are common. In one case, in Canterbury, Kent, a priest was exorcising Allison Fairley, an eighteen-year-old secretary, and, holding up the crucifix, called upon a demon to identify himself. Back came the snarl, 'Satan! And you bring out that puppet?'

Still holding up the cross, the priest cried, 'In the name of the Virgin Mary!'

In reply, the voice of Satan mocked, 'Madam! Oh Madam!'

Another priest, carrying out an exorcism in Bristol on Mrs Valerie Tranter, an unhappy woman who had parted from her husband, challenged the demon to 'talk to me about the blood of Jesus'. A deep male voice retorted, 'We hate the blood of Jesus.' The voice continued, sarcastically, 'She says she loves him.'

'Loves who?'

The cooler the priest remained, the more angry the voice became. 'You know who!', and after more fencing questions the word was spat out, 'Jesus!'

Pastor Williams tells of witnessing, as far apart as Seattle in Washington State, USA, and Salford in Manchester, cases of a Christian girl walking down the street and being suddenly rushed at by an elderly lady screaming obscenities, threatening violence and brandishing a walking stick. The older woman, obviously possessed by the Devil, had identified Christianity and the Holy Spirit in the younger in both instances.

One of the most difficult problems in recording the history of the possessed is that they often suffer loss of memory. Critics of the demonic argument point out that amnesia is usually a result of mental or physical disease or injury, especially head injury. But there are two types of amnesia: retrograde amnesia, which occurs before a head injury, and anterograde amnesia, which comes afterwards. Dr P. M. Yap, psychiatric adviser to the Hong Kong government, writing in the *Journal of Medical Science*, says, 'Complete possession is marked by subsequent amnesia.' Dr Kenneth McCall, writing on 'Demonosis or the Possession Syndrome' in the *International Journal of Social Psychiatry*, found that of thirty cases of possession, seven, just less than a quarter, 'did not know that any exorcism was taking place'.

The Reverend George Bennett of the Crowhurst Healing Mission, Sussex, tells of a woman who asked for deliverance.

> She swayed as I did so, as if she were about to faint, and then suddenly collapsed. I helped her to a chair and laid my hands on her, praying the Holy Spirit to flood her whole being. Two or three days later she asked me what had happened as she could not remember much of our conversation or the ministration. She [then] became a regular member of her church and was soon preparing for confirmation. It is strange how such sufferers only vaguely remember the exorcism itself.

Violence in possession cases is often a prime factor, but the clergy challenge psychiatrists and psychologists, who deny the existence of possession, to explain why a person should hurl a crucifix or some other religious object, and never a secular object, at a priest or his assistants. Such selective missile-throwing has no sound or satisfactory scientific explanation.

Dr Christopher Woodard talks about a young soldier who went out of his mind, became very violent and started picking fights with fellow soldiers and trying to kill himself. His colleagues held him to the ground. The doctor was called and, seeing that he was foaming at the mouth, remembered the Biblical story of Jesus driving devils out of a man on the shores of Galilee. He called the army chaplain, who hesitated before making the sign of the cross and saying: 'In the name of Jesus Christ, I command this thing to come out of you.' The soldier immediately appeared to be all right but the padre collapsed and died. No medical evidence could prove it, but many demonologists would conclude that the hesitant padre, certainly not prepared by concentration, fasting and meditation to play the part of an exorcist, was himself overcome by the Devil. He was said to have died from natural causes, but many did not believe it.

No one should be surprised at the sheer physical force of the demons or the demoniac. St Mark's example (v, 4–5) says that 'no one could secure' the possessed man on the shores of Galilee

> because he had often been secured with fetters and chains but had snapped the chains and broken the fetters, and no one had the strength to control him. All night and all day . . . he would howl and gash himself with stones.

And in the Acts of the Apostles (xix, 16) 'the man in whom was the evil spirit leaped on them, and overcame them, and prevailed against them, so that they fled out of that house naked and wounded.'

Reverend Christopher Neil-Smith, the well-known Hampstead exorcist, received a phone call from an actor's wife at four one morning. She said her husband was going berserk, smashing up the house, and that the other occupants were in fear of their lives. When Neil-Smith arrived he found the place in absolute chaos.

> The actor was a big fellow and had smashed a great deal of furniture and was shouting and contorting himself hideously. As I entered, a china vase shattered on the wall by my head. I immediately felt the presence of demonic evil and acted accordingly, making the sign of the cross and praying rapidly for the demon to depart. The actor's eyes glazed over and he fell on the sofa in a dead faint. He was never troubled by the Devil again.

Professor T. K. Oesterreich, who taught philosophy at Tübingen University until he was hounded out of office by the Nazis for his democratic and anti-militarist views, told of a young boy who, arriving at a church for exorcism, fell to the ground, unconscious, as soon as he passed the crucifix outside. At the exorcism he let out a terrible cry.

> We seemed no longer to hear a human voice but that of a savage animal, and so powerful that the howlings were heard at a distance of several hundred metres from the convent chapel. The weak child flung the father [exorcist] to earth with such violence our hearts were in our mouths. At length, after a long struggle, he was overcome by his father, the men who were witnesses and one lay brother, and led into the presbytery. By way of precaution we had him bound hand and foot with straps, but he moved his limbs as if nothing of the kind had been done.

Establishing cases of demonic possession requires the detailed observations of those present to be analysed dispassionately. One incidence involving violence and other manifestations was the carefully recorded case of the notably pious Mary Winters of Marathon, Wisconsin. When she was fourteen years of age, blasphemous inner voices interfered with her prayers and devotions, frightened her and caused her embarrassment and shame. Over the years, doctors examined her but could find no known medical complaint, nor any symptoms of nervous disease or hysteria. Physicians said she was normal in every sense of the word. But she did display the known signs of demonic possession. She would foam at the mouth and lose her temper when a priest blessed her. When an object had been sprinkled with holy water or blessed out of her sight she instinctively knew. She could understand and speak in languages she couldn't have known.

In 1928, when she was forty years of age, Mary agreed to undergo exorcism. She was prepared for the ritual by Father Theophilus Reisiger, a sixty-year-old Capuchin monk of St Anthony in Marathon. An expert on the subject, he chose to take Mary to a Franciscan convent in Earling, Iowa, where his friend, Father Joseph Steiger, was pastor. On her first night in the convent Mary became furious when she realised that holy water had been sprinkled on her food. She purred like a cat and refused to eat until she was given an unblessed meal.

The next day, the two priests began the exorcism in the presence of the nuns. Mary was put on an iron bed and as soon as the ritual began she became unconscious. Her eyes were closed so tightly that they could not be forced open. Nor did her lips ever move. She remained in this state until the service had ended. At one point a shrill cry filled the room, loud but apparently from far off. This was followed by the din of howling wild animals coming from Mary's motionless mouth. Despite the exorcist's call to the Devil to desist, the unworldly cacophony continued. Apart from Father Theophilus, none of the others in the room could for long withstand the pandemonium nor the sight of the twisted, distorted features of this otherwise pleasantly countenanced woman. In relays, each of the others left the room for intervals.

This continued day after day, with periods in which, although Mary was existing on only a spoonful of milk or water a day, she evacuated her bowels of large quantities of excrement and vomited bowlfuls of what appeared to be shredded tobacco leaves or other offensive matter.

By incessant questioning, Father Theophilus identified one of the demons as Beelzebub, who spoke to him through Mary's lips. Another demon, Jacob, who identified himself as Mary's father, said that he had tried to force his daughter into an incestuous relationship. He had then put a curse on her so that she would be entered by devils who would destroy her chastity. Mina, a female demon who claimed to be Jacob's mistress, joined in the litany of evil and confessed that she was damned because she had murdered her four children. A fourth, appropriately called Judas, warned that he intended to drive Mary to suicide.

To test the demonic forces, the priest put a piece of paper on which was written a meaningless Latin inscription on Mary's forehead. Nothing happened. Then he replaced it with a document which had been secretly blessed and it was torn to pieces.

As the exorcism continued, the two priests, Reisiger and Steiger, disagreed about whether the ritual should be continued or indeed ever have been begun. 'Just wait until Friday,' a demon warned.

On the Friday, Father Steiger was called away to visit a sick parishioner. Driving carefully, in view of the demonic threat, he was approaching a bridge over a deep ravine when a black cloud seemed to descend and envelop the car. He could see nothing. The vehicle crashed into the bridge railings and teetered on the edge. The priest suffered no serious injuries, even though the car's steering wheel had caved in with the impact.

When he returned to the exorcism room, Father Steiger was greeted with devilish, malicious laughter. One demon jeered, 'I certainly showed him up today. What about your new auto, that dandy car that was smashed to smithereens? It served you right.' The priest had not mentioned the accident to anyone present.

Still the exorcism continued. Father Theophilus sacrificed sleep, staying awake day and night to give the demons no respite from his verbal pursuit. On the twenty-third day, he was near to collapse and the demons were complaining about his torturous exorcism. As the evening wore on, the exorcist, sensing that the moment was right, called upon the demons, in the name of the Trinity, to depart and never trouble Mary again. Suddenly she broke free from her attendants and stood up. The stiffness left her body. Demonic voices shouted the chorus, 'Beelzebub, Judas, Jacob, Mina,' over and over again, and then, 'Hell! Hell! Hell!' But Father Theophilus went calmly on. 'Depart ye fiends of hell! Begone, Satan! The Lion of Judah reigns!'

It was all over. Mary, still conscious, said, 'My Jesus, mercy! Praised be Jesus Christ!'

Few exorcists ever witness such detailed and lengthy rituals. The extended rites are never quite the same, nor are the individual features of the possessed. For instance, levitation is now somewhat rare. The act suggests supernatural powers, but what of the ability of 'mind over matter' occultists and professional entertainers to achieve levitation?

Levitation in the theatre has been described as a trick. A rope is thrown into the air and to all appearances remains rigid enough for a man to climb it. Critics say that the rope is hooked on to a concealed cord and suspended so that the climber can hoist himself into a horizontal acrobatic position and remain there.

The ability to rise and float in the air was originally, in Christian history, the prerogative of saints like Francis of Assisi. His biography, *The Little Flowers of St Francis*, says that he was seen to rise at one time three or four cubits (a cubit being the length of the forearm); at another to the height of a beech tree and at another so high that the monk who recorded the feat could hardly see him.

Saint Teresa of Avila on more than one occasion, and sometimes during communion, found herself raised in rapture half a yard from the ground. In humility, she ordered her nuns not to speak about it. Both she and Saint Joseph of Capertino have been depicted in religious paintings engaged in such feats. When Saint Joseph saw ten workmen struggling to erect a heavy cross he 'rose like a bird in the air' and set it in its proper place without assistance. Maria of Agreda had a horror of being considered holy and resisted her ecstatic levitations so fiercely that she injured herself.

Although it is not regarded as any blanket proof of spiritualism, Daniel Dundas Home, a Victorian medium, had from the age of nineteen been witnessed and tested as he rose in the air. On one occasion he went out of one window in a room and re-entered through another. Sir William Crookes (1832–1919), the English chemist and physicist who discovered the element thallium and who went on to become President of the British Association for the

Advancement of Science, witnessed and attested that Home's feat was not achieved by trickery.

> On three occasions, Home lifted himself off the ground, once while sitting in an armchair, once while kneeling on a chair, and once while standing upright, when he levitated eighteen inches. Generally, this levitation phenomenon took place rather slowly. Home used to pull his feet up to the seat of the chair and raise his hands up in the air. The levitation phenomenon could also be transmitted to observers on the scene. Once, Lady Crookes, together with the chair she was sitting in, was levitated.

The evangelist Maxwell Whyte recalled that the first time he heard a demon speak through the mouth of someone possessed, the command was given for the demons to depart. To his astonishment, the man shot vertically into the air and came down with his mouth shaking from side to side like a dog with a toy in its jaw. After coughing, vomiting and writhing, the demons started to speak. 'We had read about demons who spoke to Jesus, but we had never heard of anyone in our day hearing demons speak to us. We knew differently then.'

Levitation at exorcisms is believed to be a demonstration by the Devil that he is capable of performing the feats of saints through people he has demonised. The voice of demons, however, is something else again.

24

Reading Stars, Seeing Spirits

A strong fascination with astrology can bring anyone into bondage and fear about their future.

Reverend Tom Walker, *The Occult Web*

Cleland Thom, a thirty-seven-year-old journalist from the East End of London whose work took him into many oddball situations, should have had no fear of the Devil or his influence. He may not have had the old-fashioned characteristics of a newsman, the face of brass and the hide of a rhinoceros, but he was tempted into the occult for the most understandable of reasons – family influence, childish inquiry and boredom.

His parents were both spiritualists and his father was a widely known spiritualist preacher. When Thom was eight years old he and his ten-year-old brother would regularly hold their own seances. 'We were absolutely fascinated by it all. It was like an adventure to us. As a family, too, we used to hold seances to seek messages from the spirits.'

Because of his long-standing involvement with such occult practices he began hearing voices.

> Things were getting worse. My personality, my sexuality, my mental and emotional state were being destroyed. I went from being a rosy-cheeked outgoing boy to someone who was moody, introverted who locked himself away in his room and would not talk or see anyone for long periods.

Cleland's interest in the supernatural was also very much stimulated by Dennis Wheatley's novels about black magic, which he read at school. Intrigued and excited by the occult, Cleland and a friend made a blood pact – cut their fingers and mixed their blood – and recited vows to Satan. Years later he found his life slowly deteriorating into depression and illness. By his mid-twenties he had twice tried to commit suicide and was convinced he was going mad. Looking back, he said:

> Entering spiritualism was like signing my own death warrant but having it happen by instalments. Many people enter spiritualism because they want comfort. But it is a false comfort that carries a curse.

Unfortunately, many who hear of such disturbing experiences – particularly those of people close to them; relatives, neighbours and friends – dismiss them as one-off incidents. They are not. There is a mass of evidence to show that they are far from being unique. And those of devout nature will say, 'Just read the Bible.'

Time and time again, the warnings are given in revised versions. In the Old Testament, in Leviticus, the third book of Moses, God tells us, 'Do not turn to mediums or seek out spiritists; for you will be defiled by them' (xix, 31). And 'I will set my face against the person who turns to mediums and spirits to prostitute himself by following them, and I will cut him off from his people' (xx 6). Deuteronomy, the fifth book of Moses (xviii, 11–12), advises:

> Let no one be found among you who practises divination or sorcery, interprets omens, engages in witchcraft, or casts spells, or who is a medium or spiritist who consults the dead. Anyone who does these things is detestable to the Lord.

The prophet Isaiah (Isaiah xlvii, 13–15) said:

> Let your astrologers come forward, those stargazers who make predictions month by month, let them save you from what is coming upon you. Surely they are like stubble; the fire will burn them up. Each of them goes on in his own error; there is not one that can save you.

Still the warnings come. The Reverend J. A. Sargent, pastor of the Worthing Tabernacle, Sussex, wrote in 1983 in *Christianity Today* that the Bible 'sternly forbids' Christians to dabble in astrology because it is basically polytheistic and 'a prostitution of revealed religion [which] reduces men to the level of a pawn.'

Yet daily millions of British newspaper readers pursue their horoscopes according to their birth signs. Of course, they say, 'It's only a bit of fun, not to be taken seriously,' but occasionally their belief in astrology, about which the ancients warned, leads to grief and even disaster. Nor is there any claim or guarantee of accuracy.

Historians have told many times how the British Secret Service, on Winston Churchill's insistence, hired Louis de Wohl, a Hungarian refugee, to cast Adolf Hitler's horoscope to determine day by day what the Führer was being advised, in the hope of predicting the enemy's strategies during the 1939–45 war. Only at the end of the war was it learned that Hitler had had his stargazer imprisoned as long ago as 1941, when the practice of astrology was forbidden throughout the Reich.

The Queen's abdication was in the stars for 1986, according to the television astrologer Russell Grant, and ten years previously, in 1976, *Old Moore's Almanack*, which has been in continuous publication since 1700, also predicted that the Queen would step down to be succeeded by her son. Not only was the first prediction inaccurate but the subsequent one is in some doubt. Grant also predicted 'money hassles' for Joan Collins, the actress, in the year her income actually reached £2 million.

The American *Ladies' Home Journal*, which has been published since 1883, hired the British witch, Sybil Leek, to write their horoscopes. Maurice Woodruff, the well-known British astrologer, predicted that in 1961 England would produce a world-beating super weapon; Castro, Nehru or Nasser would be assassinated, and Khrushchev would be ousted from power in the Soviet Union. No such weapon appeared. Fidel Castro is still alive and running Cuba in 1995, thirty-four years later; Jawaharlal Nehru, Prime Minister of India from independence in 1947, did not die until 1964; Gamel Abdel Nasser survived until 1970 and Khrushchev until 1971.

When Muriel Mackay, wife of Alick Mackay, a director of the *News of the World*, was mistakenly kidnapped in 1969 instead of the wife of Rupert Murdoch, the newspaper's proprietor, and held for ransom, members of her family were so convinced of Woodruff's powers that they hired him to predict where she would be found. Neither he nor the police ever found her body, which is believed to have been fed to pigs on Rooks Farm at Stocking Pelham, Hertfordshire.

In America, in 1977, the third Psychic Fair attracted a hundred prognosticators and five leading exponents of the art of prediction and concluded that 'a huge airliner will crash around 20 December of this year, Idi Amin will be murdered before 1978 is over, Prince Charles of Great Britain will have a sex change, the Leaning Tower of Pisa will collapse and saboteurs will blow up the Alaska pipeline.'

Curious support for astrology came from the respected Institute of Psychiatry at the Maudsley Hospital, Camberwell, south-east

London. Beverley Steffert conducted a three-year study, in which over 500 couples cooperated, which showed that marriages are happiest when partners are born under the same astrological sign. Steffert said she changed from being a sceptic to a believer in astrology as a predictor of personality. But she also had to concede that her limited statistical survey was further restricted because all the couples who took part lived in Scotland. Predictions are supposed to depend on the actual hour in which a person is born, and in the UK only Scottish birth certificates give such details.

The fact that astrology, with particular reference to showbusiness and other famous personalities, feeds the vanity of fans and is overwhelmingly and consistently wrong comes as no surprise. After all, 'everybody knows' that horoscope predictions in newspapers and magazines and on the radio and television are 'only a bit of fun'. But there is a case for arguing that there is nothing at all funny about something that trivialises human destiny.

There is an understandable attraction in being able to turn to a few words of vaguely generalised prediction that offer some interest and excitement on the horizon. But, on the negative side, the churches say that astrology reinforces the belief that there is no personal God who wants people to entrust their personal lives to His hands. It is, in short, a challenge to established religion.

Horoscopes, as we have heard from the marriage study at the Maudsley, ask us to believe that the chance and random moment of birth has a determining influence on our future; that our personalities, characters and futures are at the mercy of wherever the planets happen to be spinning at the moment we are born. Such an idea has been roundly discredited, not least by a detailed study at the University of California. There, 256 volunteers had their personalities defined by means of a long-established 'personality inventory'. Then twenty-eight astrologers were each given a birthdate and asked to correctly match it to one of three personalities randomly selected from the inventory results. Their success rate was no better than that of guessing.

One French psychiatrist listed 50,000 character traits that typified 16,000 people. He then compared these traits with the characteristics that astrologers claimed should match their birth signs and found absolutely no connection.

Despite their flawed basis, astrology and horoscopes are still capable of inflicting damage. As Dr David Enoch, an eminent consultant psychiatrist, says, 'If people's lives are controlled by such devices then it causes confusion and perplexity and can lead to disaster.'

While there is scant evidence of anyone having been hurt

through checking their stars in a newspaper, there is the danger that for some this will create an interest in seeking to know their future through more direct involvement with the occult. As the Reverend Tom Walker says in his book, *The Occult Web*, 'A strong fascination with astrology can bring anyone into bondage and fear about their future.'

There are inescapable boasted links between astrology and spiritual forces. Russell Grant, the television astrologer, helped to found the British Astrological and Psychic Society and on his nationwide Zodiac telephone line he advised Capricorns, 'If you've always wanted to study psychology, the occult or the paranormal, then now's the time to begin.'

The Evangelical Alliance cites the possible consequence. Paul Heather knows the danger to be true. In his late teens he became immersed in astrology, believing that cosmic waves influenced a person's psyche and in some situations predetermined people's lives. Through complicated mathematics and calculations he sought to bring his life into line with the cosmic influences. Paul went on to become deeply involved in many other aspects of the occult world – fortune-telling, extrasensory perception, hypnosis, psychokinesis (mind over matter), spirit-writing, thought-transference and more.

As a result, he suffered harrowing experiences when he tried to give up his interest. These included being 'beaten up' by spirits during an out-of-body experience, the psychic state during which a person is aware of the existence of an exteriorised counterpart of his or her physical body. Paul had no doubt afterwards that 'Astrology is basically witchcraft. If you are an astrologer you are dominating people's lives. Astrology becomes a controlling force.'

All this seems a long way from demonic possession, but the attraction, according to clergymen, leads – as it did in the case on which the film *The Exorcist* was based – to demonisation. This is why the Evangelical Alliance monitors such cases as the following.

A childhood fascination for the supernatural launched Robert Rustridge down a road paved with Tarot cards, crystal balls and spells. Twenty years later, he needed a church exorcism to free him from the spirits that bound him. Seemingly innocent 'fun' activities have preyed on other unwary souls in the same way.

The headmaster of an Essex school was confronted by a dozen terrified fifteen-year-olds who were seeking help after playing with home-made ouija boards, which they believed were a simple way to communicate with outside forces.

Teachers at another school in the county were shocked at the behaviour of some pupils, which included another fifteen-year-old boy who stood bolt upright during a geography lesson, shouting at a spirit to get off his shoulder, before running out of the classroom and out of the school grounds. A girl claimed to have woken in the night and seen a spectral person in her bedroom. Another child told how, after a ouija session in a block of recreation-park toilets, he was barred by a spirit from leaving the building.

Only through the help of local clergymen could these problems be resolved through prayer. The children said that they felt as if a huge weight had been lifted from them. One girl slept peacefully through the night for the first time in weeks. A clergyman likened the ouija-board craze to inviting a child to build sandcastles on a beach laid with landmines.

The case of Clive Manning, a Nottingham accountant, indicates how serious the 'harmless' game can become, even for the skilled and intelligent adult. Ouija, together with books on magic and the supernatural, was the bait in the trap for him. As a teenager, he said, 'I would read anything I could lay my hands on concerning magic and superstition.' His childhood interest in ouija boards extended to include Tarot cards and spiritualism.

> It offered me something other-worldly, and naturally my girlfriend and I became involved. Then I became plagued by constant fear of what would actually happen next, never knowing for certain.

Clive's girlfriend started to hallucinate and hear voices. The frightened couple sought release from their fearful dreams and noises, but became more and more entangled in the occult web. They tried meditation and a spiritual healer, but things worsened. Clive's girlfriend began speaking in 'other voices', which left them both terrified. The talking in tongues, said to be evidence of the Holy Spirit or possession, frequently occurs in cases of crisis, as we shall see. It led to Clive's girlfriend being admitted to a mental institution.

Clive, now in his mid-thirties, says:

> All these experimental games of our youth, ouija boards, Tarot cards and other such things, are far from harmless. If you are prepared to contact forces outside yourself, then you will do so. But many of these activities, including palmistry and astrology, can be like conveyor-belts. Once you are on them you can't get off. They are not a game. They are highly dangerous.

Children and teenagers who admit to dabbling or complain about the effects of their experiments often ask, with refreshing honesty,

'If spiritualism is wrong, why is it such a respected religion?' The answer is that it is one of the innocent faces of the occult. There are some 52,000 spiritualists in Britain compared with nearly 8 million known Christians. Yet people's attention – and particularly that of the bereaved – is regularly captured by those claiming to bring messages from beyond the grave.

Doris Stokes, the famous spiritualist medium, became a national celebrity. Her paperbacks sold in millions and she could sell every seat in the London Palladium at twenty-four hours' notice. Meanwhile, Britain's spiritualist churches and meetings report a 100 per cent growth in attendance over a five-year period.

Can they be phoney? Do they really bring messages from those who have died? Much that happens at a 'sitting' or seance can be the result of the medium using intuition and observation. Some have been accused of doing their homework on clients prior to the gatherings. But in some cases, the unexplained can be attributed to fraud for financial gain – or to demonic deception, with evil spirits communicating actual information about people who have died, even to the extent of impersonating their voices.

When I was a young reporter, the journalist Hannen Swaffer, the 'Pope of Fleet Street', was head of the spiritualist movement in succession to Sir Arthur Conan Doyle, the creator of Sherlock Holmes. In 1944 Swaffer invited me to hear him give evidence on behalf of a medium charged at the Old Bailey with witchcraft.

An explanation is necessary: Helen Duncan and three others were charged that they

> conspired to pretend to exercise or to use a kind of conjuration, to wit that through the agency of the said Helen Duncan, spirits of deceased persons should appear to be present and that the said spirits were communicating with living persons then and there present contrary to Section 4 of the Witchcraft Act, 1735.

Curiously, the Witchcraft Act was put on the Statute Book in the reign of George II not to enable people to be prosecuted for witchcraft but the opposite: witchcraft was an imposture which did not exist, and anyone who pretended to perform it must be a fraud. Times had changed since James I's obsession with witches, which the enlightened Georgians thought was all nonsense. It was ridiculous to prosecute people for practising the utterly impossible, like sorcery, enchantment and spells, or turning a poor village idiot into an animal, or something like that, when they could not possibly do so.

The act punished those found guilty of such fraud with automatic imprisonment. Even so, to this day spiritualists claim – and are believed – to create conditions in which invisible spirits may be heard rapping out messages; to put their vocal cords directly at the service of spirits whose once-familiar voices may be recognised by living friends and relations; and/or, when in a trance and under the control of their guides, to materialise the actual physical form of a spirit, not in flesh and blood, but in a strange, semi-physical, semi-spiritual substance known as ectoplasm which exudes from their bodies.

Christians will cite St Luke's Gospel xvi, 26 where Jesus taught that the spirits of dead people do not have the capacity to make contact with those who are still alive. He told the parable in which he made it clear that 'a great chasm has been fixed' between heaven and earth so that no one can 'cross over from there to us'.

There was a very good reason why the Witchcraft Act was resurrected. The offences which occupied the Old Bailey in 1944 occurred in naval Portsmouth during the Second World War, a time when parents, children, wives and girlfriends were anxiously seeking news of their lost ones, missing and presumed dead at sea. Money, too, raised its ugly head: the Crown was incensed that anyone should charge admission to any entertainment or exhibition at which someone claimed to produce the spirits of the dead.

What actually happened was that Lieutenant Stanley Worth, RN, who was curious about spiritualism, took a friend who was sceptical, Surgeon Lieutenant Elijah Fowler, RN, to a seance given by Mrs Helen Duncan. They paid 12s 6d (62½p) admission each and inadvertently switched places in reserved seats.

Mrs Duncan's guide, 'calling out' the spirits with whom she was in contact, offered 'a lady who passed over with some trouble to the lower part of her body' to the naval officer whom she thought was Fowler, the doctor, but was in fact Worth, who had taken his seat and knew nothing about such a lady. Worth was then offered 'your sister', but his sister was alive and well and driving an ambulance in London. When he queried this, he was told that she was a prematurely born sister who had died, but when Worth checked with his mother she was quite sure she had not had any prematurely born children who had passed over to the other side.

There were also produced spirits of a naval gentleman in uniform who saluted smartly, an ectoplasmic parrot (recognised by a lady in the audience as 'my dear old Bronco who used to say, "Pretty Polly" ') and a policeman so devoted to discipline and duty that he retired from the seance scene because he had forgotten his helmet and returned wearing it.

All this was too much for Lieutenant Worth, who informed the police. Officers went with him to another seance, at which a sailor in the audience claimed that a spirit's voice was that of his mother. She duly appeared carrying a dead baby who was supposed to be the claimant sailor, an only child, very much alive and sitting in the audience. Police got a hand to the ectoplasm, which turned out to be white cloth, whistles were blown, the constabulary marched in and arrests were made.

The jury took twenty-four minutes to find the defendants guilty. Mrs Duncan, who had two previous convictions for fraud, and made £112 a week – a very substantial sum in those days – conducting seances, was sentenced to nine months' imprisonment. The Witchcraft Act was never used again: such offences were subsequently dealt with under the ordinary laws against fraud.

Much more recently, Joan Williams was drawn to spiritualism following the death of her parents and her brother. She desperately wanted to make contact with them. Acting on advice from spiritualists, Joan and several friends from a Welsh village near Swansea where she lived held a meeting. 'As we sat there I could feel my chest bulging and I could see people from the past, too. From that time on I had the power to bring people back from the grave,' she said.

News of Joan's new-found abilities spread among her friends and neighbours and they would visit her, requesting contact with departed relatives and friends. Joan described how she used to 'make contact'.

> I just sat there and I would go cold. I would have a vision of the person who was dead. Then I would take on their little habits, gestures, manners of speaking and movements, symptoms of sickness, and I would speak in their voices.

The voices spoke to Joan, passing on information or perhaps making a request. During one session the voice of a woman who had died of a stroke asked to be taken to her previous home in the village. 'It was as though I were her eyes,' Joan recalled. She believed that she was a vehicle for good and performing a valuable service. But one terrifying experience convinced her otherwise.

> I was contacting a young boy who had fallen off the back of a lorry and died from a fractured skull. All of a sudden my head began to hurt. And it looked like it was covered with blood from the accident I was reliving.

Joan was so shaken that she decided then and there to give up her role as a medium. That night she began to hear voices in her head, speaking to her and threatening her. Today she is unequivocal about what happened to her.

> I wasn't in touch with the dead. It was Satan. The spirits inside me knew a great deal about the people I was trying to contact. They were using me to produce familiar voices and habits.
>
> Satan plays on people who have lost someone dear and would love to make contact with them. By taking part in all that you are lending yourself to Satan. He is evil and has no pity for you at all.

Are people like Joan Williams possessed by the Devil? Should they be exorcised? If so, who shall decide and on what grounds? That is the argument which has literally bedevilled the whole issue since the clergy first tried to interpret Christ's teaching.

The evangelists think it is tempting to believe that those living 2,000 years ago, in Biblical times, had a primitive and superstitious outlook on life and that, as a result, they blamed spirits and the Devil for illnesses that defied explanation. It has even been suggested that in ignorance the early disciples put the condition of epilepsy down to demonic possession. However an examination of the facts shows that this could not possibly have been true.

According to St Matthew's Gospel iv, 24, people brought to Jesus all who were ill with various diseases, those suffering from severe pain, the demon-possessed, the epileptics and the paralytics, and he healed them. Here it is shown that Jesus and his disciples made a sophisticated distinction between disease, pain, demonic possession, epilepsy and paralysis. One of their number, remember, was Luke, who was a doctor, so the explanations should not be so surprising.

True believers accept that Jesus and his disciples believed that and behaved as though there really was an unseen spirit world which had malevolent intentions towards the human race. The Church, in combating that evil, propounds a lifestyle which seems to have less and less relevance to the lives of an increasing number of people, particularly where matters relating to sexuality and personal relationships are concerned. While the Roman Catholic Church denounces contraception, divorce and homosexuality more strongly than the Anglican Church, many of the people involved will resolve their feelings of guilt thus induced by rejecting the Church. Yet rejecting the Church means more than merely dispensing with its moral codes. It also means abandoning the spiritual hope and comfort it provides and which many people seek.

A free moral code plus a kind of sustenance is what the near fringe of the occult, like parts of the New Age, seems to offer, and this in part explains its popularity. Generally, occult practices, in their bid to seem harmless, take the stance of the 'old religion' that existed before Christianity. Nudity, sexual freedom and removal of inhibition all play a significant role which may well be magnetic to those oppressed by Christian-induced guilt.

Left in the middle, between the discipline of the Christian Church and the indiscipline of the other groups, are those vulnerable to demonic influence and the possessed. And there is the rub. Some churches and some priests have laid on exorcisms as a matter of course; others will only consider them in extreme cases.

Monsignor Luigi Novarese, the official Roman Catholic exorcist for Rome, estimates that he has exorcised only about sixty people during a career spanning thirty years. Father Dominic Walker of Brighton, who heads the Anglican Church's perpetual study of possession and exorcism, believes he has come across only seven genuine Satanists in his wide and varied career.

Other priests and exorcists vary in their estimates and many Protestants will not use the exorcism ritual, insisting on 'deliverance' through simpler prayers, counselling, discussion and ministry. They admit to no failure and seem not to have come across cases where the troubled person remains possessed and might need to be passed on to a more experienced priest or even to a psychiatrist.

Driving out demons was known to primitive peoples. It belonged to the realms of magic and witchcraft. The concept of possession and exorcism as we know it is essentially Christian. Contemporary Judaism, Islam and Buddhism have an equally divided credence for demons, some claiming they belong to a distant mythical past.

Possession must have a psychological or perhaps a physical cause. With this in mind, sympathy for the sufferer's religious beliefs is generally regarded as helpful. But counsellors, advisers and friends are all faced with the crucial question: what constitutes possession? Literally, the definition is simple enough – obviously, it is when an individual is, or feels he or she is, taken over by an alien personality.

Anthropologists know that the idea is universal and age-old, occurring in virtually every culture, religion and society known to man. Often the idea of being possessed is avidly sought and taken as a sign of approval by the gods. Drugs, sexual activities and physical endurance rites have been developed to encourage a state of possession in places as far apart as the Amazonian jungles, the deserts of North Africa, the plains of India, the forests of Alaska and the jungles of Borneo. The famous possession rituals of Haitian voodoo have been made on occasion into a touring theatrical show.

Here we are only concerned with individual demonic possession.

Symptoms have been listed through the centuries, and because the diagnosis of possession has been so often mistaken through human error, epileptics have been treated as possessed. Writhing, foaming and convulsive fits do occur in possession cases, and other physical symptoms do look like a horror tale, as we have seen.

During the past fifty years there have been a handful of recorded cases which have included some, but by no means all of the symptoms. In Britain, few cases involving spectacular physical behaviour are recorded. Those that are tend to lean towards violent and anti-social rather than extraordinary behaviour. Mostly they involve girls or young women who step out of character and become abusive, angry, foul-mouthed, suicidal and neglect themselves.

Sex and sexual activity, or lack of it, play a prominent part in possession cases. Not untypical, apart from the fact that the demon was the spirit of a dead pop star of some note, was the case of a teenage girl exorcised by the Reverend Bob Whitfield. She claimed she had contacted the star through a ouija board. She assumed sexual fits and convulsions and at times managed to produce a voice similar to that of the dead performer. At the end of the exorcism, Whitfield said, 'The evil has been lifted. But the longing for the enjoyable side of her evil – a sexual longing – is still with her.'

Sexologists may well query whether a 'sexual longing' can really be seen as a 'side of evil'. But there is often a sexual cause for the behaviour encountered in possession cases and it is an important aspect of the whole subject.

Historic church records contain remarkably few cases of men being possessed, but there are hundreds involving women and pubescent children. A constant characteristic of demonic possession in convents over the centuries is the sexual nature of the women's behaviour, involving display of the genital organs, masturbation, the assumption of coital positions and streams of foul, blasphemous, obscene and explicit sexual language.

It would be a mistake to think that because of the limited number of violent cases of demonic possession and exorcism on record they are not increasing. They are, and in alarming numbers.

In 1986, Cardinal Ballestero, the Archbishop of Turin, shocked the city by appointing six specially trained priests to deal with the growing demand for exorcism from people who believe they are possessed by the Devil. The fact that the Devil is making himself felt in Italy's greatest industrial city, rather than in some old centre of mediaeval learning or a city traditionally tied to ideas of pleasure and licence, accounted for the sense of shock. Indeed, Turin has a reputation for being rather puritanical.

The cardinal said that the problem was very real. He described as incredible the number of people who attributed their troubles to the Devil or felt themselves to be possessed. His team of new appointments was drawn from priests with wide experience of exorcism. 'It would be a mistake,' he said, 'to regard them simply as priests armed with holy water. They are expert theologians, anthropologists and psychologists.'

Again, he blamed it all on the falling off of religious faith. 'When faith declines, people look for substitutes.'

Meanwhile, in Britain, the Archbishop of Canterbury, Dr Robert Runcie, was so alarmed at the growth of Satanism that he directed again that every diocese should have a trained exorcist and that three bishops should supervise the whole problem.

25

Satanic Child Abuse

The victims of child abuse are the little ghosts . . . They are invisible. They are voiceless. I weep for the mothers and their children.
Esther Rantzen, television presenter and founder of Childline

The epidemic of ritual child-abuse scandals in Britain can be traced to early 1988, when several social workers with a fundamental charity became concerned about ritual abuse after reading some American materials about the so-called 'signs' of such offences. The panic spread through several channels, including the evangelical Christian movement, the books and testimonials of 'survivors', 'deliverance' ministries and 'experts' from the United States, who circulated the message through the media and on conference circuits. Particular channels of preaching and believing were the Christian organisations such as the Association of Christian Psychiatrists and the Social Workers of the Christian Fellowship, individual churches, anti-occult campaigners and 'born-again' survivors of Satanic abuse.

Some British social workers went to the United States to be trained in how to identify ritual abuse. Back in England, they organised several conferences on the topic, first at Reading University, in September 1989, and then elsewhere. This helped more than anything to popularise what became a Satanic cult conspiracy.

American 'experts' in ritual abuse, Chicago police detective Robert 'Jerry' Simandl and 'ritual abuse' counsellor Pamela Klein, who had met at a police conference on the subject and had gone into business together, were brought in as guest speakers. Ms Klein was behind videotapes used by social workers to detect abuse in San Diego, where faulty findings caused an uproar. In the USA, she had identified a total of fifty-two children who, as a result, had been taken from their parents and made wards of court for a period of time, ultimately being returned to their families when no evidence of ritual Satanic abuse could be found.

Klein had lived in England for six months between July 1985 and January 1986, during which time she set up in business with Norma Howes, an English social worker, as a 'consultant' for cases of sexual abuse. Howes claimed to have identified eighteen cases of Satanic ritual abuse in England between 1987 and 1990. She was the interviewing 'therapist' in the first English case of Satanic cult abuse in Kent in 1988, in all cases using the same Klein-imported indicators.

The Reading conference was also attended by Maureen Davies of the British Reach-Out Trust, who described hardly believable scenes of blood-drinking and cannibalism said to be part of Satanic rites. The seminar was followed by a series of organised 'teach-ins' during which participants passed on information to local social workers and childcare specialists.

The English social workers, who felt that the Americans were more informed about how to detect these crimes, then went about 'uncovering' cases of ritual abuse in England. Some of the children's stories were traced by investigative journalists and police detectives to child-protection workers who had attended the Reading conference, and from them back to Simandl and Klein. These American 'experts' had, for instance, claimed that babies in the US were being cooked by Satanists in microwave ovens. Similar bizarre stories were heard soon afterwards in Britain, allegedly from the mouths of children being interviewed intensively by the child-protection workers.

Six months after the Reading conference, on 13 March 1990, the National Society for the Prevention of Cruelty to Children (NSPCC) announced that Satanic child abuse was common in Great Britain. Sexual perversion, animal sacrifice and the drinking of blood were among the bizarre rites which were supposed to be adding a shocking new dimension to the abuse of the young.

On 14 June 1990, social workers began raiding homes on a poor housing estate in Rochdale, the old cotton-manufacturing town that has been absorbed by Greater Manchester. Police and social workers took away seventeen children from their parents, placed them in protective custody and interrogated them for signs of ritual abuse.

For six months, by means of court injunctions, the authorities kept journalists from reporting the case. Finally, on 9 September, the *Mail on Sunday* launched a series of scathing attacks on the affair. An initial complaint came from teachers of one six-year-old boy who, they said, was telling bizarre stories of black magic and the killing of babies. The children were made wards of court and put into foster care, without parental visits being allowed, while social workers questioned them. After weeks of interrogation the social workers claimed that the children were all victims of a secret Satanic cult which had abused them in sexual rituals.

This diet of sex, sadism and occult religion was meat and potatoes to the more sensational sections of the media. Gradually, through serious investigative journalism, the picture that emerged was one of deep concern that the children had been unjustly taken from their parents by a bureaucracy that was either possessed or obsessed with Satanic ritual abuse.

The social workers defended their positions but the cases the Rochdale authorities brought against the parents were finally made the subject of a judicial inquiry set up to investigate the charges themselves as well as the practices of the social workers. Mr Justice Douglas Brown ordered the children to be returned to their parents on 8 March 1991, nine whole months after they had been seized. He severely criticised the police and social workers for needlessly traumatising the children. He noted that no evidence had ever been produced of missing, dead or mutilated babies and that the worst the parents had done was to allow young children to watch horror videos like *The Evil Dead*. The day after the court case, Gordon Littlemore, the director of Rochdale Social Services Department, resigned in disgrace.

By then, Rosie Waterhouse in the *Independent on Sunday* magazine had suggested:

> Evangelical Christian groups are also largely responsible for spreading stories last year that children were being sexually abused by Satanists in black magic ceremonies, and that teenage girls were being used as 'brood mares' to produce foetuses for sacrificial rites. No evidence of these practices has been found by the police.

The foetuses, according to other observers, are required for their blood, which, along with that of babies, is alleged to be drunk at orgiastic ceremonies. Where did the social workers get these ideas? Norman Cohn traces these accusations with great thoroughness in his work *Europe's Inner Demons* through 2,000 disgraceful years. He points out that early Christians, dissident Christian sects and witches in the Middle Ages were all in turn accused of engaging in orgies of sex, baby-killing and cannibalism in the service of evil. Originally, secular cults were blamed for it, but the mediaeval church reinterpreted the traditional libel and slander by blaming the worship of demons.

Academic Dr Gillian Bennett, the editor of the folklore journal *Dear Mr Thoms*, noted that these proceedings were said by Cohn to take place in underground tunnels, a feature of the accusations in so many British cases. She said:

> I am not in a position to judge whether the children of Rochdale or other places were abused. (I suspect that child cruelty of all kinds including incest and child abuse is much more common than we would like to think.) But I am confident that, if they were abused, it was not in the context of Satan-worship, murder or cannibalism. I believe that the notion of obscene and deviant sex (such as the abasement of one's own children) is by 2,000 years of tradition so bound up with notions of ritual murder, cannibalism, Devil-worship and subversive conspiracies by groups of people outside the pale of 'normal' humanity that it was almost inevitable that sooner or later the whole complex would be politicised in our own time.
>
> It's quite hard in this [Rochdale] case to assess which is the target group of the libel, child-abusers or Satanists. Judging from the extent to which modern pagans are now lobbying MPs, it looks as if it is Satanists who feel themselves to be the victims and Christians who are the accusers. Though the popular perception would seem to be different – here it is [incestuous] parents who are seen as the targets and social workers who are the accusers.
>
> Why people should want to believe such vicious and incredible lies of any group at all is, of course, another question altogether.

Just as the social workers were retreating back to their headless department in Rochdale and the whole affair was dissolving amid public criticism, another disgraceful episode was looming in the far north of the country.

In the Orkney Islands, where one child in ten is in council care, a group of social workers in St Margaret's Hope on the island of South Ronaldsay were investigating another so-called child-abuse ring. Ironically, according to Ernest W. Marwick in *The Folklore of Orkney and Shetland*:

> The Devil, although not unknown in the north, was regarded more as a theological hypothesis than as a personage who might come to transact his business in a visible, much less a theatrical manner.

The social workers focused on what was later described as 'Family

W.'. The father of the family had previously been convicted of sexual abuse and three children were still in care. According to statements made by these children in February 1991, incidents of ritual sexual abuse had taken place near a quarry outside St Margaret's Hope, involving them and nine other children from families designated as 'M.', 'B.', 'H' and T.'.

According to one of them, the rituals were conducted by a man called Morris, who wore 'a long black cloak with a hood and a mask covering his eyes'. Children dressed in white robes ran and danced in a circle of gas-lamps around him while music called 'The Power of the Night' was played from a stereo in a caravan nearby. Then he would hook one of the children with a shepherd's crook and have sexual intercourse with her. One of the children also recalled that Morris sometimes dressed as a turtle.

Social workers identified the leader as the Reverend Morris Mackenzie, Church of Scotland minister on South Ronaldsay, who had previously been linked to sexual abuse by another of the children of Family W.

Social workers in the city of Glasgow, more experienced in such matters, expressed misgivings about the children's testimony from the start. But the island's social work director, Paul Lee, organised a task force to raid the four families' homes at 7 am on 27 February and removed nine children aged between eight and fifteen from their parents and the island. They were not allowed to take personal belongings with them because toys might carry a 'possible symbolic meaning' that could limit their ability to describe their experiences. For the same reason, messages from parents to children were intercepted and letters from children were never delivered. The parents said their telephone lines were tapped. Even Easter eggs sent by parents were broken open to see if they concealed messages or anything else.

Medical evidence revealed no physical signs of sexual abuse but three children from three families gave accounts of being dressed in turtle suits and abused by a man in a black cloak whom they called the master or the prime minister. Later accounts added that children were sometimes dressed as Brownies or Boys' Brigade members and that two of the families' mothers also made love to the Reverend Mackenzie, one dressed as a cowboy and the other as a white ghost. One social worker noticed that when two of the seized children were parted, they gave each other 'a masonic handshake'.

Mackenzie's lawyer suggested that these stories were influenced by the cartoon series, *Teenage Mutant Hero* or, as it is known in the United States, *Teenage Mutant Ninja Turtles.* One social worker noted that in three of the W. children, memories of the ritual abuse were triggered by a poster of the characters. During the official inquiry she was asked, 'Have you heard of a turtle called Splinter, an old wise turtle, who carries a stick and wears a robe? Is that news to you?' The social worker replied, 'That's news to me.'

Master Splinter, the turtles' good Ninja mentor, is in fact a mutant rat who does not normally wear a robe or carry a stick. The 'master' to whom the children could have been referring was the evil arch-enemy in the popular British TV fantasy series *Dr Who*. In episodes screened as recently as spring 1990, he sometimes did wear a black robe. And in an early episode, 'The Daemons', the Master did carry out a quasi-Satanic ceremony to summon a powerful alien. Even though he did not carry a stick, could this not have been the image in the children's minds?

The cases were much criticised, largely by members of the South Ronaldsay community, who supported the parents' attempts to regain custody of their children, even though none of them were native Orcadians, but had recently moved to the area for the away-from-it-all lifestyle. Islanders ridiculed the claims that such rites could take place without attracting local attention. South Ronaldsay became known as 'Devil's Island'.

The cloud of suspicion dismayed the God-fearing islanders who went to church to pray for deliverance from the blight of scandal. The kirk criticised the social workers.

After a month of agitation, the case was heard by Sheriff David Kelbie. In Scotland, the sherrif presides over a children's panel in a judicial capacity in cases involving delinquent youths and the care and welfare of the young. Sheriff Kelbie ridiculed the Satanic abuse evidence and asked, 'What is ritualistic music?' It could be from Australian pop star Kylie Minogue or from *Phantom of the Opera*. On 4 April, the very day the Rochdale case collapsed, the sheriff threw the case out as 'fatally flawed' after one day of testimony. But social workers insisted on appealing against the decision. Conceding that media attention had made it impossible to re-prosecute the cases, they insisted that they had followed proper procedures and denied that they had been influenced by seminars or other cases involving 'Satanism'.

When Sheriff Kelbie threw out the case, angry parents stormed the offices of Paul Lee, head of social services. 'It's criminal what they did,' said one mother as she joined others in a call for resignations. The judgement dismayed the Royal Scottish Society for the Prevention of Cruelty to Children (RSSPCC). There were other calls for the protection of children, not from Satanism but from excesses of official zeal.

The RSSPCC backed the police and social workers in the appeal.

But the children still went home. 'Hip, hip hooray! I'm going home today,' they sang. 'Why did they keep putting words in my mouth?' asked one literate child. But a top social worker warned of a backlash. Professionals and parents took up their stances and the situation was left in turmoil.

On 12 June, Kelbie's peremptory dismissal of the case was unanimously overturned by the Scottish Appeal Court, which found that the sheriff had passed judgement on evidence that had not yet been presented to the court. The appeal judges held that:

> He allowed himself to form views about the content of the productions [of the social workers] which would have made it impossible for him to bring a fair and balanced judgement to the issues which were before him when evidence was being led. The effect of what he did was incalculable.

Continuing public controversy, however, initiated an official inquiry into the handling of the affair which was convened on 26 August in Kirkwall by Lord Clyde and continues to the time of writing.

The whole issue left a nasty taste in the mouths of many. The Orcadians were enraged by the removal of their children, a child-abuse file had been created and island parents feared every knock on the door – and in a place called Hope! Meanwhile, other ministers on the island rallied round the Reverend Mackenzie. One moment it appeared that the islanders were trapped in a nightmare as child abuse, once a subject not talked about, came out into the open. The next, as Orkney parents asked the Prime Minister to intervene, the pendulum seemed to swing the other way.

Social workers admitted that they had made mistakes. A respected Orkney GP complained that he 'was not consulted'. The Orkney action group rapped the methods of inquiry and the angry debate was not helped by the arrival of a group of white witches to join the fray.

Three weeks had passed before it was revealed that all the allegations came in the first place from three local children. There was an immediate call for change in the rules of evidence for sex-abuse cases but the care order for the children to be kept away from their families was maintained. The role of the reporter, the official to the children's panel, was criticised.

Television presenter Esther Rantzen, who had set up a charity to combat child abuse, went to Scotland to lead a newspaper investigation into what she called 'the little ghosts of Orkney. They are invisible. They are voiceless. I weep for the mothers and their children.' But 'tabloid hysteria' was attacked as the full hearing into child-abuse claims began. Lawyers argued that the care orders could not remain in place while the custody of the children was being debated in court in the absence of the children.

Obsession with Satanism had put families through a living hell and unanswered questions were to haunt them for a long time to come. As one parent said, 'One nightmare is over but another is just beginning.' The sheriff's criticism of the Orkney officials revealed loopholes in a system which parents had believed had much tighter safeguards. Orkney social services officials had taken the ritual fears to heart and now they sought an advisory council to protect them from possible error and judicial attack. But no one was really satisfied.

Four families believed they had been failed by the system. They took their children home to a normality that hid dark anger. The Orkney decision was lauded and lambasted. While officials called for protection and a redirection of criticism, the children were almost forgotten. An appeal was made for specialised teams on child abuse and an official government promise that dawn raids to snatch children would be a last resort. All this helped play down the trauma.

Meanwhile, another chapter had been added to the professional history of American Pamela Klein, who was believed to have influenced the hysteria. A legal judgement disputed her qualifications in a criminal case involving allegations of ritual child sex abuse in which she appeared as a 'therapist' for the child. On 13 February 1991, in Illinois, Cook County judge R. Morgan Hamilton ruled that 'Pamela Klein is not a legitimate therapist as defined by Illinois law' and dismissed her from the case. Affidavits presented to the court revealed that Klein had exaggerated or falsified some of the qualifications included in her *curriculum vitae*.

The case involved a five-year-old child who had started to cry during a police presentation about child abuse. Taken by police to be interviewed, she told how she had been sexually touched on her clothed genital organs the previous day by John Fittanto, her friend's stepfather. Fittanto was arrested on the strength of the girl's accusations. By order of the court his stepdaughter was taken from him and his wife and placed in the custody of her natural father.

After being interviewed by Pamela Klein repeatedly in the weeks following the initial complaint, the child elaborated her story with tales of extremely bizarre events. The girl claimed, among other things, that Fittanto committed various sexual acts with her with other men present while the acts were being videotaped; that he deliberately cut himself with scissors and smeared blood on his face and made drawings with the blood; and told her that the Devil would kill her brothers if she told anyone.

A medical examination found no evidence that the girl had had sexual intercourse. The case against Fittanto was dismissed by the trial judge on 23 August 1991, for lack of evidence. His step-daughter was returned to him and his wife after a period of eighteen months. As sociology professor Jeffrey S. Victor says, 'There is no way of determining the exact circumstances and perceptions which led to the child's initial allegations. However, the stories of 'ritual abuse' have been shown to be obvious fabrications.'

In a later case involving Pamela Klein, affidavits were provided by Illinois state child protection officials stating that Klein had been involved as a consulting 'therapist' in at least three other cases in which children also made allegations of sexual abuse. The affidavits stated further that Klein used questionable methods of interviewing, asking 'legal' questions, and drawing conclusions not based on facts. In none of the cases was anyone found guilty of the accusations against them.

26

The Twenty-One Faces of Sarah

[Multiple personality disorder] is a very, very rare condition. Because of TV talk shows it has become the fashionable disease of the month and the plea of the year.
Dr Darrold Treffert, director, Fond Du Lac Healthcare Centre

Margaret Hilton is forty. She sometimes speaks like a child of four. She was taken to the London Healing Mission at Notting Hill, which isn't a church in the usual sense of the word. It shuts on Sundays – its services are held midweek. An average of one hundred people attend. Some are in need of private help, which the missioners call deliverance, not exorcism. The sufferers are blessed, there may be a laying-on of hands, a question about belief and trust in and love of the Lord. Such deliverances from minor demons may last something like a quarter of an hour. Margaret's deliverance lasted much longer, something like sixteen hours. By diligent but friendly, persistent but encouraging questions, there emerged this Satanic history.

All the women on Margaret's mother's side of the family have been high priestesses. Her grandmother and her mother hoped she would take their place. Margaret started early – she was brought into a Satanic group at the age of four. She was raped at the same age. She was tied to an upside-down Satanic cross. The cult, like some other Satanic groups, keep a private zoo. They injected a puma with a sleeping drug, nailed the animal to the cross, slit its belly down the middle and put Margaret inside.

As a result of this and other experiences in a Devil-worshipping environment she has developed multiple personality disorder. She has five distinct personalities. In one character, the girl of four, she still talks about the puma as a big brown pussy-cat.

During her deliverance she told how she was constantly being told that she was dirty. 'Dirty girl' is an admonition she frequently uses as if she is repeating an adult reprimand over and over again. She was so dirty she was put in a black box. Her four-year-old persona did not know the word ‘coffin’. Hours had to be spent invoking the power of the Holy Spirit to break her memory and habit of repeating stories of the ‘brown cat’, ‘dirty girl’ and the image of the ‘black box’ and release her from her sense of guilt.

Margaret was blessed with holy water. She suddenly said – still in the voice of a four-year-old – ‘I like that.’ Again and again she repeated ‘dirty girl’ and began washing herself with the holy water. Fully clothed, she washed her hands, arms, neck, between her legs and all over. ‘I like it. Water tastes lovely. I love water.’

Mrs Arbuthnot, the pastor’s wife, said to her, ‘If you like it, why do you not make some yourself? When you have a bath tonight, bless the water in the name of the Holy Trinity, ask God’s help, and wash yourself with it. He would like you to do that.’

The Reverend Andy Arbuthnot recalled that the session ended when the forty-year-old woman with the voice of a four-year-old kept staring wide-eyed at each bare corner of the room and saw big angels in the first three. To a child all adults are big. The angels stretched from the floor to the ceiling. She stared at the fourth corner and said, ‘I know who that is. That’s Jesus.’ She described him in detail, the beard, the smile, the holes in his wrists and his hands stretched out to her. Then she turned up her nose and said, ‘There’s something else on the floor there, dark . . .’ She shuddered. Arbuthnot demanded in the name of the Lord that the darkness, another spirit, image or representation of the Devil, the stain on the floor, depart. And it did.

That is Arbuthnot’s story of Margaret Hilton, but could she not be schizophrenic or a sufferer from multiple personality disorder. Arbuthnot held a responsible post in a City of London finance house but gave up mammon to found the London Healing Mission and deliver the masses from the Devil. He is dogmatic, has no time whatsoever for psychiatrists, believing that while he, by prayer and laying on hands, can successfully bid the demons depart, psychiatrists can only incarcerate the patients in mental hospitals and feed them with drugs without cure or hope.

Curiously, while some churchmen accept that there is multiple personality disorder in some cases of demonisation, some psychiatrists disagree. They acknowledge the presence of schizophrenia, the most common major psychiatric disorder, reckoned to affect about 1 per cent of the population of the western world. Schizophrenia is not a disease in the normal medical sense and the diagnosis is based entirely on the behaviour and statements of the affected patient. Schizophrenics are said to have delusions, hallucinations, disordered thinking and a loss of contact with reality. They indulge in non-logical reasoning, mix up literal and metaphorical expressions and use invented words. The cause has never been established, but case histories suggest that schizophrenics find life intolerable and adopt an alternative reality as a means of escape. In addition to the environmental theory, there is an argument that the illness can be inherited. Patients can be treated to conform with normal social behaviour by anti-psychotic drugs. Psychoanalysis, a help in many mental disorders, is of no value in the treatment of schizophrenia.

Now, if psychiatrists accept the split personality of schizophrenia and clergymen think the other personality may well be the Devil, why does the same not apply to multiple personality disorder? It may well be that the two disorders are the same, only one more complicated than the other. It is important to be aware of the danger, for MPD is much more often associated with crime, and crime of a kind which suggests to some demonic influence.

MPD sufferers may have all the symptoms of schizophrenics but they are expressed through different ages and, of course, different voices. They cannot fit into ordinary acceptable social behaviour, cannot communicate or get on with their fellow human beings and believe themselves to be social and occupational failures. Some are quite oblivious to the fact that there is anything unusual about them. They may be eccentric, histrionic, suspicious, cold, have an excessive or erotic interest in themselves or be otherwise preoccupied with themselves. They may have exaggerated self-importance, undue dependency on others, extreme lack of self-confidence and rigidity of habits. And, according to doctors, counselling or behavioural therapy is seldom very successful in MPD patients.

The greatest difficulty in diagnosing such spiritual or medical complaints – or are they both medical and spiritual? – arises from the fact that the evidence comes almost entirely from the behaviour and explanations of the sufferer himself. An examination of the classic cases illustrates the point.

Ever since the phenomenon of multiple personality was first described by an American doctor called Mitchill in an article published in 1816 entitled 'A Double Consciousness, or a Duality of Person in the Same Individual', it has aroused argument and scepticism among doctors and driven an even greater wedge between doctors and clergymen. It confuses the questions 'mad or bad?' and 'sad or mad?' Fiction drew attention to the argument but did not provide the answers. At the time Robert Louis Stevenson was writing *The Strange Case of Dr Jekyll and Mr Hyde*, which was based on, but over-dramatised, the real-life case of Deacon

Brodie, a respectable professional man by day but a burglar of the Royal Mint by night. His night-time activities resulted in him being hanged.

Neurological wards were filled with young ladies with bizarre paralyses. Morton Prince, a well-known neurologist, described the famous case of Miss Beauchamp, a prim, self-righteous, moralistic young lady who eschewed the pleasures of the flesh but developed an aggressive other self. Then, under Prince's hypnosis, there emerged a third personality, Sally, who mocked Miss Beauchamp's ladylike ways, although Miss B. knew nothing of Sally.

In the years since the heyday of hysteria and the theories of Freud, such cases have, according to records, declined. Not one of the 250 known incidences has been recorded outside Europe or North America. This may be due to the more sophisticated health care of those regions, but another viewpoint is that the way of life in other parts of the globe is less complicated, more spiritually sound, demands are fewer and therefore less mental health care is necessary or available.

While many doctors believe that MPD is the invention of the attention-seeker and the malingerer and some clergy are cautious, public attention is quite often drawn to some eye-catching stories. The best known is that of Christine Sizemore, on which was based the 1957 film from 20th Century-Fox, *The Three Faces of Eve*. Her illness was discovered and treated by psychiatrists Corbett H. Thigpen and Hervey M. Cleckley. Film star Joanne Woodward was called on to play the three personalities: a drab, colourless housewife; a mischievous, irresponsible sexy adventurer and a sensible, intelligent and balanced woman. The psychiatric sessions in the film, while possibly authentic, could easily confuse the layman. Entertainment, based on but not entirely comprising fact, is often thus.

In 1993, Joan Frances Casey, a psychotherapist working with an MPD patient, published *The Flock*, which deals with this bizarre and fascinating psychiatric condition. She said of one patient:

> I usually see Renee and Jo during each appointment, and I can tell when a personality switch is occurring. There's always a pause, a lowering of eyelids. Then Renee comes in a flash – bright, gay and immediately orientated. Jo comes slowly, seemingly dazed, fuzzy, almost drugged . . . Sometimes the transformation period, which lasts no more than half a minute, brings yet someone else in. Those same eyes, so pleading and full of pain in Jo, so twinkling and merry in Renee, grow cold and full of contempt.

Dr Ray Aldridge-Morris, psychologist author of *Multiple Personalities: A Case of Deception*, thinks MPD is an illusion. Experiments do take place in which patients are encouraged to fake other personalities. This can be achieved under hypnosis which is being conducted for a totally different reason. In cases of hysteria, hypnosis is used to draw the focus away from the symptoms. In their place the patient concentrates on one fragment of his personality and magnifies it to produce another personality.

'MPD is a very, very rare condition. Because of TV talk shows it has become the fashionable disease of the month and the plea of the year,' according to Dr Darrold Treffert, director of the Fond Du Lac Healthcare Centre. 'It's a condition fairly easily induced in a very suggestible patient.'

MPD patients are said by some critics to be encouraged to play the parts of their fragmented personalities – which may include the overpowering mother, the colonel, the trickster, the prostitute and more – but they are not real personalities, just actors. So the debate returns to whether or not the screen and the stage might be the proper niche for MPD rather than serious medical or spiritual study.

Robin Skynner and John Cleese, in *Families and How to Survive Them*, explained that there are demons that couples keep hidden behind their mental screens which sometimes take charge of their daily lives with disastrous results. But is that a case of MPD, which is being argued by psychiatrists, or demonisation, which is being debated by clergymen?

Before Hollywood gets its hands and cameras on more cases of MPD, the champions of the different points of view should study again the following cases.

In 1990, Mark Peterson, a thirty-one-year-old bespectacled, fair-haired grocery worker from Oshkosh, Wisconsin, strolled up to a group gathered on the bank of a fishing pond in Menominee Park. He sat down beside a twenty-six-year-old woman who called herself Franny. During the next few minutes Peterson noticed that her personality underwent several profound changes.

He asked her if she would like to go out dancing. She agreed. Some friends of hers in the park told Peterson that her real name was Sarah. They explained that she suffered from MPD and had twenty-one personalities. Undeterred, Peterson telephoned 'Franny' and invited her out. According to her story, they drove to a coffee shop, where Franny told Peterson about Jennifer, another personality, whom she described as a 'twenty-year-old female who likes to dance and have fun'.

When the couple got back into Peterson's car, he summoned

Jennifer and asked her, 'Can I love you?' She answered, 'OK.' Later, Jennifer said she thought it was an invitation to go dancing.

Peterson stopped near a park, lowered her seat back and started sexual intercourse. During the act, the personality of a six-year-old girl, Emily, suddenly intruded. Peterson told Jennifer to tell Emily to keep their amorous activities 'a secret'. Instead, Franny and Emily 'told' Sarah, the predominant personality. Sarah subsequently told the police that she had been sexually assaulted.

Did a crime actually take place? Which personality said yes to sex? Which personality later said no and complained? Peterson was charged with rape and the subsequent case broke new ground. Until then criminal cases which had involved MPD sufferers had been confined to those who committed crimes themselves. They pleaded that their own original personality was not involved but that one of their other selves was responsible. They could, under the McNaghten rules, plead that they were not responsible for their actions by reason of insanity or that they were mentally unfit and incompetent to stand trial.

In Sarah versus Peterson, for the first time, the evidence of a victim claiming to have the disorder, it was thought, could result in Peterson being sent to jail for rape for up to ten years. Sarah's claim was that she was mentally ill and as a result was unaware of having sex with the defendant. That meant that she was, she said, sexually violated.

During one hearing, three of Sarah's personalities had to take the oath separately. In each instance, she closed her eyes, paused, then opened them again to speak and act as different people. At one point the judge asked that a glass of water be given to the witness. Later, another personality did not remember having taken that drink.

The jury faced the issues: was Sarah mentally ill at the time? Was she able to evaluate Peterson's conduct at the time? Did Peterson know of Sarah's mental condition?

Peterson's defence was that Sarah was not mentally ill nor mentally deficient. She appeared to be perfectly normal and there had been sexual contact between consenting adults. There is absolutely nothing illegal about that. Unfortunately for Peterson, he had admitted to the police that he knew Sarah had several personalities and that six-year-old Emily was 'peeking' while they had sex.

The prosecution set out to demonstrate that Sarah was mentally ill and therefore had been victimised. Peterson had learned about her disease, then called upon Jennifer, the personality who most wanted to have sex, 'the twenty-year-old female who likes to dance and have fun'. He even told that manipulative personality to keep it their little secret.

Peterson was found guilty of engaging in sexual intercourse with a person he believed to be mentally ill and who could not assess his conduct. But the case did nothing to solve the belief or disbelief in MPD. Nor did it answer the question whether a demon in Sarah tempted Peterson.

John Parry, director of the American Bar Association commission on the mentally disabled, says, 'There's a great deal of disbelief about this disorder, a concern that people are faking.' And Dr Frank Putnam of the National Institute of Mental Health says that while people with the disorder are no less honest than anyone else, 'They may have trouble with memory of some facts, since amnesia is one of the complications of the condition.'

MPD, used in that case for the prosecution, has generally been used as a defence. Terror stalked the Ohio State University campus when four female students were abducted, forced to cash cheques or use bank or credit cards to obtain money, then driven to some lonely country place and raped. Acting on a mysterious anonymous telephone tip-off, and a mug-shot identification by one of the victims, police arrested twenty-three-year-old William Milligan.

Milligan had been physically abused as a child, cashiered from the navy after only one month and was constantly in trouble with employers and the police. He was sent to a psychologist and during the session she addressed him as Billy.

Milligan replied, 'Billy's asleep. I'm David.'

Psychiatrist George T. Harding Junior was called into the case along with Cornelia B. Wilbur, the psychoanalyst who melded the sixteen personalities of a patient known as Sybil, an achievement which was later the subject of a film and a stage play. In the Milligan case, Harding came to the conclusion that William or Billy had multiplied himself into ten different people, from Arthur, a twenty-two-year-old rational Briton who tried to repair the damage done by other personalities, to Christena, a vulnerable three-year-old.

Milligan's personalities used different voice patterns and different facial expressions, scored different IQ levels and, when given pencil and paper, turned out very different artwork. Ragen, aged twenty-three, spoke with a Slav accent and was almost devoid of concern for others. Danny and Christopher were decent, quiet teenagers, but Tommy, who was sixteen, and had enlisted in the navy – and who had some similarities to Milligan himself – was depressed, withdrawn, socially isolated, cold, aloof and sometimes eccentric.

What shook the experts more than anything else in this case was that the personality who abducted the girls, forced them to obtain cash and then raped them was a woman. Milligan said she was Adelena, who was nineteen and a lesbian.

Among the others he identified was Allen, a talented eighteen-year-old artist and the only personality who smoked, and David, a frightened and abused child who may have made the telephone call which led to Milligan's arrest. The police telephone number had been found on a pad next to Milligan's phone when he was arrested.

Billy, however, was the core personality, guilty, suicidal and 'asleep' for most of the previous seven years while the others took over. When Wilbur, the psychoanalyst, first summoned up Billy, Milligan jumped off his chair and declared, 'Every time I come to [when another personality is called up] I'm in some kind of trouble. I wish I were dead.'

Psychiatrists believe that Milligan's MPD is a desperate attempt to handle conflicting emotions by parcelling them out to different 'people'. Its roots are in a warped childhood. Milligan was the illegitimate son of two entertainers from Florida. When he was three his father committed suicide. His stepfather physically abused his mother and sodomised young Milligan, threatening to bury him alive if he told anyone. As a teenager, Milligan fell into trances and walked the streets in a daze. He was imprisoned twice, for the very same offences for which he was now under arrest, rape and robbery.

Whether Milligan should stand trial was in this case a moot point. The court held that the personalities were sufficiently fused to a point where Milligan should be tried. Confinement in prison on remand, however, produced a new problem. Milligan confronted his lawyer with a picture he had drawn of a rag doll with a noose round its neck, hanging in front of a cracked mirror. Doctors and others thought he was out of control, but was that picture not truly representative of his mental condition?

Others thought he was in control three days later when he questioned his attorney about how certain he could be that his other personalities would be protected and get a fair trial. Christena, writing beside a drawing partly believable as the work of a three-year-old, said:

Why do I gotta stay in a cage and can't got out to play
Do you like I luv Sam
Mr A— say you going to help us
A great big hug an a kiss for Miss Judey

The table, butterfly and vase of flowers beneath the writing was a trifle too symmetrical for a child of that age and 'From Christena' was a little too well spelled. But a different message came out of the prison cell from Tommy, the sixteen-year-old schizoid:

I'm sorry I took your time
I am the poem that doesn't rhyme
So just turn back the page
I'll waste away
I'll waste away.

If the owners of the various personalities already recounted were not in need of exorcism or deliverance, what are we to make of the twenty-seven faces of Eric, also known as Charles, and by twenty-six other names?

Dazed and bruised from a beating, twenty-nine-year-old Eric was discovered wandering around a shopping mall at Daytona Beach. He had no identification on him and acted so oddly that an ambulance crew, who took him to a nearby hospital, assumed he was retarded. After six weeks he was transferred to the Human Resources Centre, where he began to talk to doctors in two voices. One was the infantile voice of a young Eric, the other the measured tones of an older Eric.

According to the older personality, his immigrant German parents had died and a harsh stepfather and his mistress had taken him from his native South Carolina to a drug-dealer's hideaway in the Florida swamps where, Eric said, he had been raped by several gang members and had watched his stepfather, David, murder two men.

Nearly two months later, a counsellor saw Eric's face twist into a violent snarl. He spat out a stream of obscenities which reminded Malcolm Graham, the psychologist directing the case, of a scene from *The Exorcist*. 'It was the most intense thing I have ever seen in a patient,' he said. Graham diagnosed MPD, which often follows a severe trauma. Again the Devil or demons were not mentioned.

During the ensuing weeks, the other personalities emerged. Dwight was quiet, middle-aged; Jeffrey, a hysterical blind mute; Michael, an arrogant athlete; Tina, coquettish, regarded by Eric as a whore; Mark, a menace; Philip, an argumentative lawyer. Malcolm Graham explained: 'Philip was a pain. He was kind of obnoxious, always asking about Eric's constitutional rights.'

Gradually, Eric revealed his twenty-seven different personalities, which included three females, one of whom was a lesbian. They ranged in age from a foetus to a sordid old man who kept trying to persuade Eric to fight as a mercenary in Haiti. In one therapy session, Eric shifted personality nine times and the psychologist, who had eleven years' clinical experience, said, 'I felt I was losing control of the sessions. Some personalities would not talk to me and some of them had much insight into my behaviour as a psychologist as well as Eric's.'

Most of the personalities interacted. Cye, a religious mystic, once left a comforting note for Eric. Michael, the pushy athlete, who loved rock music, hated Eric's classical records so much that he yanked the wires from a stereo. Eric defended Mark the menace, saying, 'Mark never hurt anybody. He is just there to scare other people off when they get too close.'

Eric referred to his troupe of personalities as his 'talking books'. Another was Max, a librarian, who occasionally announced a change of personality by saying, 'A book fell off the shelf.'

All the personalities knew about Eric's terror of David, his stepfather. When Eric said he had seen a member of his stepfather's drug gang near the therapy centre, Graham protected his patient by establishing a new legal identity for him as Michael Eric Sontag.

Within six months, Graham's therapy, conversation and hypnosis had apparently rid his patient of many of the personalities. Suddenly, there appeared a new one, a sophisticated, overbearing male, known only by the initials T. K., who threatened to expose Eric's new legal identity to the drug gang. That night T. K. 'committed suicide' by drinking a single beer. The next morning a friend found Eric in what appeared to be a drugged state.

When he awoke, he announced yet another surprise. He gave his real name, which the psychologist agreed to keep confidential. He suggested that Eric called himself Charles and when they parted they exchanged home phone numbers and addresses. The patient chose that moment to tell the psychologist that the German parents, the wicked stepfather and the Florida drug ring were all fiction. But he insisted, and showed, that he still suffered from MPD.

He came from a middle-class home, had once been captain of the high-school swimming team, sports editor of the school newspaper and a bright student. He told the centre clinical staff that he had a nervous breakdown in his senior year caused by his failure to prevent his girlfriend having an abortion. He said, 'I've lived through hell. I'm surprised I didn't go crazy, except perhaps I was already there.'

After nine months, Charles moved out of the centre to live in an apartment, taking the personalities with him. They seemed to have an uneasy pact. He was sore all over for three days because Michael, the athlete, went for a fifteen-mile jog. He talked openly about his personalities. 'I can see they've really had fun these last nine months. They have been fighting amongst themselves and not worrying about me at all. They let me shave and then they leave me alone and go out.'

But whenever Charles tried to walk to a library where he could research MPD he blacked out and changed into one of the other personalities. Eric has read *I'm Eve*, the book of the film *The Three Faces of Eve*, and leaves a copy in his flat, but Charles won't read it. 'I want to get rid of all of them but I don't want to upset them either. I'm afraid one of them will come out and won't let me come back.'

Psychologist Graham has been encouraged by the success of his therapy. He began talks with his patient's real parents. Then Eric emerged and wanted to quit the treatment for good. 'I feel so lonely now,' he complained. But Graham, who once thought that Eric was the core personality, is cautious. Who is the real one? It may be Charles. After all, the third face of Eve, the sensible, intelligent and balanced personality, turned out to be a sham. And Christine Sizemore, the real Eve, went through seventeen more years of torment from nineteen other personalities before she was finally cured in 1974.

Where there is no permanent cure or solution in medicine the Church may have the answer. When the Reverend Andy Arbuthnot is asked whether deliverance is the answer to the problem of demonisation – he does not accept the word possession – he says:

> There must be hundreds of thousands of women incarcerated in psychiatric wards drugged up to the eyeballs who will never be able to get it right. The only way to treat the problem is by the ministry of deliverance. I have met only two clergymen who were also psychiatrists. I think they have two masters, medicine and the Church.
>
> In twelve years we have referred only two people to a Christian psychiatrist and in both cases he has destroyed their faith. In an abstract way the doctors accept the existence of the spiritual. The whole essence of our faith, the answer to the problem, is a love of the Lord. The answer to the whole thing. Body, soul and spirit. If the medical profession leave the crucial spiritual side of man's nature out of their work there is going to be a defect in their approach. If the clergy is too imbued with theologically liberal ideas they shrink it. They either don't understand it or are frightened of it.
>
> My wife and I were talking to an Anglican bishop and we told him about some of the more hairy cases that the Lord sends our way. I said there are not that number of clergymen who are into this. His instinctive reaction was that they would not dare to be.
>
> Even with the 1963 Church of England commission and the idea that there must be thorough psychiatric and priestly

examination, there will still be disasters on both sides. The archbishop's rules are completely impractical and crazy. The rules are that if I am faced with someone we both recognise as demonised I must make an appointment with the diocesan exorcist and with a practising psychiatrist one or two months before I can do anything. If I have someone in my chapel after a service who is manifesting demonisation, in nine cases out of ten it is a perfectly simple deliverance. Whatever the problem, we get down to it right away. In this mission there may be two or three cases of deliverance going on simultaneously.

But are psychiatrists in many hospitals not trying to do the same thing, under a different name, in a different way, but with the same goal – the peace of mind of the patient?

27

The Possessed Priest

The exorcist must be as certain as possible . . . that his assistants will not be weakened or overcome by obscene behaviour or by language foul . . . they cannot blanch at blood, excrement, urine.

Malachi Martin, ex Jesuit professor,
***Hostage to the Devil,* 1976**

Few people can explain better in layman's language just what goes on during the Rituale Romanum exorcism of the Roman Catholic Church than Malachi Martin, former Jesuit priest, former professor at the Pontifical Biblical Institute in Rome and former Vatican diplomat. Although the Church of England at one time banned exorcism, many Anglican priests continued to practise a form of that rite. In his 1976 work *Hostage to the Devil*, Martin tells of a possessed woman whose evil spirit hides behind her innocent, disarming grin. Then there is the evil spirit which attacked the exorcist and horribly violated his body so that he had to spend weeks in hospital, a parallel to the true story behind the film *The Exorcist*, in which one priest was slashed from shoulder to wrist and required a hundred stitches, as we saw in Chapter 11. A top radio announcer was possessed, as was a leading university parapsychologist whose exorcist was gifted with psychic powers which enabled him to free the possessed from the Devil.

Eyebrows were raised when Father Martin told how even a priest can be possessed. The words turned out to be prophetic. The priestly author was himself an example of his own warning: he was alleged to have been involved in scandal, had a love affair with a journalist's wife, quit the priesthood, moved to New York where he became a television guru on religious matters.

Father Martin is a specialist in the Dead Sea Scrolls and holds a doctorate in Semitic languages, archaeology and Oriental history. He studied at Oxford and at the Hebrew University and is versed in the study of Jesus through Jewish and Islamic sources as well as Christian ones.

The Jesuits (Society of Jesus), to which he once belonged, were founded by Ignatius Loyola in 1534 to fight the Reformation and preach to the heathen. They became so thoroughly disciplined, organised and secretive that they attracted both civil and religious enemies. They were suppressed by one Pope, reconstituted by another and had their influence and power severely limited by the current Pope, John Paul. Because their theology resolved many problems of conscience and duty by false reasoning, the words 'Jesuit' and 'Jesuitical' became synonymous with a deceiver or prevaricator. This has done much to mask the positive achievements of the order.

Before Malachi Martin quit the Jesuits, his works were much respected and the truth in them survives to this day (though one Jesuit father asked me whether the words of Martin I was intending to quote were uttered before or after he quit the ministry before he would give priestly comment or approval).

Malachi Martin defined the ideal exorcist as follows.

> Usually he is engaged in the active ministry of parishes. Rarely is he a scholarly type engaged in teaching or research. Rarely is he a recently ordained priest. If there is any median age for exorcists, it is probably between the ages of fifty and sixty-five. Sound and robust physical health is not a characteristic of exorcists, nor is proven intellectual brilliance, postgraduate degrees, even in psychology or philosophy, or a very sophisticated personal culture. Though, of course, there are many exceptions, the usual reasons for a priest being chosen are his qualities of moral judgement, personal behaviour and religious beliefs – qualities that are not sophisticated or laboriously acquired, but that somehow seem always to have been an easy and natural part of such a man.

The Christian rite of exorcism is very short, consisting chiefly of Scriptural commands to Lucifer to depart. But the actual time it takes to drive out a demon can vary enormously, as we have seen. The exorcist is allowed to use his judgement to decide whether or not or how long to carry on fighting the Devil and driving him out.

Circumstances may differ widely, as is shown by contemporary written and voice recordings of exorcisms. They do, however, have some things in common. First, there is an all-pervading awareness of non-human evil, often, as in many of the cases covered here, manifested by an icy chill, temperature and stench. The evil spirit will pretend that he is one and the same person as the subject of the exorcism. The priest will by exhortation try to get the Devil to reveal his presence, so that the Evil One often speaks through the mouth of the possessed in an unfamiliar or even unnatural voice. The paranormal Devil, on the other hand, will, using that other voice, even reveal the otherwise unknown sins of the exorcist and his assistants, as in the case of Judy Backworth in Chapter 23.

One of the characteristic ploys of the Devil is that he impersonates the possessed by using 'I' as if they were one and the same person. When he is unmasked by the exorcist and named as the demonic power, he uses the first-person plural, 'we'. While beforehand he speaks only through the mouth of the human being, he then seems to come from anywhere or nowhere in the room, and certainly not from the usually tightly closed mouth of the subject. An example of this is the experience of Mary Winters, covered in Chapter 23.

Exorcists have described this dismembered voice as unnerving. Here is a priest trying to drive out the demonic spirits from a human being, which requires concentration, piety, quiet and prayer, and there is a constant Babel of voice or voices interrupting and trying to put him off. To win, the exorcist must silence the Devil.

The moment the voice falls silent, the demon must be directly challenged, in the name of Jesus Christ, His power, His cross, His blood. At this moment comes victory or failure. The exorcist and the possessed at that point are said to be tortured by unbearable mental and physical anguish and torment. Exorcists have been known to die during this clash of good and evil. When this occurs the exorcist's priestly assistant must immediately take his place in the fight.

Exorcism can take place in stages, even over several years, but what must be understood is that no person can be possessed without their consent. That is the essential concept of possession. A person is tempted by Satan, succumbs of his own volition and must be rescued. It would be unthinkable and defeatist for a Christian to suggest that anyone could be possessed who surrendered themselves up to the Devil.

What is not generally appreciated is that possession and exorcism are universal, common to all religions and beliefs at all times and places. Demonic possession has always been misinterpreted and sometimes dismissed as derangement. Very often there are both medical and spiritual problems. Exorcism is one of the means used to restore the afflicted person to normal behaviour. And this treatment was provided by priests long before it was performed by psychiatrists.

The perceived fundamental disagreement between priests and psychiatrists has now become blurred. Psychiatrists have become priests and priests have taken up psychiatry for precisely the same reason. The comparison can be taken a stage further. A psychiatrist is himself often expected to undergo psychoanalysis. A priest, before he may become an exorcist, must have experienced some form of demonisation before he can be permitted to fight the Devil to exorcise others.

According to *L'histoire des diables de Loudun* (1716) – the history of the devils of Loudun – 'Exorcists almost all participate, more or less, in the effects of the demons, by vexations which they suffer from them, and few persons have undertaken to drive them forth who have not been troubled by them.' Unfortunately, the horrors of priestly inquiries into mediaeval witchcraft were worsened by the behaviour of priests and exorcists who were themselves probably possessed by the Devil at the time.

More than one historian has compared the pagan and the Christian ideas of possession. The difference, in Catholic demonology, is that possession by any evil spirit must be possession by a Christian Devil. Only a Christian Devil will obey the commands of the exorcist on behalf of God and His Church. Christian rites of exorcism, however, are not fundamentally different from similar ceremonies performed in other religions against possession by demons of those religions. Exotic differences include the rituals of the Hindu Indians, who blow cow-dung smoke, burn pig excreta, pull the hair of the possessed or cut and burn it, wedge rock salt between their fingers, or tie a blue band round the neck of the afflicted. Other Orientals offer the Devil sweets and other gifts as bribes to encourage him to depart. Only the Roman Catholic Church holds to an adaptable written ritual.

Even poltergeists, which are not held to be vulnerable to Christian exorcism, are to this day driven from houses and, as wits are wont to point out, even from bridal suites.

As the New Testament provides so many lessons, instructions, examples and explanations on the question of casting out devils, it was hardly surprising that the Christian Church introduced exorcism at a very early stage. Exorcists formed one of the four minor orders of the priesthood. In fact, the whole Christian faith, its progress and success, owes much to their reputation. Justin Martyr, whose death in the second century provided the first account of martyrdom, wrote in his *Apology*:

> For many of our Christian men exorcised numberless demoniacs throughout the whole world and in the city of Rome and in the name of Jesus Christ. They have healed and do heal them, rendering the possessing devils helpless and driving them out of the men, who could not be cured by all the other exorcists or by those who use incantations and drugs.

From this we can see that as early as the second century, those regarded as phoney exorcists or 'doctors' with drugs were perceived as the necessary opponents of Christian exorcists. In those days there was a simple service of petitions, prayers and the laying-on of hands. This took from the third to the seventeenth century, much more than 1,000 years, to crystalise into the three-chapter Rituale Romanum of the Roman Catholic Church. Despite its verbiage, its essential message is in the power of calling up Jesus – as Origen, the second-century Greek theologian said –

> whose name has already been seen, in an unmistakable manner, to have expelled myriads of evil spirits from the souls and bodies of men, so great was the power it exerted upon those from whom the spirits were driven out.

One version of the Roman ritual is reserved for exorcising geographical places and specific buildings possessed by demons. In the early days it extended to animals. The New Testament tells of the Devil passing into the herd of Gadarene swine. St Jerome's fourth-century *Life of St Hilary* recalls that:

> Brute animals were also daily brought to him in a state of madness, and among them a Bacterian camel of enormous size, amid the shouts of thirty men or more who held him tight with stout ropes. He had already injured many. His eyes were bloodshot, his mouth filled with foam, his rolling tongue swollen, and above every other source of terror was his loud and hideous roar. Well, the old man ordered him to be let go. At once those who had brought him as well as the attendants of the saint fled away without exception.
>
> The saint went by himself to meet him, and addressing him in Syriac said, 'You do not alarm me, Devil, huge though your present body is. Whether in a fox or a camel you are just the same.'
>
> Meanwhile, he stood with outstretched hand. The brute, looking as if he would devour Hilary, came up to him, but immediately fell down, laid its head on the ground, and to the

> amazement of all present showed suddenly no less tamenes than it had exhibited ferocity before.
>
> But the old man declared to them how the evil, for men's account, seizes even beasts of burden; that he is inflamed by such intense hatred for men that he desires to destroy not only them but what belongs to them.

Even in 1995, priests of all faiths hesitate when asked, how do you know, how do you tell, that a person is possessed by the Devil or by demons or by evil spirits? Explanations seldom seem entirely satisfactory and it is clearly a matter of deep faith and belief which cannot be explained in logical and material terms.

The German scholar Vincentius von Berg, wrote the mediaeval *Enchiridium* (handbook) on exorcism and defined the test: the person must have fled at the sign of the cross, holy water, the name of Jesus, etcetera; said anything against the Catholic faith; excited the mind of the possessed to pride, vainglory, despair, etcetera; refused to discuss the possession with the priest; appeared with a loathsome or dejected appearance; departed leaving a stench, noise, frightfulness or injury; or approached mildly, but afterwards left behind grief, desolation, disturbance of soul and clouds of the mind.

This list has lasted until very late in the twentieth century. Berg was asked to list 'indications by which it could be ascertained if anyone were bewitched into possession'. He listed the following symptoms:

> The bewitched desire the worst food. They are unable to retain their food, are irked by continual vomiting, and are unable to digest. Others experience a heavy weight in the stomach as if a sort of ball ascended from the stomach to the gullet, which they seem to vomit forth, yet nevertheless it returns to its original position.
>
> Some feel gnawing in the lower belly; others feel either rapid pulsation in the neck or pain in the kidneys. Others feel a continuous pain in the head or brain, beyond endurance, on account of which they seem oppressed, shattered or pierced.
>
> The bewitched have trouble with their heart, which feels as if torn by dogs, or eaten by serpents, or pierced by nails and needles, or constricted and stifled.
>
> At other times, all parts of their head swell up, so that throughout their body they feel such lassitude that they can scarcely move. Some experience frequent and sudden pains, which they cannot describe, but they shriek aloud.

> In others the body is weakened and reduced to a shadow on account of extraordinary emaciation, impotency of vigour, and extreme languor. At other times their limbs feel whipped, torn, bound or constricted, especially the heart and bones. Some are accustomed to feel something like the coldest wind or a fiery flame in their stomach, causing the most violent contractions in their entrails and intense and sudden swelling of the stomach.
>
> Many bewitched are oppressed by a melancholy disposition. Some of them are so weakened that they do not wish either to speak or converse with people.
>
> Those injured by witchcraft may have their eyes constricted, and the whole body, especially the face, almost completely suffused by a yellow or ashen colour.
>
> When witchcraft has by chance befallen the sick, he is generally attacked by some serious trouble, seized with fear and terror; if he is a boy, he immediately bewails himself and his eyes change to a dark colour, and other perceptible changes are observed. Wherefore the discreet exorcist takes care to disclose the recognised signs of this sort to the relatives and those present to avoid scandal.
>
> It is especially significant if skilled physicians are not sure what the affliction is, and cannot form an opinion about it; or if the medications prescribed do not help but rather increase the sickness.
>
> Sometimes the only indications of bewitching are considered circumstantial and inferential, as employing witchcraft for hatred, love, sterility, storm-raising, ligature or harm to animals.

The exorcist has always been free to carry out the ritual at his discretion, particularly where 'skilled physicians are not sure what the affliction is'. That explains the historic antipathy between medicine and the Church and the present-day mingling of medical doctors who are also clergymen. But who, even within the priesthood, can possibly explain how he knows a person is possessed, whether or not to perform an exorcism and which type of exorcism it should be?

Most stories about exorcism concentrate on the sufferings of the possessed. Little is ever said about the pains of the exorcist. He undertakes terrible risks when he takes on the Devil. Not only does he isolate himself perhaps for months, often fasting, before the ritual itself, but he must be prepared to have his own personal secrets, and those of his family, exposed and their voices mimicked, by this paranormal Satan. He, like the possessed he has been called upon to help, may also suffer the feelings of guilt that he, too, is demonised.

The Church, knowing that exorcism has such dangers and is not to be undertaken lightly, imposes a number of safeguards, such as the presence of witnesses, especially where women are to be freed, because the Devil often encourages women to seduce the exorcist and anyone else present. It is also essential that the priest is forbidden to say or do anything 'which [unwittingly] might provoke obscene thoughts'. There is no doubt that in some of the barely believable exorcisms of the Middle Ages, in which exorcists came to such improbable conclusions, they too must have been diabolised, as in the case of the nuns of Loudun in Chapter 4.

Although the rite of exorcism is itself very short, the questioning to establish who are the individual possessing demons may take time. The individual devils are asked their names, how they are demonising the sufferer and whether they propose to stay in possession for a limited time or forever. And the exorcist is required to ask the exact time the demon entered the body and the precise time he will leave.

Only then, when the last devil is ready to depart, does the priest invoke the traditional exorcism rite, 'I, —, Minister of Christ and the Church, command you, unclean spirit, to depart.'

The witchcraft delusion which caused so much unnecessary anguish and death was an excuse to complicate the rite of exorcism and more than half a dozen additional features were added, including whipping, as a means of identifying which party, devil or possessed, enjoyed flagellation.

Today, the place of the exorcism is always prepared. Because the Devil is violent, all movable objects are removed. Not only ornaments, table lamps and similar smaller objects, but all unnecessary furniture is taken away, for chairs, tables, dressers and even wardrobes have been known to be flung about. Usually there only remains a bed on which the possessed may lie and perhaps be restrained and a small table to hold a crucifix, candle, holy water, prayerbook and other religious paraphernalia necessary for the ceremony. It will include salt, which represents purity, wine, which typifies the blood of Christ, and strong-smelling herbs, like hellebore, a plant that was once supposed to cure madness, attar of roses for remembrance and rue for penitence.

Because of the dangers, the exorcist will never work alone. He will always be assisted by one or more junior priests, preferably including a trainee exorcist. The principal assistant acts as a guide and monitor, keeping the exorcist to a logical agenda so that he is not misguided by the perverting voices and antics of the demons.

He will provide physical aid if necessary and if the exorcist is physically attacked or collapses under the strain of the ceremony the assistant must take his place and not abandon the necessity of getting rid of the enemy. Malachi Martin defines the position:

> The exorcist must be as certain as possible beforehand that his assistants will not be weakened or overcome by obscene behaviour or by language foul beyond their imagining; they cannot blanch at blood, excrement, urine; they must be able to take awful personal insults and be prepared to have their darkest secrets screeched in public in front of their companions.

The idea that exorcism is necessarily a guaranteed permanent answer to possession is not encouraged. The demonised are nowadays usually advised to keep in touch with their medical advisers as well as the priest, to beware the return of demons, voices, temptations and interference by keeping busy, concentrating on work, hobbies, reading, sports, listening to the radio and watching television, all to prevent the possibility of a recurrence of demonic distraction.

Why then, if the so-called possessed person cannot always be cured spiritually, can he not be left alone to be cured by medical doctors?

Despite the modern blending of therapeutic and spiritual minds, many fundamentalist priests maintain that demonic possession is one thing and epilepsy, hysteria and multiple personality disorder are another. Many doctors still hold that what the church and sufferers call possession is a misperception or an hallucination. Those in the middle believe that doctors in the name of medicine can cure one ailment, clergymen in the name of Christ can cure another. They work together to try to discover which malady belongs to which professional cure. This is why chaplains permanently attached to National Health Service mental hospitals are paid salaries by the state.

If we take the extreme medical view, symptoms of 'possession' can be caused by epilepsy, hysteria and multiple personality disorder. During a convulsive seizure a person with epilepsy, for instance, can experience extreme muscular rigidity and foam at the mouth and is sometimes subject to rapid backward and forward head movements which are not unlike those of the 'possessed' person who twists the head through 180 degrees.

The 'belly-speaking' and other strange, guttural noises unlike the subject's normal voice may be produced in an epileptic by a spasm of the throat muscles. Epileptics, immediately before a seizure, experience strange sounds and voices, hallucinate and are subject to distortions of the other senses. Most epileptic seizures last no more than five minutes.

Exorcists maintain that these symptoms occur in the demonically possessed and that the attacks last much longer. The muscles are lively rather than rigid and the muscular reflexes are not weak but strong. And, as we have seen, other symptoms of possession, defined in the Rituale Romanum – such as speaking in tongues, divulging future and hidden events and other powers beyond the subject's age and natural condition – do not fit any medical diagnosis.

Earlier this century, Professor Paul Richter of La Salpêtrière, the famous Paris hospital for the mentally disturbed, was treating eighteen-year-old Mademoiselle Madeleine Russier and seeking a diagnosis when, suddenly:

> We heard loud cries and shouting. Her body, which went through a series of elaborate motions, was either in the throes of wild gyrations or catatonically motionless. Her legs became entangled, then disentangled, her arms twisted and disjointed, her wrists bent. Some of her fingers were stretched out straight, while others were twisted. The body was either bent in a semi-circle or loose-limbed. Her head at the time was thrown to the right or left or, when thrown back with vehemence, seemed to emerge from a bloated neck. The face alternately mirrored horror, anger and sometimes fury; it was bloated and showed shades of violet in its colouration.

No doctor, taking all these symptoms into consideration, would automatically dismiss the suggestion that possession is all mediaeval superstition and ignorance without offering an alternative diagnosis. What the French doctor observed was an unusual simultaneous combination of all of the symptoms of demonisation. The body 'bent in a semi-circle' is known as the hysterical arch and is frequently seen in cases of possession. All the other symptoms he described have occurred during carefully monitored and recorded exorcisms. Livid marks on the skin, even when they resemble bites, or even letters or graphic symbols interpreted as 'demonic writing', can also be produced by hysterics.

So, faced with identical symptoms, how else can we distinguish possession from illness? The most frequent determining factor is the religious context in which the symptoms occur. Most, if not all, demoniacs who are candidates for exorcism have a background, active or inert, in religious worship, although the connection may not be with the church from which they seek help.

If their symptoms arise in tandem with a hatred of religious objects, which they would normally respect, and are accompanied by other phenomena – clairvoyance, knowledge of hidden holy objects, understanding of languages never learned or levitation – then the Church is most likely to decide that they are manifestations of a demon resident within. That is possession.

Since psychiatry is an interpretive discipline, some practitioners may well argue that these extraordinary symptoms are due to faulty recognition, even hallucination; even that the exorcist may have been in a trance at the time. The less sceptical may view them as parapsychological while still denying the existence of the Devil or demonic work. The Church will still insist that whatever the doctors say, when all or any of these symptoms occur at the same time in a normally Christian person who is displaying an uncharacteristic hatred of all things and persons religious, then he or she is demonically possessed.

28

Deliverance Not Exorcism

Even if our belief in individual demons . . . has long faded, the Christian priest . . . is still faced with people whose sickness can be understood only in the New Testament terms of possession.

Reverend John Richards,
***But Deliver Us From Evil,* 1974**

In the last decade of the twentieth century, the existence of demonic possession has been questioned more and more frequently by churchmen and women. Can a person be possessed by something which has no form and cannot be seen? If a person can be possessed by the Devil or by demons or their agents, can they be freed from that control by exorcism?

In Chapter 26 we met the Reverend Andy Arbuthnot, missioner at the London Healing Mission in Notting Hill, west London, who does not use the word 'possession' because he believes it is misleading. He says:

> The Lord, in His wisdom, has chosen to send to this mission for ministry a succession of people who have been deeply caught up on the other side and, in several cases, have been actual leaders of quite large Satanic groups, if not leaders of Satanism internationally.
>
> Yet we have never met anyone, however deeply they may have been on the other side, who has not ultimately been in a position to exercise their free will and to choose to come out.
>
> It can be desperately hard for them. Of that there is no doubt. I remember the first witch we dealt with. She told us that she was the ninth woman to try to get free

> from that community and that each of the eight before her had finished up committing suicide.
>
> It can be desperately hard for them to come out but, in our experience, there is always the element of free will left to the person for them to make the choice and, if they really want to, to get free.
>
> This being the case, I think the word [demonic] possession is misleading for, to the lay mind, to be 'possessed' means that one no longer has the option to get out.
>
> Furthermore, the very word 'possessed' is a mistranslation of the Greek text which came in with the Authorised Version of the Bible, so there is, I believe, no Biblical basis for it. The Greek word is almost always *daimonizo*, meaning to be affected by demons or, in other words, to be demonised.
>
> At the same time, we are aware here of the almost desperate need among Christians for balanced books on deliverance which are both Scriptural and which, at the same time, draw on the practical experience of those who (sometimes against their own wishes!) have been drawn into this ministry.
>
> Jesus's words to His followers are so clear – 'preach the gospel, heal the sick, and drive out unclean spirits' – and the sin of omission on the part of the main-line churches in not having the courage to teach on deliverance has the result of leaving the field wide open for the enthusiastic amateur who will barge in on a deliverance situation without being led by the Holy Spirit and will thereby often do very real harm.
>
> From the enthusiastic amateur exorcist, Good Lord, deliver us!

This view is shared by the preacher Michael Harper, who says the word 'possessed' in ancient Greek means 'having a spirit'. Bishop John Robinson, an eminent New Testament scholar, says it does mean to be possessed, and he cannot see how it can mean anything else. 'To have a spirit' and 'to be possessed' are represented by two different words in that language. Even though the classical Greek word for deity has been translated in the New Testament as demon, it is not necessarily wrong, for the demons are the gods of sex, of money, of wine, of drugs and so forth.

Andy Arbuthnot at once raises a number of other important issues. He uses the word 'witch' as if such a person is an agent of the Devil, yet, as we have seen, the popular conception of witchcraft today is much more likely to be considered an imposture. Was it not always an impossible craft, an invention of the clergy to keep their flock in fear, faithful and obedient; a delusion and therefore an imposture on the religious and intellectual life of the people for centuries?

Even if the word 'possession' in the Authorised Version of the Holy Bible is a mistranslation, it is still very much relied upon in Christian teaching. The man in the tombs who was chained and fettered because he was thought to be possessed by the devil was released by Christ. And St Luke's Gospel viii, 36 says, 'They which also saw it told them by what means he that was possessed of the devils was healed.'

Dictionaries, encyclopaedias and books of Christian teaching still use the word 'possessed' to mean possession by a demon or evil spirit; 'to possess' being to occupy and dominate, control or actuate. Many will hold that even if it were a mistranslation, the meaning could still be accurate as understood through the ages. Nor is this altered by the fact that a demonically possessed person can be so controlled voluntarily or involuntarily. Does the Devil not take advantage of the voluntary experimenters as well as the weak and defenceless? Freeing a voluntarily possessed person who does not want to be separated from the Devil might prove difficult, however.

A totally different view is taken by the Reverend John Richards, who was for nine years secretary of the Anglican Bishop of Exeter's study group on exorcism. He says:

> Even if our belief in individual demons with names and describable characteristics has long faded, the Christian priest or minister is still faced with people whose sickness can be understood only in the New Testament terms of possession. There are kinds of behaviour which are otherwise unaccountable and seem to result from control by an alien or evil power. These things are realities.

Psychology, often cited as the scientific enemy of religion, has not denied this. But sufferers from hysteria; those who are withdrawn, solitary, socially isolated, cold and aloof and sometimes eccentric; and those who have delusions but whose intellect and reasoning capacity remains unimpaired, can be treated by psychiatrists.

Richards believes that the clergy can recognise possession states, but there is no technique of healing which can be studied and practised and put into effect 'Cure,' he says, 'is by the Church in the name of Jesus Christ and the exorcist has authority and faith, not superior knowledge or any acquired power.'

Somewhere in between Arbuthnot and Richards come the pragmatists. Dr David Ashby, who teaches theology to tomorrow's

Methodist preachers at Cliff College, Calver, Derbyshire, takes a practical viewpoint.

> If I am faced with a person who thinks he or she is possessed, and that person is writhing on the floor like a snake, or behaving in the traditional physical way of the possessed, and I do not think it is genuine then I will leave the room. I will tell them that I am going to the loo or to make a cup of tea. When I return they will probably be sitting meekly but comfortably on a chair.

This illustrates the need to treat each case individually. A family doctor looks at each patient separately, and so should a parson. Exorcism may be the proper course to cast out demons, but in some cases the laying-on of hands and similar lesser forms of deliverance may be more appropriate and far less traumatic.

The use of the word 'vibrations' or 'vibes' in popular culture has done much to put across the idea of the presence of good, which religion identifies as the Holy Spirit ('good vibes'), and the existence of evil, the Devil or demons ('bad vibes'). The *Daily Mirror* magazine described the exorcisms of the Reverend Christopher Neil-Smith:

> He uses his hands [like a water diviner] instead of a twig. If there is an evil force, he feels it in his hands as a tingle or a sharp sting. After commanding the evil spirit to depart, he makes the sign of the cross and lays his hands on the possessed person, and as he does so he feels a very strong vibration which shakes the pair of them until the evil has gone. It appears that one is having a struggle with the person but it is not that at all. It is the evil force in the person having received the impact of the power of God through his hands.

Soon after the tragic Barnsley case, reported in Chapter 12, in which the subject of an all-night exorcism promptly murdered his wife, the Methodists began to tackle the conflict in Christian attitudes towards possession. They found that there are three currently held views. The first is that the process of exorcism involves the casting out of an objective power of evil which has gained possession of a person. This stance includes the conviction that the authority to exorcise has been given to the Church as one of the ways in which Christ's ministry is continued in the world. Some who hold this view believe in the reality of evil spirits while others prefer to speak of people as being overpowered by a personal force of evil.

To others, the process of exorcism is a necessary or at least an effective psychological means of reassuring those who believe themselves to be possessed. Whatever the minister's personal beliefs, he must accept the psychological reality that the sufferer believes him or herself to be possessed.

A third opinion is that a belief in demons is explicable sociologically and psychologically. It is undeniable that there are people who claim to believe in demons, but – since demons do not exist – it is that belief with which we should deal, not demons. In such cases, exorcism would be inappropriate since what is to be dealt with is a false belief. To pretend to accept a situation which is false is not a means of bringing people to the truth. Those who take this view stress that normal ministry with the appropriate pastoral care can deal with these situations. Fears and anxieties can be dealt with by the assurance and presence of Christ and the necessity of exorcism is excluded.

All three attitudes encompass the ministry of healing. Other views may be in conflict but not in practice. Remember, in the Barnsley case, it was a Methodist who felt in the first place that the exorcism which ended so tragically should not go ahead. The Anglican priest, on the other hand, claimed he had authority from the New Testament to carry out the ritual. As the Methodists point out, some think that the language and thought of the New Testament world belong to a bygone culture and cannot be transferred to ours, so there is no reason to assume that in our time a Christian should claim the power to 'drive out demons'.

The differing opinions also raise the questions of individual responsibility for evil and whether a rational view of providence can exist side by side with the practice of exorcism. Perhaps the most important result of that Methodist report was that its authors, after giving guidelines for the supervision of exorcism, insist that the pastoral care, save in exceptional circumstances, should always include close collaboration with those qualified in medicine, psychology and social services. Such a service as exorcism should not be carried out when a person is in a highly excited state. It should not be unnecessarily prolonged. Publicity must be kept to a minimum.

Just as the churches' attitude towards possession and exorcism has changed over the centuries, so have the behavioural fashions of the people, each phase bringing a new culture. In the aftermath of the Second World War came the rival gangs of Teddy Boys, dressed in mock Edwardian clothes: velvet-collared overcoats, long double-breasted jackets, string ties, short peg-topped trousers revealing expanses of fluorescent sock and thick-soled shoe. Behind them came the rival Greasers, Hoods and Socs, Mods and Rockers.

Then the young picked up, from the behaviour of pop singers like The Beatles, the fascination for the East, the power of Zen, the Buddhist self-contemplation to understand the universe, the teachings of the Maharishi Mahesh Yogi, the 'flower power' of the Hippies, the musical *Hair* and its principal theme, the song 'The Age of Aquarius', made popular by Shirley Maclaine, and the music of John Denver. That heralded the New Age philosophy.

To the instant analysts, New Agers are defined as the unwashed drop-outs who, often with young families, travel in large numbers in unsafe, broken-down, unlicensed vehicles, squatting, urinating and defecating on other people's land, and attend pop conferences, all in search of a better world. New Agers are, however, around us in every facet of life. More concerned with the soul and spiritual matters than the material side of life, followers are interested in a number of fashionable beliefs: reincarnation, spiritualism, out-of-body and near-death experiences; Eastern faiths, practices and mysticism; crystals and pyramids; new physics and electrical and magnetic forces. They focus on Mother Earth and female values and thought. They perceive male values as dominating and brutalising women and, by extension, exploiting nature. Harmony, wholeness and unity are crucial to the New Age.

Methodists have concluded that the New Age movement appeals by and large to prosperous or relatively prosperous people in the West with no vested interest in changing the existing political and social structures. Its beliefs and practices should be taken as a challenge and stimulus to orthodox Christianity. The Methodists have decided that they must engage in a critical dialogue with the New Agers: a more confrontational approach would neither encourage New Agers to examine the claims of the Christian faith, nor bring to the Methodists the challenges and concerns the New Agers present to the churches.

Like so many suddenly fashionable beliefs, the New Age movement is by no means new. It owes much to Eastern religions, to the founding of the Theosophical Society in 1893 and other historical roots. They even practise Wicca, popularly known as witchcraft, but which they insist is not Satanic. The New Agers, like so many, are dissatisfied with the old religions and the interpretations they have been given. They feel we have been over-taught the holiness of God without the love of God, which has left people with an over-burdened sense of their own unworthiness and overwhelming guilt.

They do not want to change the world, but what is unfortunate is that, well-educated and highly intelligent though they might be – and some of them are former successful 'yuppies' – they are regarded merely as 'drop-outs'. How will they deal with wickedness, with all-consuming evil, with demonic possession?

Like all new or revived cults, the members – even though they are concerned with environmental matters, with sexism, racism and similar contemporary issues – spend much time experimenting. Among the subjects of their investigation is the occult, matters beyond the bounds of ordinary knowledge, which is where we came in.

Index

INDEX

INDEX

INDEX

INDEX

INDEX